PAPERS ON ISLAMIC HISTORY

I.

THE ISLAMIC CITY

PAPERS ON ISLAMIC HISTORY: I

THE ISLAMIC CITY

A Colloquium

EDITED BY

A. H. HOURANI and S. M. STERN

PUBLISHED UNDER THE AUSPICES OF

The Near Eastern History Group

Oxford

and The Near East Center

University of Pennsylvania

University of Pennsylvania Press

Library of Congress Catalog Card Number: 75-105944

ISBN: 0-8122-7634-5

Printed in the United States of America

Table of Contents

PREFACE

For the last few years the " Near Eastern History Group ", an informal association of Oxford scholars concerned with Islamic history, has been meeting regularly to discuss problems connected with the subject. In 1965 the Group organized a small colloquium on the Islamic City, held at All Souls College from June 28 to July 2. A number of talks were given and discussed, and the speakers were asked to revise their papers in the light of the discussions and with a view to publication. Hence the long delay before the appearance of the present volume.

A second colloquium, on Islam and the Trade of Asia, was held at All Souls from June 25 to 30, 1967. It is hoped that the papers given at it will be published with rather less delay.

The holding of the first colloquium was made possible by the generosity of All Souls and St. Antony's Colleges and the Board of the Faculty of Oriental Studies at Oxford. The University of Pennsylvania has made a grant towards the publication of the present volume. The organizers of the colloquium, and all those who participated in it, wish to record their grateful thanks to their benefactors.

Introduction

THE ISLAMIC CITY IN THE LIGHT OF RECENT RESEARCH

by

A. H. Hourani

I

When we speak of the " Islamic city " we can mean several different things, and it is best therefore to begin by making some distinctions. A town or city comes into existence when a countryside produces enough food beyond its requirements to enable a group of people to live without growing their own crops or rearing their own livestock, and devote themselves to manufacturing articles for sale or performing other services for a hinterland. When these goods and services are relatively simple or are sold to the region lying immediately around the town, it is a market town. But it may produce a wider range of goods and sell them to a wider market, or perform more than the simplest services, and if so we may call it a city. But here also we must make distinctions. There are cities with a special function: desert or river or sea ports, for example, which devote themselves to the carrying rather than the making of goods; or holy cities, centres of worship, pilgrimage or religious learning. But there are also cities with many functions: which both make and transport many types of goods, which are centres of secular as well as religious activities, and so on. Among these again we may distinguish some which are centres of administration, the collection of taxes, the control of armies and the dispensing of justice; some of these are dependent or provincial centres, but others are metropolitan, the seats of autonomous or independent governments.

This is one type of division, but of course it is possible to think of others. One which has sometimes been made in recent years is that between " spontaneous " and " created " cities: those which have grown up over a long period, because of a particularly fertile hinterland, good natural communications, or some quality of enterprise in their people;

and those which have been founded by deliberate act of a ruler or dynasty, to be royal residences or pleasances or centres of government. But an essay by Pauty[1] has shown that this distinction is more apparent than real. However a city comes into existence, it can only survive by taking on some permanent social or economic function. Created cities must become " spontaneous " if they are to remain alive. Political power by itself will not maintain them: it must be used to create a permanent economic activity (for example, by diverting trade routes), so that, once the power vanishes through a change of dynasty or the destruction of a state, the citizens will be able to maintain themselves. For similar reasons, the distinction which might be made between cities created in Islamic times and those which have survived from an earlier period does not signify much; it may be, as we shall see, that some traces of an earlier time can still be found in the street plan of some Islamic cities, and it is not impossible (although this is more doubtful) that there is some continuity of institutions, but if so the reason is not simply that streets or institutions were inherited from the pre-Islamic past, but that they still performed some function in the Islamic age, and it is this function which will most concern us.

There is however another type of distinction which must not be left out of sight: that based on differences of time and place. What we might call the " Islamic city " existed in some sense from the seventh century A.D. until the emergence of a single world-wide society in our own times. Even allowing for the slow pace of change in what we regard as " traditional societies ", it is clear that change did take place, and in the life of cities which existed throughout most or all of this long period several phases must be distinguished, in each of which the city, whether we look at it as a group of buildings or a community of people, had a rather different form. In his book on Aleppo Sauvaget distinguishes five main periods: those of the early Caliphate, the anarchy which came when it disintegrated, the " Turkish " dynasties, the Mamlūks, and the Ottomans.[2] Such distinctions will vary from one city to another, but we must always make them; and we must be careful not to think of the Islamic culture and society of the last period, that of the great empires—Ottoman, Ṣafavid, and Moghul—as being the " traditional " Islamic society or culture, that which it has always been.

Again, what we call " Islamic cities " are to be found in different parts

[1] E. Pauty, " Villes spontanées et villes créées en Islam " in *Annales de l'Institut d'Études Orientales*, ix (1951), pp. 52–75.

[2] J. Sauvaget, *Alep* (Paris 1941).

of the world: in Spain and North Africa, Egypt, Syria and Asia Minor, Iraq, Iran, Central Asia, and the Indian sub-continent. We cannot expect that urban life should have taken the same form in all these regions, not so much because of supposed differences of "national character" as because of varying soils and climates, different inheritances, and involvement in various commercial systems. We might perhaps distinguish the cities in the western half of the Islamic world, with their common heritage from Greece, Rome and Byzantium, and their life passed between the Mediterranean and the steppe or desert where the Arab tribesmen lived, from those in the area of Iranian culture, lying between the Indian Ocean and the steppe or desert where Turkic tribesmen lived; and those again from the cities of the Indian sub-continent. But within each area we should again have to make sub-divisions: between cities of North Africa, the Nile valley, and the Levant; and between cities of Mesopotamia, the Persian plateau and Transoxiana. The danger of not making such divisions is the greater because research has not been evenly distributed. Most study in depth has been done by French scholars in North Africa and Syria. We have one detailed study of a Turkish city, not much of any value on Egypt until work now in progress is completed, virtually nothing on Iran. Until some of these gaps have been filled, we should beware of applying a North African or Syrian model to Egypt, or one drawn from the region of Arabo-Turkish culture to that of Irano-Turkish culture.

II

By a tacit agreement, most of the papers in this volume are confined to certain among these various types of city, and so will our introduction be. We shall be concerned more with large cities than local market towns, more with the western than the eastern Islamic world, more with the period before the rise of the three great empires than with the period after, and (because the sources are more readily available) more with the second half of that period—the age of the Fāṭimids, Seljūqs and Ayyūbids, the Mongols and the Mamlūks—than with the first, the age of the Islamic conquests and the undivided caliphate. Even as thus defined our field is a broad one, and it is the very breadth and variety which give rise to the problem with which our colloquium was most concerned. Over this wide area of the world and these many centuries, can we really speak of something called the "Islamic city"? Did cities in the Muslim world have any important features in common, and if so can they be explained in terms of Islam, or must we look for other types of explanation?

A generation ago the answer to these questions seemed clearer perhaps than it does to-day. A number of scholars, who combined vast knowledge of detail with imaginative power and artistic sensibility, had put forward various ideas in the light of which it appeared that cities in the world of Islam did have a common character. The brothers Georges and William Marçais, working in North Africa, suggested that the shape of the Islamic city was determined only in part by the exigencies of power (which decided, for example, where the citadel, the walls and the gates should be), but in part also by their being Islamic; or, in other words, by the fact that the city is necessary for Islam, since it is only there that the virtuous life as Islam conceives it can be fully lived. The congregational mosque in the centre of the city, the religious schools beneath its shadow, the hierarchy of *sūqs*, whose position in relation to mosque and schools was determined by the religious role of the goods they sold or the attitude of the *sharī'a* towards them, the residential quarters with their ethnic or religious solidarity, the cemeteries and shrines of saints outside the walls: all these, they suggested, existed and were where they were because the city was a Muslim city.[3] Massignon, going a stage further, asserted that there was one type of socio-religious institution above all which dominated the life of the Islamic city: the professional corporation or guild, going back beyond Islamic times into the Sasanian empire, encouraged by the Ismā'īlis, having a religious basis and sanction expressed in rites of initiation and the cult of patron saints. Such corporations created within the framework of the *ṭuruq*, the brotherhoods of mystics, provided (Massignon believed) the basis of urban society in the Muslim world: of solidarity between man and man, and of individual self-respect, the craftsman's belief in the worth of his own labour.[4] Yet another French scholar, Sauvaget, studying first the physical shape of cities and through it the human community, showed by close research in Syria that the physical shape of what we usually call the Islamic city was that of the Greco-Roman city which had preceded it, but somewhat changed by the dynamic forces of Islamic society. The classical cities planned by the Seleucids and embellished by the Romans, with their broad colonnaded avenues, temples, market-places, and rectangles of streets, were slowly

[3] W. Marçais, " L'Islamisme et la vie urbaine " in *Articles et Conférences* (Paris 1961), pp. 59–67; G. Marçais, " La conception des villes dans l'Islam " in *Revue d'Alger*, ii (1954–5), 517–33, and " L'urbanisme musulman " in *Mélanges d'Histoire et d'Archéologie de l'Occident Musulman* (Algiers 1957), i, 219–31. Cf. G. E. von Grunebaum, " The structure of the Muslim town " in *Islam, Essays in the Nature and Growth of a Cultural Tradition* (London 1955), pp. 141–58.

[4] L. Massignon, " Ṣinf " in *Encyclopaedia of Islam*, first edition, iv, 436–7.

transformed but kept traces of their first state. When the Arabs came, mosques and palaces gradually took the place of temples and cathedrals or were built on the *agora*; a certain lack of grandeur in the Islamic conception of the city, and the emphasis of Islamic law on the individual, led to the gradual encroachment of shops and dwellings on to the broad avenues, and when the period of anarchy succeeded that of the early caliphate, the insecurity of life caused the population to withdraw into the city-quarters, small units where the ties of neighbourhood were reinforced by those of common religious allegiance or ethnic origin. With this, the city ceased to exist as a moral unity.[5]

The very clarity and precision with which such theories were stated revealed the problems inherent in them. From the writings of a Marçais or a Sauvaget there emerged a vivid sense of the "personality" of an Islamic city, of the continuous tradition of civic life in Damascus or Aleppo or Fez, of a "spirit" which had made it possible for the city to assert itself again and again as a force in Islamic history. In those of Massignon one could find an explanation of how this spirit had persisted and expressed itself: for him, Islamic society was essentially corporate, and urban Muslims had some special power of organizing themselves, maintaining their communal existence in the face of political power, and giving it a religious sanction. But if we compare the Muslim cities with those of western Europe in the same period, a different and even a contrasting impression emerges. Max Weber suggested that there were five distinguishing marks of the city in the full sense: fortifications, markets, a court administering a partly autonomous law, distinctively urban forms of association, and at least partial autonomy. In this sense, Weber maintained, the city had fully existed in Europe, never in Asia, only in part and for short periods in the Near East.[6] His definition does more or less correspond to what Europeans would think of as a city, and if we accept it then we must also accept his conclusion that Near Eastern cities are not cities in the full sense. Of his five marks two at least are missing in the Islamic city. It would usually have a market and a wall; if Massignon was right it would have distinctively urban forms of association; but it had no legal privileges conferred by the state, for the *sharī'a* recognized no privileges for one group of believers above others; nor, apart from some

---

[5] J. Sauvaget, *Alep*; "Esquisse d'une histoire de la ville d'Alep" in *Revue des Études Islamiques*, viii (1934), pp. 421–80; "Le plan de Laodicée-sur-Mer" in *Bulletin d'Études Orientales*, iv (1934), 81–114.

[6] M. Weber, *The City*, tr. D. Martindale and G. Neuwirth (Glencoe, Ill., 1958), p. 88.

rare exceptions (some short-lived municipal bodies in Spain and North Africa), did it possess autonomy.

Thus we seem to be faced with a paradox. How was it that the " Islamic city " was able to maintain its personality, its power of collective action, throughout Islamic history, when it never possessed municipal institutions in which that personality could be formally embodied, or a municipal law which would at once express and legitimize it? How was it that urban Muslims showed—once more, if Massignon is to be believed—such a power of corporate organization in other ways, but were unable to create *this* kind of institution?

III

In the light of recent research as revealed in the papers published here, it is clear that in some respects the problem has been falsely presented. So far as the physical shape of the Syrian city is concerned, Sauvaget's work stands in principle unshaken, although Elisséeff's paper corrects it in certain important ways. But Massignon's view of the corporate nature of Islamic society can scarcely be maintained. The exact opposite indeed might be nearer the truth: in the Islamic view of the world there was the individual believer and there was the whole community of believers, but in between there was no stable grouping regarded as legitimate and permanent. Islamic law did not recognize corporate personality except in a limited sense, and the whole spirit of Islamic social thought went against the formation of limited groups within which there might grow up an exclusive natural solidarity hostile to the all-inclusive solidarity of an *umma* based on common obedience to God's commands. Not only did corporations have no moral or religious basis, it is not certain that they ever existed. Cahen's paper throws doubt on Massignon's theory of the professional corporations and shows that they were not " guilds " in the medieval European sense, but, in so far as they existed, were instruments of state control. It was only at a late period, he suggests, that they acquired a life of their own. (Here we may carry his doubts further and ask whether even the " guilds " of Ottoman times had so much of an independent life as we may be tempted to think. Except in a few specialized occupations did they exist in a fully articulated and autonomous form? Can we find more than a chief—*shaykh, amīn*—whom the government recognized as responsible for his fellow-craftsmen, but whose independence and authority may have been limited; a certain community of feeling and interest among those who practised the same craft, often in the same part of the bazaar; and certain ceremonies, in particular at the moment when an apprenticeship was completed, of which the importance is difficult to assess?) More generally, Stern suggests that the absence of professional organizations is only one example of the absence of organizations in Islamic society. Seen in this light, the lack of municipal institutions is not an exception which needs to be explained, but a further example of this general rule, and to be explained in the same way as other examples, by those features of Islamic law and theory already mentioned, and also by the fact that the power of the state was rooted in the city and this made it difficult for autonomous institutions to grow up.

It is clear moreover that the autonomous cities of the classical world and of medieval Europe, privileged corporations within a larger state, or city-states themselves, are not the norm to which all cities at all times have tended to approach, but an exception which itself needs to be explained. Here as in other matters we may be misled by Weber's insistence that his ideal types were " value-free ". His main problem was always to explain the emergence of the rational, bureaucratic, industrial society of modern Europe; he himself was conscious that special conditions had been present which enabled Europe to develop in such a different way from other societies, but it is easy to draw the inference from his writings that this unique society is the norm and others have been arrested or diverted in their natural development towards it. Very special conditions were needed to produce the chartered city of medieval England or the urban republics of northern Italy: in Italy, for example, the disintegration of Roman authority while urban life and trade continued, and in northern Europe the growth of monarchies based on a rural economy and society. These conditions did not exist in medieval Europe before the eleventh century; they ceased to exist fully in Europe when the nation-state and the modern bureaucratic government developed; they never existed in most of Asia and the Muslim world.

It would not however be true to say that, because municipal privileges never existed, urban life never existed. As Aubin points out, the city in the Islamic world resembled other Asian cities in its lack of formal institutions. This lesson is driven home by Gernet's paper from which it appears that, at least until the growth of a commercial bourgeoisie in the Sung period, the urban conglomeration had no recognized existence at all in China. In the vast sedentary empire, where the hand of the imperial government lay equally on all, a city was simply a piece of land where the population was particularly thick (and not always even that); it had no special government or administration, no special function in Chinese society. In one way the picture is like that of the city in the Muslim world, but in others very unlike; they are alike in the absence of municipal institutions and autonomy, but unlike in the quality and volume of public life. The Chinese city is passive beneath imperial rule, but the Islamic city is active, even disturbingly so, whether its activity takes place within the confines of a political system willingly or unwillingly accepted or tries to break out of it. It is this positive feature of public activity, rather than the negative one of not possessing what European cities possessed from the eleventh century onwards, which poses our real problem. How did this activity express itself? Why was it that Islamic cities were able to maintain it so continuously? To what extent, in this respect, did they differ from the cities of China, India, the Byzantine Empire and western Europe in the same period?

IV

If we are to understand this or any other aspect of the Islamic city it may be best to begin not with the city in isolation but with the settled area of which it forms a part. The fact from which Near and Middle Eastern history starts (or started before the technological revolution of our age) is the fragility of settled life. West of the Indian sub-continent, the regions in which Islam took root were those in which scarcity of water or the threat of the nomadic pastor made agriculture precarious (but we should not of course build on this fact any general theory about Islam being a faith specially adapted to such regions). The peasant could not maintain himself unless such water as existed could be stored and canalized, or unless there were some natural or human obstacle against the coming in of the nomad. For both these purposes a division of labour was needed, there must be some technical skill or military strength greater than the village itself could provide. The village needed the town; but the town could not exist without the food produced by the peasant and delivered to the urban market, whether for sale or in payment of taxes. The basic unit of Near Eastern society was the " agro-city ", the urban conglomeration together with the rural hinterland from which it drew its food and to which it sold part at least of its manufactures.

This basic unit can be analysed in one way, into town and countryside, but also in another, into two mutually dependent components, government and society. The countryside needed a ruler, with an army and administration, to hold back the nomads; the town too needed him to maintain its hold over the countryside and thus ensure its food-supply, and to maintain also the system of laws which harmonised private interests and without which a complex urban life would not have been possible. But the government needed the wealth of the "agro-city"; it could only exist, on any but the smallest scale, in an area where the production of food and manufactures was so far in excess of what the producers needed as to carry the burden of a palace, an administration, and an army.

There existed then a basic harmony between government and "agro-city", or at least those elements in it which had an interest in a prosperous and settled life: craftsmen and merchants, scholars, those cultivators who had a safe tenure of their lands, and those who, although not themselves cultivators, had been able to establish a claim to part of the produce of the land and whom we call (by an analogy with western Europe which may be misleading) the "landowners". The mutual dependence was all the closer as the city grew in size and the government in strength. A large city had to have not only an immediate agricultural hinterland, but a larger commercial hinterland as well; it had to be an organizing centre, a stage, or a terminus of trade-routes, and this would make possible a diversification of products, a division of labour, a standard of living, and a growth of population such as could not otherwise exist. For all this too the city needed the power of the government, not only in order to protect existing trade-routes against pirates, nomads, mountaineers, foreign governments and mercenary armies, but even to create new trade-routes; as Aubin remarks, the power of the government could be used in various ways to draw towards its capital or provincial centres trade and wealth which formerly had followed other courses. On the other hand, the bankers, merchants and craftsmen of a great city, producing goods for a wide market and financing or organizing international trade, would bring in revenue and enable the government to maintain a more complex administration and a more powerful army.

Such a relationship between government and settled urban society had existed in the Near and Middle East before the rise of Islam. In the Islamic period it was given a distinctive shape by two factors: first, the virtual monopoly of political power over most of the Muslim world, after the 'Abbāsid caliphate disintegrated, by politico-military groups of mainly Turkic origin, Islamized but not always deeply so, and standing at a certain distance from the Arabic or Persian-speaking peoples whom they ruled; and secondly, the close connection between the commercial bourgeoisie and the *'ulāmā'*, those learned in the law and other religious sciences, belonging to or grouped around the mosques and schools. This connection had several aspects: members of bourgeois families took to learning, men of learning married into such families, the *'ulamā'* possessed a certain economic and social power through their control of the *awqāf*, and both groups shared an interest in a stable, prosperous and cultivated urban life. Members of the great bourgeois families and of the *'ulamā'* together provided an urban leadership: their wealth, piety, culture and ancient names gave them social prestige and the patronage of quarters, ethnic or religious groups, crafts, or the city as a whole.

This relationship between government and urban society may help to explain the forms and limits of activity in the Islamic city. If we look at the city so to speak from above, from the point of view of the ruler, we may have the impression of a passive society on which a hierarchy of control has been imposed. At the apex stood the ruler and his " household ", a group closely identified with him, almost in fact an extension of his personality: his family, his harem, his palace officials, his personal army whether " slave " or " free ", with a professional *'aṣabiyya* oriented towards maintaining him in power. Beneath the ruler lay a whole system of control: the governor and his household, the secretaries in the government offices, the *ṣāḥib al-shurṭa* or *muḥtasib* who maintained order, the *qāḍī* who administered justice, other functionaries who supervised public acts of worship, the heads of quarters, of villages, of crafts, and of non-Muslim communities, whom the government held responsible for the payment of taxes and the maintenance of order and obedience. All these could be regarded as emanations of the ruler's personality, as possessing an authority derived from his and existing to carry out his orders and wishes. But on the other hand they had a connection, which could be a close one, with the urban society they controlled, and this not only exposed them to pressures from it, but also made it possible for them to have a social power and influence independent of the ruler. Some of those exercising functions in or for the government might themselves be drawn from the urban population. This would be true of the *shaykhs* of quarters, villages or crafts; it might be true of higher officials also—as Ashtor-Strauss has shown,[7] a *ra'īs al-balad*, responsible for police and order in the whole city, was often found in Syria before the Ayyūbid period. In the same way, many of the holders of posts connected with law or worship would be drawn from the local *'ulamā'*, and so too might be the *qāḍī*. Even those who were not by origin from the local urban society might be drawn into it. They had at least the tie of religious faith; they might be closely connected, by the necessities of their work if not by blood or marriage,

[7] E. Ashtor-Strauss, " L'administration urbaine en Syrie medièvale " in *Rivista degli Studi Orientali*, xxxi (1956), 73–128, and " L'urbanisme syrien à la basse-époque " in *Rivista . . .*, xxxiii (1958), 181–209.

with leading families of the city; the holders of religious posts would have some connection with the local *'ulamā'*; officials or soldiers who were given land-grants or held tax-farms would be drawn into the economic life of society and might partially control the exchanges between town and countryside. More generally, the ruler and his subordinates could not lightly ignore the wishes of those groups in the city with which their interests were bound up.

When formal institutions do not exist and the exercise of power is not defined, political roles tend to be ambiguous. The " notables ", the leaders of the bourgeoisie and the *'ulamā'*, obeyed the government not only from fear or self-interest, but from concern for peace and security, from that preference for social peace at almost any price which was the principle of later Islamic society, and from the final need of the city for political power and authority, to bring in the food-supply from the rural hinterland and to keep the trade-routes open. But they were also " leaders " responsible to the urban population. At times they could use their independent power over it to mobilize urban forces and put pressure on the ruler. This mobilization was carried out through an ancient machinery of contacts between notables of the city and leaders of quarters, popular preachers, *shaykhs* of *ṭuruq*, leaders of certain crafts, and leaders of organizations of the under-employed unskilled workers, or of the peasants whom economic chance drew backwards and forwards between the rural and urban parts of the " agro-city ". In this process even those who held posts under the ruler might take part: the *qāḍī* could become a spokesman for the local *'ulamā'*, the *shaykhs* of quarters or villages could act as clients of local leaders rather than servants of the ruler.

Circumstances would decide whereabouts on the spectrum between obedience and rebellion the local leaders and their followers would be found. There were times and places when a relatively stable balance existed, when a strong government ruled in close partnership with the bourgeoisie and their leaders, and the influence of the leaders was thrown on the side of the existing order. But there were other times when the balance was shaken, and, because of a weakening of authority or the widening of the gap between the interests of the ruler and those of the townspeople, the urban leaders and notables would emerge as organizers of protest or even of rebellion. But it did not often happen that such a movement was taken to the point of an overturning of authority. Throughout most of our period, the social norm remained that of close cooperation between men of the sword and notables of the city. As Stern points out, it was in general only at moments of interregnum, when a dynasty or state had collapsed or been defeated, that the local leaders came forward as a provisional government: they would administer the city for a time, until one of them emerged as ruler, or until they must hand it over to its new master. Lapidus explains why it was that, such rare exceptions apart, the local leaders could not take the place of the rulers. On the one hand, the popular forces which they could use or manipulate were themselves divided: the only effective popular associations were those based on the quarters, there were no effective professional or " political " organizations on a city-wide basis, except for certain " marginal " and " anti-social " associations whom the higher orders of the city could only control and use up to a point. On the other, the active leadership tended to be in the hands of the *'ulamā'*, the religious element in the upper bourgeoisie, and they, because of their very conception of society and of their place in it, were not able to integrate the various elements of the city into a political whole. This could only be done by the military rulers; hence the long predominance of " Turkish " or Mamlūk ruling groups, acting both as rulers and as patrons or local leaders, until much later the decline of Ottoman authority led to the re-emergence of local leaders in the provincial cities.

At times indeed the " popular " forces, the instruments of political action, could escape from the control both of the government and of the urban leaders and throw up their own leaders. Hence those long-lived bodies which both Lapidus and Cahen have studied—*'ayyārūn, ḥarāfīsh*, and so on. They might continue to exist for centuries, but, as Lapidus has shown, their basis was not the city as a whole but a small unit, the quarter or group of quarters, and their aims were essentially non-political. They could trouble ruler and urban leaders alike, but could not take their place.[8]

V

It would be a mistake to try to see the physical shape of the Islamic city simply as an expression of its social structure—of such factors as these: the predominance of a commercial bourgeoisie linked with the upper *'ulamā'*; the distinctive religious institutions of Islam; the ethnic difference between ruler and people; and the moral distance between

---

[8] In addition to the papers by Cahen and Lapidus in this volume, cf. C. Cahen, " Mouvements populaires et autonomisme urbain dans l'Asie musulmane du moyen age " in *Arabica*, v (1958), 225–50, and vi (1959), 25–56, 223–65; I. M. Lapidus, *Muslim Cities in the Later Middle Ages* (Harvard 1967).

the ruler's household and the society around it. A city cannot be just an external sign, in stone or wood or mud-brick, of a system of social ethics or social institutions. Aubin reminds us that there are many factors which affect the shape of a city, and first of all there are physical factors. A city must have an adequate supply of water, it must have an adequate hinterland of cultivable land, its streets and buildings will follow the contours of the land on which it is built. Apart from these physical factors, its shape will be affected by an uncounted multiplicity of individual choices not always known as such.

With such reservations in mind, it may however be possible to construct a picture of what a " typical " Islamic city would look like. To do so is of course a dangerous task, as innumerable variations will be found in so large an area and over so long a period of time. But, speaking very roughly, we may say that we should expect to find such features as the following. First, there would be a citadel, very often placed on some natural defence work, and serving indeed to explain why there is a city at all in that place; Sauvaget for example has shown that Aleppo is where it is because of a natural *tell* dominating the countryside around, and Elisséeff suggests where the *tell* of Damascus must have been. Secondly, there might be a royal " city " or " quarter " which would have grown up in either of two ways, as shown in the difference of emphasis between the papers of Lassner and El-Ali about the origins of the Round City of Baghdad: it might be a royal enclave implanted in an already existing urban conglomeration, or it might be a new foundation on virgin soil and around which a conglomeration later grew, attracted by the power, wealth and prestige of a court. However it began, it tended to be more than a palace: it would be rather a " compound ", grouping royal residence, administrative offices, places for the bodyguard or personal troops. Its situation, shape and size depended largely on the relations of government and society. In disturbed times, the compound might also be the citadel, the strong point of defence; in times of ease and confidence, of prosperity and a sure control of society, the court might move to more spacious surroundings, out of a desire for peace and tranquillity, for solitude, or magnificence; and when it moved it tended to draw the government after it. Rogers' study of Sāmarrā shows how difficult it is to disentangle motives or to discern the exact nature of a royal foundation, which may have been pleasance, palace, and administrative centre at once.

Thirdly, there would be a central urban complex, which would include the great mosques and religious schools, and the central markets with their *khāns* and *qaysāriyyas*, and with special places assigned for the main groups of craftsmen or traders. The great houses of the merchant and religious bourgeoisie would be in this district, although, as Raymond has shown,[9] the houses of the " military aristocracy " would be near the centre of political power, wherever that might be. To explain why religious and commercial buildings should be close together, we may refer partly to that alliance of bourgeoisie and *'ulamā'* of which we have already spoken, but also, at least in cities of Greek or Roman origin, to a process analysed by Sauvaget. The Muslim conquerors planted themselves in the complex of *agora*, central avenue and temple or church which stood at the heart of the Greek city; the mosque replaced or stood near the church or temple, the central bazaars and what went with them took over the avenue and *agora*.

Fourthly, there would be a " core " of residential quarters, marked by at least two special characteristics: the combination of local with ethnic or religious differentiation, and the relative separateness and autonomy of each quarter or group of quarters. The development of both these characteristics again is not hard to understand. As a new city developed or an old one expanded, the immigrants—soldiers, merchants, peasants, nomads—tended to settle in compact groups: Massignon has shown how this happened in Kūfa,[10] and it can be seen to-day in the *bidonvilles* of the great cities of the Near East and North Africa. Methods of administration and tax-collection strengthened and perpetuated the separateness of these groups: it was simplest and most satisfactory to hold each group collectively responsible, and recognize one member of it as local chief.

The separateness was still further strengthened when the authority of the ruler weakened, both because the quarter provided a viable unit of defence, and because of that " ambiguity " of leadership which has already been mentioned: chiefs of quarters would have more of the character of " subordinates " when the government was strong, more that of " leaders " when it was weak. But it is doubtful whether the autonomy of the quarters reached the point where, to quote Sauvaget again, the moral unity of the city dissolved; as Scanlon's paper shows, there must always at the least have been some kind of general arrangements for traffic, water-supply, the removal of refuse, and so on.

Fifthly and finally, there would be the " suburbs " and outer quarters,

---

[9] A. Raymond, " Essai de géographie des quartiers de résidence aristocratique au Caire au XVIIIème siecle " in *Journal of the Economic and Social History of the Orient*, vi (1963), 58–103.

[10] L. Massignon, " Explication du plan de Kūfa (Iraq) " in *Opera Minora* (Beirut 1963), iii, 35–60.

where recent and unstable immigrants would live and certain occupations be carried on: in particular the " caravan " quarters spread out along the main roads. Here whatever planning the city centre showed would leave little trace; even in the cities of Roman and Byzantine Syria, there must have been such " Semitic " conglomerations around the central core. Some of these would be outside the city walls, built around the shrines of holy men, and touching the great cemeteries which surrounded the cities. Outer suburbs and cemeteries might—as Scanlon shows to be true of Fusṭāṭ—lie outside the jurisdiction of the urban authorities, and be the home of outlaws.

VI

How far are such features as we have described, in the city as human community and as physical entity, peculiar to the Muslim world, and how far are they to be explained in terms of Islam? Both Cahen and Aubin warns us that it is more correct to talk of cities in Dār al-Islām than of Islamic cities. Cahen shows that many of the characteristics of what we call the " Islamic city " are in fact those of the " medieval " city: of the Byzantine city, of the Italian city before the eleventh century, even of the Chinese and central Asian city to some extent.[11]

Even some of the features which seem to be peculiar to the city in Dār al-Islām may not be due to Islam as a religion. Ought we, for example, to explain that special balance between military élite and bourgeoisie, between authority and rebellion, by the Islamic theory of politics? It is tempting to do so but it may be dangerous. We must at least ask whether there are not other explanations, economic or political: the conditions in which settled agriculture was carried on in the Near East, the need for irrigation and urban capital; the pressure of Arab and Turkish nomads on the countryside and the trade-routes; and so on.

But when all this has been said, there still remains something which may be explained in terms of Islam. To say that " Islamic civilization was urban " may be commonplace but is still valid to some extent. The Islamic institutions were concentrated in the cities: mosques, schools, *zāwiyas*. They possessed a kind of prestige and strength which neither rulers nor bourgeoisie could ignore, and it was for this reason that they provided a framework for urban life. Through them the ruler's acts could be legitimized, the city-dwellers could take corporate action, and the two

[11] " Mouvements populaires . . ." in *Arabica*, vi, 255–60.

could be morally linked. The close connection of the *'ulamā'* with the bourgeoisie gave a distinctive shape to the urban society of the Islamic world.

Islamic law too helped to shape the city. As we have said, it did not recognize the corporation, only the individual and the community of believers. In the interests of the community, the ruler had a duty to intervene in order to regulate the relations of individuals, to prevent one individual infringing the freedom of others. It was in this way, as Brunschvig has shown[12] and as Scanlon reminds us, that the existence of the city was given a kind of indirect recognition by the *sharī'a*: regulations had to be made for roads, drainage, the burial of the dead, and so on. But otherwise, all the emphasis was on the freedom of the individual to seek the goods of this world and the next in his own way, and to dispose freely of them. Both Brunschvig and Sauvaget have pointed out that this tension between the freedom of the individual and the rights of his neighbour, with the balance weighted in favour of the first, is relevant to the problem of how the classical was transformed into the medieval " Islamic " city.

The individual, in Islamic law, belongs to the *umma*, but he is also enclosed within another unit, the family, the basic and irreducible unit of social life, the possessor of property. What is in essence a much older conception of the family was carried by the spread of Islam to regions where it may not have existed, and was strengthened and sanctified by the *sharī'a*. The right of the family to live enclosed in its house led, as Torrès Balbas has remarked,[13] to a clear separation between public and private life; private life turned inwards, towards the courtyard and not towards the street; in the thoroughfares, the bazaars, and the mosques, a certain public life went on, policed and regulated by the ruler, active and at times rebellious, but a life where the basic units, the families, touched externally without mingling to form a *civitas*.

---

[12] R. Brunschvig, " Urbanisme médievale et droit musulman " in *Revue des Études Islamiques*, xv (1947), 127–55.

[13] L. Torrès Balbas, " Les villes musulmanes d'Espagne et leur urbanisation " in *Annales de l'Institut d'Études Orientales*, vi (1942–7), 5–30.

THE CONSTITUTION OF THE ISLAMIC CITY

by

S. M. Stern

Nowadays, the proposition that Islamic civilization is a predominantly urban civilization, has become a commonplace. There is no need to insist on it, since it is generally admitted. This statement, however, is somewhat devoid of meaning; for all civilizations—or let us be cautious and put it thus—most civilizations are urban civilizations. It is more profitable to pass immediately beyond this simple statement and ask about the specific character of civic life in Islam, and to examine the constitution of the Islamic city which distinguishes it from the cities of other civilizations. "Constitution" in the sense of character and structure, not in the narrower sense of the word, since one of the main points which I wish to make is that the Islamic city has not constitution in this sense. The comparison of the Islamic city with those of other civilizations can be made from various points of view. J. Sauvaget has contrasted the regular plan of the ancient cities and the tortuous streets of their Islamic successors, and showed by suggestive examples how the straight, porticoed streets of antiquity were gradually encroached upon by shops and houses in the Islamic period, resulting in a new townscape.[1] His observations were confirmed by L. Torres Balbás, insofar as he showed that the Islamic cities of Spain offer the same kind of street-net as those of the East; this tradition, imported into Muslim Spain, can be considered characteristic of Islamic civilization. He also contrasts the Muslim cities of Spain with the cities founded in Christian Spain.[2] The characteristic landmarks of the

---

[1] "Le plan de Laodicée-sur-Mer", *Bulletin d'Etudes Orientales*, 1934, pp. 99–102, reprinted in *Mémorial Jean Sauvaget*, i, Damascus 1954, pp. 124–5; idem, *Alep*, pp. 78–9, 104–5.

[2] L. Torres Balbás and others, *Resumen Histórico del Urbanismo en España*, Madrid 1954. Eliséeff suggests in his communication that this development antedates the Islamic period. Thus classical town-planning is not continued in Islam, because it had disappeared by the time of the Islamic conquest; just as I shall try to show that classical civic institutions were not continued, for the same reason.

Muslim city—the mosque, the market, etc.—have also been repeatedly described. It is not with the material, topographical, aspects of the Islamic city that I wish to deal, but with its inner structure. I should like to suggest that one of the most essential characteristics of the Islamic city is the looseness of its structure, the absence of corporate municipal institutions.

FROM ANTIQUITY TO ISLAM

Since Islamic civilization was in many respects the heir of Antiquity, and since, more concretely, many of the cities of the caliphate had possessed in Antiquity civic institutions, this absence needs an explanation. There is no more typical Greek institution than the sovereign city-state, which was already diffused over in the Eastern Mediterranean lands before the reign of Alexander the Great. His reign marks, however, a new epoch. In its course and under his successors Hellenism penetrated deeply inland, and with it the Greek political institutions. A great number of Greek cities were founded by—or under the reign of—the kings of the various dynasties, and though the process was slowed down after the conquest by the Roman Republic, this set-back was only temporary, since under the Roman Empire the creation of new cities was again vigorously pursued. It is true that the cities, incorporated into the Hellenistic kingdoms and then into the Roman Empire, lost their political independence, but they preserved a high degree of internal autonomy. They retained the traditional constitution of the Greek city, with its assembly, council, and magistrates. If some of the towns were organized as Roman colonies or obtained the privileges of a Roman colony, this made little difference since the colonies too had their autonomous civic institutions.[3]

Islamic civilization did not, however, inherit the municipal institutions of Antiquity, because, owing to their gradual decline, there was by the time of the Muslim conquest of the provinces of the Roman Empire nothing left to inherit. The process of decline was gradual and complicated.

> Since the beginning of the second century A.D. and perhaps earlier the vitality of city life had been imperceptibly ebbing, and the anarchy of the third century had accelerated its decline. The emperors had perforce, since they were unable to arrest the decay of local government, to introduce more and more direct control, but they strove by legislation to infuse new life into the cities. They had been

[3] The standard work on the subject is A. H. M. Jones, *The Greek City from Alexander to Justinian*, Oxford 1940.

in the past very useful institutions—they had collected the taxes, maintained public security, built the roads and performed countless other functions for the imperial government—and if they could retain sufficient vigour to perform these tasks, so much the better. Despite the efforts of the imperial government the growth of the bureaucracy absorbed more and more the strength of the cities during the fourth and succeeding centuries. But this movement only added another motive for endeavouring to maintain local self-government. The bureaucracy as it grew became more and more unwieldly and less and less obedient to its master; the officials became a class whose interests were far from identical with those of the empire they served and pursued those interests without scruple. The only effective check on their depredations was to give the provincials whom they oppressed more effective power to resist them, and some of Justinian's measures show that he realized the value of local autonomy as a means of curbing the bureaucracy.

The emperors thus had practical motives for maintaining the cities, and indeed for promoting the growth of city life where it did not hitherto exist. But it would be unjust to assume that the Byzantine emperors were moved by practical reasons only. It was still in this age, despite the actual decay of civic institutions, accepted as an axiom that civilization meant cities, and it is probable that many of the emperors genuinely felt that in their efforts to sustain and promote city life they were the champions and missionaries of culture.[4]

One sees that the measures taken and the motives behind them were far from being simple, so that the process of decadence were also not one which can be described in simple terms. New cities were founded by Justinian, and a military post in eastern Syria was granted city rank as late as A.D. 573.[5] " Though qualitatively city life was degraded, the area in which it prevailed was substantially increased by the Byzantine emperors . . . In the lists of Hierocles and Georgius Cyprius cities are the almost universal units of government." Nevertheless, the decline of the " quality " of city life is decisive from our point of view. " The cities had in the nine hundred years which passed between the reigns of Alexander and Justinian sunk from independent states which resented submission to any external authority, to organs of local administration ".[6] The *curia*, the class of leading citizens represented on the council, was degraded into a group whose main function was to serve as hostages for the taxes imposed on the city, obliged to make good any deficit from their own pockets. Membership of the council was a hereditary obligation incumbent on the rich, it was a heavy burden which people tried to avoid by all means, even by absconding. The emperors resorted to harsh legislation in order to prevent the members of the " ruling " classes from shirking their duty. Also, while in the hey-day of civic life the leading

---

[4] The quotation is from Jones, pp. 85–6.

[5] See Jones, p. 89.

[6] The quotations are from Jones, p. 94, and p. 155.

citizens took a pride in providing their cities with public buildings such as theatres, amphitheatres and gymnasia, in the Byzantine period they had neither the means nor the willingness to do so. The domestic services of the cities also tended more and more to depend on the initiative of the imperial governor. It would seem that by the end of the third century the administration of justice had passed from the city court to the provincial governors. The old magistrates gave way to new officials, such as the *curator* and the *defensor civitatis*, which were originally appointed by the imperial authorities, though it is true that they were gradually transformed into civic offices. If Justinian, finding the cities useful organs of administration, tried to prevent their decay, " the attempt was doomed to failure. The vigorous spirit of civic patriotism which had once inspired the cities had been allowed by the emperors to die for lack of anything to feed upon, and now that it might have been useful to the emperor it could not be revived by a stroke of his pen ".[7] Alongside the Imperial government, the Church also played a role in making the city government superfluous by taking over many of its functions.

There can be no doubt that after Justinian the process of disintegration continued apace. The curial class, which only survived " as a caste, responsible for the performance of certain menial tasks, principally, it would seem, the collection of taxes ", disappeared even in this capacity long before Leo the Wise, in order to tidy up the law by eliminating obsolete statutes, formally revoked all those referring to the decurions, motivating his measures, characteristically enough, by saying that now all matters depended upon the emperor and his administration.[8] In the provinces retained by Byzantium after the Arab conquests the strictly centralized military provincial government (the system of the *themes*) must have eliminated all municipal autonomy if it lingered on as long as that. We may quote the sentences in which the prevalent view of the historians of Byzantium is summarized:[9] " There is no doubt that even in the late-Roman period the old municipal organization began to decay. This process was not only continued, but intensified in early Byzantine times, until, with the introduction of the theme system, municipal government was altogether destroyed. The most important towns of the Byzantine provinces became the seats of the *strategi* and centers of their military and civil organization. In becoming the nerve center of the

[7] See for the preceding: Jones, chapters xi–xii (pp. 170–210). The quotation is from p. 155.

[8] Novella 46 (ed. Noailles-Daim, Paris 1944, pp. 183–5).

[9] G. Ostrogorsky, " Byzantine Cities in the Early Middle Ages ", *Dumbarton Oaks Papers*, 1959, p. 65; following G. I. Bratianu, *Privilèges et franchises municipales dans l'empire byzantin*, Paris 1936.

Empire, the new military and bureaucratic machinery stifled the last remains of city autonomy." Since the decay of the civic institutions was a long established trend there is no need to refer to external events. Nevertheless it is possible that the Persian occupation of Syria and Egypt at the beginning of the seventh century, lasting some fifteen years, might have given the *coup de grâce* to the last vestiges of such institutions. At any rate, it does not seem likely that any of them survived at the time of the Arab conquest, thus there was nothing for the Arabs to imitate.[10] It may be noted, incidentally, that the Arab commanders negotiated either with the Byzantine military and provincial authorities, or with the bishops as the spokesmen of the towns. We have pointed out that in the Byzantine age the clergy acquired great influence in the life of the cities. This explains also the role of the church in the self-government of the Christian minority communities under Muslim rule.

If the formerly Byzantine provinces were not able to pass on municipal institutions to the Muslims, the provinces conquered from Sāsānid Persia were obviously even less able to do so. In the distant past there had existed some cities in Persia possessing Greek political institutions, but all memory of these institutions must have been lost. Our evidence for the internal history of the Sāsānid empire is not very rich, but one can say with some confidence that the Persian cities did not enjoy autonomous institutions.

If I say that Islamic civilization did not inherit municipal institutions from Antiquity, I have in mind juridical, political, institutions. It is evident that on the whole urban life in the Muslim cities owed a great deal to the traditions of Antiquity. I intended to discuss a few examples illustrating this statement, but the posthumous publication in the meantime of a book by U. Monneret de Villard[11] dispenses with the need for this. In that book the author examines with his customary acuteness and learning the roots in Antiquity of some of the main features of the Islamic

[10] Ashtor (*Rivista degli Studi Orientali*, 1956, p. 74), in order to document his statement that " the ancient institutions of municipal autonomy survived at the beginning of Muslim domination " quotes Husaini's " conclusions " that in many of the towns conquered by the Muslims there were municipal councils (*dīwān al-shūrā*) whose presidents were called *ṣadr* and members *amīn*. I think however (see below, p. 31 note 13) that all this is entirely unfounded. For the survival of municipal institutions in Spain after the Arab conquest Ashtor refers to I. de las Cagigas, *Los Mozarábes*, Madrid 1947, i. 57; but it has been shown by C. Sánchez-Albornoz, *Ruina y extinción del municipio romano en España e instituciones que le reemplazan*, Buenos Aires 1943, that the autonomous institutions of the Christians in Muslim Spain do not represent survivals of the ancient municipalities.

[11] *Introduzione allo studio dell' archeologia islamica*, Venice 1966. See chapters iv–vi.

city: the bath, the market—the chapter on it including the *qaysāriyya*, covered market hall, and the inn—and the wall and gates. This is a fundamental contribution to the study of the origins of Islamic civilization. Other aspects of its links with Antiquity have hardly been studied at all. There can be no doubt that the craftsmen in the old cities conquered by the Arabs continued their work according to their traditional routine; the techniques of the various crafts and the question how far they continue traditions of Antiquity offer fields of study which have hitherto been almost entirely neglected. Presumably the organization and the social framework of industry and trade in the cities was also not brusquely interrupted but survived to some extent; the trouble is that we do not know what was the situation at the moment of the conquest, or how much the further development was influenced by the passing of the cities under Islamic domination. I shall come back to the problem of the organization of crafts and trades; to sum up our discussion about municipal institutions, we may say that as in other fields, Islamic civilization could take over and develop what existed at the moment of the transition; but since municipal institutions had ceased to exist at that moment, Islam could not borrow them from Antiquity.

While the Islamic empire inherited many ancient towns in the previously Byzantine and Persian provinces, a great many new ones were founded by the Arabs. In the first instance these were originally garrison cities (*amṣār*) established for the Beduin warriors, their families and retinue, on the organization of which tribal society left its strong imprint: the various tribes were settled in their own quarters and preserved for some time their coherence under their tribal chiefs. Max Weber attributed the absence of municipal institutions in Islam to the tribal traditions of the Arabs.[12] The survival of these in the garrison towns is well observed—though he does not seem to have realized that this survival was of comparatively short duration. At any rate, when the tribal organization disappeared, it did not result in a municipal organization, and there was no reason why it should have resulted.

ABORTIVE GROPINGS TOWARDS MUNICIPAL AUTONOMY

Thus at the point of departure of its history the Islamic city had no municipal institutions: the old cities going back to pre-Islamic times

[12] M. Weber, *The City*, tr. D. Martindale and G. Newirth (Glencoe, Ill., 1958), p. 100.

used to have them, but lost them, whereas the new foundations never had them. If Islamic society did not inherit municipal institutions from antiquity, neither did it develop any on its own account. The first Islamic centuries saw a splendid development of urban civilization, the like of which was possessed by no other contemporary civilization, China and Byzantium not excluded—not to speak of Latin Europe, where urban life was in almost total eclipse. But this intense civic life did not produce formal, juridical, civic institutions.[13] This was a period of comparatively speaking stable central government (for our purposes it matters little whether it was wielded by a caliph whose writ run through the whole Empire, or later by territorial military rulers), and so it was not particularly propitious for the rise of municipal autonomy.[14] At periods when the control of the central authorities relaxed, there were gropings towards inchoate forms of self-government, which did not, however, lead very far.

The contrast with Latin Christianity is arresting. In Western

---

[13] The picture drawn of the Islamic cities by S. A. Q. Husaini, *Arab Administration*, Madras 1949, pp. 217–18, stands in direct opposition to my conclusions: "Many of the towns were governed by a council of notable citizens (*Dīwānu 'Sh-Shūrā*). The members were nominated by the Government; and the council was presided over by an elected president (*aṣ-Ṣadr*). In the East each town with its dependencies administered its own affairs, levied its own taxes and paid the fixed revenue to the state. Only if there was a dispute with the neighbouring towns, the Government interfered.

"The cities with their dependencies formed so many semi-independent principalities and resembled in many respects the free cities of Europe.

"Each of the commercial cities had a merchants' guild or syndicate which supervised commercial transactions and suppressed frauds. This body was presided over by the most influential and outstanding merchant of the city who was called *Ra'īsu 't-Tujjār*. The members were called *Amīns*.

"Thus, in matters of administration, trade, and social relations, the towns were almost self-sufficient and most of the functions of the Government, such as the collection of taxes, maintenance of order, administration of justice, regulation of trade and commerce and looking after all the civic amenities were performed by the citizens themselves."

No evidence whatsoever is quoted, and it seems to me that this false picture is mainly due to the transference of descriptions of the Western European conditions to the Islamic world. Since the book is on the whole an uncritical and superficial compilation, I would not have quoted it at all, were it not that Ashtor referred to it as evidence for the survival of antique municipal autonomy into the Islamic period (see above, p. 29 note 10).

[14] We have seen that the centralizing tendencies of the Byzantine state was the cause (or perhaps we should rather say: one of the causes) of the final decline of the ancient municipal institutions. Cf. the words of Bratianu about the Byzantine period (on p. 43 of the book quoted above, p. 28 note 9): "Il semble donc . . . téméraire d'y rechercher les éléments d'une autonomie, d'une franchise municipale, si contraires aux conceptions administratives de la monarchie absolu du Bas-Empire", which can be applied to Islamic civilization.

Europe the gap between the civilization of Antiquity and that of the Middle Ages was in many respects more profound than in the heart lands of Islam. The Arab conquests were swift and as far as everyday life was concerned disrupted the routine of the existing societies of the conquered territories less profoundly than did the protracted process of the Germanic invasions, or the anarchy caused in the ninth century by the Viking, Hungarian and Saracen raids, in Western Europe. Thus Islamic civilization in many senses directly continues the traditions of late Antiquity: the centralized bureaucratic administration so characteristic of Islamic society, and, to remain even closer to our theme, its active urban industrial and commercial life, are direct legacies of the preceding epoch. This continuity of social life did not obtain in the Latin-Germanic West, where different circumstances brought about the rise of feudalism instead of the centralized state, and the disappearance of towns, instead of a thriving urban life. Thus in Western Europe the Roman traditions of municipal life (and we must remember that from the very beginning urban life in the western Roman provinces north of the Alps are much weaker than in the eastern provinces) were extinguished more thoroughly than in the East, since not only did municipal organization disappear, but apart from Italy, where cities survived (though in much reduced form), there were hardly any cities left at all. When, however, from the eleventh century onwards the economic life of Western Europe resumed momentum, trade, and with it the city, revived. The phenomenon is accompanied by an astonishing efflorescence of corporative municipal institutions. We find conjurations of citizen bodies pledging common help against their feudal lords, a process culminating in the twelth century when the communal movement spreads with varied intensity over Europe. The cities gain their autonomy, acquire councils, elect the magistrates. Not all of them become independent republics like Venice or Florence, or acquire commercial power like the cities of Flanders or of the Germanic Hansa—but Europe is filled with innumerable cities which possess internal autonomy, even when remaining subjects to their territorial princes or the strong monarchy which exists in England. The privileges of the cities—the most important among which is to live according to their own law—are guaranteed by charters granted by their princes. Within the towns, the merchants and artisans (and sometimes, in Italy, even political parties) are organized as corporations. Civic squares and buildings stand as outward expressions of this highly articulated civic life.

That nothing of the sort, no corporate civic institutions, ever developed within the framework of Islamic civilization, which started with an incomparably more advanced urban life than Western Europe, is paradoxical, but it is undeniably true. There were within Islam some gropings towards urban autonomy, but they led to nothing comparable with the results of the communal movement in Western Europe. In recent years these gropings have gained the attention of historians such as E. Ashtor and Cl. Cahen; the latter's study bears in its title the operative words: popular movements and urban autonomy.[15]

Ashtor has pointed out the turbulence of Syrian and Mesopotamian cities which in the course of the eight–tenth centuries repeatedly rose against their governors. These tumults do indeed recall the revolts of European cities against their lords, incidents which formed the prelude to the movement of civic independence. The Muslim cities did have its " patrician " elements, mainly the great merchants, and there was a feeling of solidarity among the citizens, or at least amongst the inhabitants of a quarter; though it is important to rememberer that the division among confessional lines, so prominent in the Islamic city, had hardly a counterpart in Western Europe, where the only non-Christian minority, the Jews, had less importance than the considerable Christian and Jewish communities of the Islamic cities. The various quarters had their own chief men, and the towns also had their *ra'īs*, their chief. At the time of the decline of government authority, the city bourgeoisie, led by their chiefs, stepped into the breach and controlled the cities de facto, often through organized bands, the *'ayyārūn* or *aḥdāth*, which sometimes came near to forming a kind of city militia.

Similar situations also arose in other parts of the Islamic world and in other periods. Let us look somewhat more closely at particular instances. After the collapse of the Umayyad caliphate of Cordova, Seville was governed by a group of local notables: Muḥammad b. 'Abbād, kadi of the city, a son of the famous philologist al-Zubaydī, and the sons of a certain Yarīm.[16] That the kadi should occupy the leading position

[15] E. Ashtor, " L'administration urbain en Syrie médiévale ", *Rivista degli studi Orientali*, 1956, pp. 73–128; idem, " L'urbanisme syrien à la basse-époque ", ibid., 1958, pp. 181–209; Cl. Cahen, " Mouvements populaires et autonomisme urbaine dans l'Asie musulmane au Moyen Age ", *Arabica*, 1958, pp. 225–50; 1959, pp. 25–56, 223–65.

[16] The principal account is by the contemporary Ibn Ḥayyān, who is quoted by Ibn Bassām (in R. Dozy, *Loci de Abbadidis* i, 220 ff.); Ibn al-Khaṭīb, *A'māl al-A'lām*, ed. Lévi-Provençal, Beirut 1956, pp. 152 ff.; Ibn Khaldūn (Dozy, ii 208). Muḥammad b. 'Abbād's father when owing to an illness he resigned the kadiship in favour of his son, " retained the leadership (*riyāsa*) of the city and the charge of the council of the elders (*tawallī ra'y al-mashyakha*) ". (Add this meaning of *ra'y* in Dozy, s.v. who has examples of related uses.) Muḥammad is called *'amīd* (=*ra'īs*) of the city and is said to have " shared the rule with the notables of the city and the eminent members of its great families until he ousted them

in a city, conforms to the general pattern of Islamic city life. It is more remarkable that the government of the city, once rid of its overlord, should have been put into the hands of a committee. It is, however, characteristic of the monarchic tendency of Islamic political life that the plurality of rulers should have been a purely ephemeral phenomenon, and that the character of 'Abbādid rule should soon have reverted to the normal type of a military amīrate, albeit that Ibn 'Abbād, after ousting his colleagues, did retain for some time the simple title of Kadi. That a leading member of the urban patriciate should emerge as the monarchical head of his city, could and did happen in Christian Europe; what is characteristic for Islam is that the collegial rule of city notables in Seville and in comparable cities was of short duration, and was not accompanied by the development of corporative municipal institutions.

A century later, when the Almoravid empire was fatally weakened, we find in Spain a number of kadis assuming the government of their cities,[17] but this inchoate urban independence was swept away within a few years by the Almohads, who, like the Almoravids before them, exemplify that other characteristically Islamic phenomenon of the large territorial empire.

In other parts of the Maghrib, in the oasis towns of North Africa, we also find at times when central government weakened, the towns attained independence under the leadership of their notables. The course of events was on the whole similar to that which we observe in Spain: one of the notables assumes the leading role and transforms collective government into personal rule. Nor do municipal institutions arise in the independent towns, which in any case tend to fall back into the hands of the territorial rulers as soon as they recuperate their strength.[18]

I have discussed these processes of the Maghrib not only because they

---

and ruled alone". Ibn Khaldūn uses the phrase: *wa-kān al-amr shūrā* between Ibn 'Abbād, Abū Bakr al-Zubaydī and Muḥammad b. Yarīm al-Ilhānī; then Ibn 'Abbād ousted them and became a sole ruler (*istabbadda 'alayhim*); see for this linguistic usage below.

[17] Cf. F. Codera, *Decadencia y desaparición de los Almorávides en España*, pp. 53 ff. (Cordova), 68 ff. (Malaga), 101 ff. (Valencia).

[18] This kind of process took place in Milyāna (Ibn Khaldūn, "History of North Africa", ed. de Slane, i, 433 = transl. de Slane, *Histoire des Berbères*, ii, 352), Qābis-Gabes (i, 604/tr. iii, 97) the cities of the Jarīd, i.e. Qafṣa-Gafsa and Tawzar-Touzeur (i, 539/tr. ii, 15; i, 599/tr. iii, 91; i, 636 ff. tr. iii, 141 ff.); Biskra (i, 625 ff./tr. iii, 126 ff.); etc. Note the pertinent observation by Ibn Khaldūn: In the thirteenth century the Banū Makkī became preponderant in Gabes through the favour of the Ḥafṣid sultan of Tunis—"when the empire was weakened . . . and its authority was not felt in the distant regions, they aspired to independence".

correspond to the state of affairs in the East and show clearly that both the tendency towards municipal independence, and the ultimate sterility of this tendency are phenomena characteristic of the Islamic world as a whole, but also because the cases alluded to come into the purview of that keen observer of the history of the Maghrib, Ibn Khaldūn, who uses in connection with them a particular terminology, which is worth our while to examine. When a group of notables is in control of a city, it is then said by Ibn Khaldūn to be governed by a *shūrā*. The preponderant member of the group is called the head of the *shūrā* and his position is described as *riyāsat al-shūrā*. Ibn Khaldūn was also perfectly aware of the process by which the leading notable of the city often succeeded in getting rid of his colleagues and assumed power for himself (*istabadda*).[19]

Two observations should, however, be made about Ibn Khaldūn's use of terms. It would be tempting to see in the word *shūrā* a term created by contemporaries in order to give a name to the government of the city by a council and the inchoate municipal authority. This would imply that the effort towards the establishment of municipal institutions and municipal autonomy may have been groping, but—since it found expression in a special term—was nevertheless conscious. I think, however, that it would be a mistake to do so. There is, as far as I can see, no evidence for this usage before Ibn Khaldūn. It seems to me very significant that in the case of Seville, which according to Ibn Khaldūn, was ruled by Ibn 'Abbād in joint *shūrā* with his colleagues until he assumed sole power, neither the author of the chief contemporary account nor any of the later historians apart from Ibn Khaldūn use the term at all.[20] I think it most probable that here—as in many similar cases—Ibn Khaldūn coined his own language in order to describe a phenomenon observed by him. Thus the word is yet one more testimony to Ibn Khaldūn's often-praised acumen rather than a pointer to the nascent awareness of the Muslim townspeople of the possibility of their gaining an autonomous political role (a possibility which was, as we know, never realized).

Secondly, it is instructive to see how this terminology is rendered in the French translation of de Slane and by Dozy in his dictionary. In order to save space, I will reproduce Dozy's relevant passages in which on the whole he follows de Slane. "Dans des temps de troubles, ces conseillers municipaux se déclarèrent indépendents et formaient une

---

[19] See the passages of the Ibn Khaldūn quoted above, p. 34 note 18. Most of the material is assembled in the remarkable article *shūrā* in Dozy's *Supplément aux dictionnaires arabes*.

[20] See above, p. 33 note 15. The term *ra'y al-masyakha* comes near to this usage.

république dont ils étaient les chefs. En parlant d'une ville où cela a lieu, on dit *ṣāra amruhā ila'l-shūrā*, ou *ṣāra ahluhum ila'l-shūrā fī amrihim*, elle se constitua (ou les habitants se constituèrent) en république ". No single phrase can perhaps be described as a positive mistake, but the several subtle misrepresentations give, I think, a false picture. " On dit "—we have seen that there is probably no question of a general usage, but of a coinage of Ibn Khaldūn. Those persons who shared in the *shūrā* can in a sense be described as counsellors and a city governed by notables can be described as—or rather be compared to—a republic. But the use of these terms give the wrong impression that in these Muslim cities these amorphous and transitory methods of government are institutions comparable to the city-councils or city republics of Europe. This superficial assimilation of ad hoc arrangements to well established institutions is even more dangerously represented in Dozy's next sentences: " Pour exprimer que certains conseillers devinrent, pour ainsi dire [this is, let it be said in Dozy's defence, a commendable saving clause], les consuls de la république, on dit: *ṣāra'l-amr shūrā baynahum*. Les chefs de la république, le consuls, s'appellent *ahl al-shūrā, arbāb al-shūrā min al-mashyakha*. Quand un d'entre eux usurpe le pouvoir et substitue sa propre autorité à celle du conseil, on dit: *istabadda bi-shūrā al-balad*, expression qui s'emploie aussi en parlant de plusieurs usurpateurs qui changent la république en oligarchie. Enfin *maḥā athar al-shūrā minhā* se dit du souverain qui rentre dans ses droits et abolit la forme du gouvernement republicain ".

To sum up. In the Islamic world there arose situations in which the inhabitants of certain towns tried, with greater or lesser success, to get rid of the control of their ruler and acquire autonomy. These aspirations sometimes resembled those of the Western European cities which resulted in the great " communal " movement. By contrast, however, the attempts within the Islamic world never assumed institutional forms and remained —perhaps for this very reason—abortive. This absence of municipal institutions is, I think only one particular case of a much larger phenomenon: the absence of corporative institutions in general in Islamic society.

THE ISLAMIC GUILDS

Before giving some examples in order to substantiate this statement, I have to embark upon a detailed discussion of a special point which stands in my way. It is widely held that guilds play a great part in the life of the

Islamic cities; now guilds are corporations (is not the French term for the guild *corporation*?) and so the thesis about the absence of corporative institutions in Islam would run into difficulties. Moreover, it could be rightly observed that if guilds flourished in Muslim cities, it is even more surprising that no municipal institutions did evolve, since the guilds would have been a natural basis for them.

The current ideas about the history of the Islamic guilds are based on the theories—or let us rather say (since it will be advantageous as well as honest to call here a spade a spade) the fancies—of L. Massignon. His article on the guild (*ṣinf*) in the *Encyclopaedia of Islam* begins with the apodictic statement: "The organization of labour and the joining of workers in guilds goes back in the Islamic cities to the 3rd/9th century and is closely connected with the half religious, half social, movement of the Ḳarmaṭians". The Qarmaṭians created the guilds in order to serve their propaganda aimed at the overthrowing of the 'Abbāsid caliphate. The theory was repeated by Massignon in various publications, but it was put in the most lucid form by a disciple,[21] so that it will be the most convenient to base our critical examination on his article. The theory, though it sounds most attractive, has in fact not a shred of evidence to support it —as it is put in the article referred to: Massignon "has not yet fully worked out his theory. As he himself says 'les matériaux sont encore à réunir'". One would be even tempted to consider a detailed refutation of these extravaganzas a work of supererogation, were it not that they are generally taken seriously.[22]

---

[21] B. Lewis, "The Islamic Guilds", *Economic History Review*, 1937, pp. 20–37. Massignon's articles on the subject are reprinted in his *Opera Minora*, i, Beirut 1963, pp. 369 ff.—not, however, the articles "Ṣinf" in the *Encyclopaedia of Islam* (1935) and "Guilds (Mohammedan)" in the *Encyclopaedia of Social Sciences* (1931).

[22] H. A. R. Gibb, *Studies on the Civilization of Islam*, pp. 19–20; "The leaders of the [Fatimid Ismaili] movement set up regular centers for systematic instruction and organized an extensive missionary propaganda; the popular masses were not neglected and in the city lodges or guilds were constituted for craftsmen"—with the footnote: "The evidence for this is inferential, but fairly convincing; see B. Lewis, 'The Islamic Guilds' in *Economic History Review*, vol. viii, no. 1, Nov. 1937." Speaking of the guilds H. A. R. Gibb and H. Bowen (*Islamic Society and the West*, i, London 1950, p. 283) write: "They are thought to date from the III/IX century", and refer to Massignon's article "Ṣinf", A. von Kremer, *Kulturgeschichte des Orients*, ii, 186, and B. Lewis, in *Economic History Review*, 1937, pp. 20–37. "Sur l'organisation professionelle, la mise au point de B. Lewis *Islamic guilds*... excellente et claire comme telle, ne peut avoir abordé les problèmes qui ne l'avaient pas été à cette date"—J. Sauvaget–Cl. Cahen, *Introduction à L'Histoire de l'Orient musulman*, Paris 1961, p. 98. C. A. Nallino, with his usual common-sense, has recognized that Massignon's theories are baseless and said so in a passage apt to be overlooked: *Enciclopedia*

What is then " the evidence in favour of this hypothesis?" " In the first place, we must note the great interest in the artisan classes displayed by the Qarmatis. A whole epistle of the Rasa'il Ikhwan us-Safa is devoted to a consideration of the manual crafts, their classification, and their essential nobility ". The Epistles of the Sincere Brethren are an encyclopaedic work of propaganda by which a certain group professing Ismā'īlism (though not that form of it which was followed by the main body of the Fāṭimid movement) tried to gain adherents to their particular brand of Ismā'īlism and philosophy; it was produced in the middle of the fourth/tenth century. In the chapter in question there is set out a rather quaint philosophical classification of crafts—since the book is designed to comprise the whole of knowledge, there is nothing remarkable that such a subject is included. Of guilds or their organization there is not a word.

Since the Ismā'īlīs are supposed to have invented the guilds, it is natural that according to the upholders of this view the organization of the guilds " found its full development in those Islamic lands which were subject to the new state which arose in consequence of the propaganda of their partisans, i.e. the Fatimid Caliphate of Cairo (4–6th/10–12th centuries) ", whereas it was hard hit by the Sunnite restoration under Saladin. This would make excellent sense—were it true. But what is the evidence for the particularly flourishing state of the guilds under the Fāṭimids? As usual, Massignon feels under no obligation to provide any, and Lewis merely echos Massignon:

A second factor [i.e. as evidence in favour of Massignon's hypothesis, after the " proof " from the Sincere Brethren] is the difference in the situation of the guilds under the Fatimids and under Sunni states. Under Sunni rule, the guilds were persecuted, submitted to a thousand restrictions, deprived of any legal rights. There was a legal functionary, the Muhtasib, whose main duty was to supervise the guilds and to nip in the bud any attempt at independent action. We possess an interesting anti-guild literature, demonstrating the distrust felt by the Sunni state for the guilds. Quite different was the position of the guilds under the Fatimids, where they enjoyed great prosperity. Recognised by the state, they seem to have possessed considerable privileges, and to have played an important part in the commercial revival that took place under Fatimid rule. It was under the Fatimids that was founded the guild of teachers which formed the great university of Al-Azhar, of which we have already spoken. In 1171 the Fatimid anti-Caliphate was destroyed by Saladin, and Egypt recovered for orthodoxy. Immediately the guilds were deprived of most of their rights and privileges, and submitted to a very strict control.

Italiana, s.v. " Corporazione ": " il Massignon che, senza prove e anacronisticamente, collega il sorgere delle corporazioni musulmane di mestiere con il movimento eretico dei Carmati ". Incidentally, the two letters of appointment from the Fāṭimid period referred to by Nallino (al-Qalqashandī, x, 360–1, 401–4) concern inspectors of army corps (*ṭā'ifa*), not of groups of craftsmen.

This is an impressive piece of historical argument, and one looks eagerly for the evidence—for instance for footnotes giving chapter and verse for the statements about the recognition of the guilds by the Fāṭimid State, the privileges granted to them, their part in the commercial revival under the Fāṭimids. One looks, of course, in vain, since the whole argument is bogus. We are in fact left with one concrete example among all these fancies: " the guild of teachers and students which formed the great university of Al-Azhar "! On closer inspection this alleged guild of teachers and students which is left to support alone the whole burden of the theory of the superior commercial role of the guilds under the Fāṭimids, also dissolves into nothingness. The Azhar was founded as the grand mosque of Cairo and under the Fāṭimids played little role as a centre of learning, which it became in after times. In any case, " the guild of teachers and students " is again mere fancy—woven it seems from vague reminiscences of the medieval western universities, which were guilds of teachers *or* students (not both!), and of modern " guilds " of students and teachers in the Azhar projected back to the non-existent Fāṭimid " university of Al-Azhar ". The persecution of the guilds by " the Sunni state " comes to this: the Islamic rulers (whether Sunnī or Shīʿite makes no difference) exercised the right of supervising through the *muḥtasib* the activities of merchants and craftsmen.[23] We shall come back to this point, which has no bearing whatsoever upon the matter in hand.

We have not yet done with the proofs. " A third factor in favour of this hypothesis is the strong trace of Qarmati influence left in the guilds long after the disappearance of Qarmatism. In thirteenth century Anatolia, M. Köprülü tells us, the guilds still have a graded system of initiation closely resembling that of the Qarmatis, and studies of different guilds in different parts of the Islamic world have revealed similar traces. An Egyptian guild-tract of the sixteenth century, studies by Thorning and Goldziher, reveals a fierce hatred of the Ottoman rule and a social messianism closely resembling that of the Qarmatis. Most significant is the interconfessionalism of the guilds, which distinguishes them sharply from their European counterparts. Muslim, Christian and Jew are admitted on equal terms, some guilds being even predominantly non-Muslim (as those of doctors, dealers in precious metals etc.) This connects the guilds very closely with Qarmati doctrine."

Let us begin to disentangle this pell-mell collection of false logic by

---

[23] That the office of *ḥisba* existed under the Fāṭimids is pointed out by Ashtor, in *Rivista degli Studi Orientali*, 1956, p. 83; on pp. 85–6, 121, and in *RSO*, 1958, pp. 186–7, however, he too succumbs to Massignon's influence.

observing that in order to appreciate correctly Köprülü's theory it must be stressed that at that time Ismā'īlism was very imperfectly known, some of the fairy-tales told about them in hostile literature—historical and theological—were generally accepted as true, and the influence of the Ismā'īlī movement upon various trends in Islam overestimated. Nowadays we know on the one hand that the "graded system of initiation" attributed to the Ismā'īlīs by Sunnite authors is largely malicious invention based on some slight foundation of fact. On the other hand initiation in the Anatolian guilds can by no means be described as "closely resembling" the initiation of the Ismā'īlīs either as it was in fact or as it appears in hostile fiction. The "close resemblance" boils down to the fact that there was some kind of initiation in the one instance and also in the other—which does not even begin to prove historical connections. In fact there is not the slightest evidence of Ismā'īlī influence in Anatolia at any time or in any sphere. The next parallel is quite fantastic. Are we to see traces of Qarmaṭian influence wherever there is a hatred of a foreign ruling class, or social messianism? The third argument: that the interconfessionalism of the guilds proves their Ismā'īlī origin, needs also no elaborate refutation, since we know now the Ismā'īlism was by no means such an "interconfessional" movement as its opponents chose to depict it in order to render it more odious.

It will have become clear, not only that the proofs adduced to support the theory about the Ismā'īlī origin of the guilds are worthless, but also that the theory was not reached at all by legitimate reasoning, but was a mere whim. Massignon was deeply interested in the organization of labour in modern Islamic countries, and also in Ismā'īlism, and linked his two interests by his reckless theory, nonchalantly waving aside his debt of proof with the words "les matériaux sont encore à réunir." Nor was the Ismā'īlī theory his last word on the subject: further wild speculations were put forward in later writings, speculations, this time, of such opacity of thought and expression that it is difficult to discuss them in a rational manner, and to try to disentangle the figments of an unbridled imagination, personal beliefs assuming the disguise of historical interpretation, and acrobatic non sequiturs, from the occasional flashes of insight.[24]

---

[24] The principal statement of the new doctrine about the origins of the guilds was published in 1952 in *La Nouvelle Clio*, pp. 171 ff. under the title "La 'futuwwa' ou 'pacte d'honneur artisanal' entre les travailleurs musulmans au Moyen Age", and republished in *Opera Minora*, i, 396 ff. The sentence about the date of the rise of the guilds, which I quote below, is on p. 401 of the reprint.

A central theological concept of Massignon was the notion of the "Abrahamic religions". This was propped up by a series of curious embroideries on such themes as Fāṭima, the *mubāhala*, Salmān the Persian, the legend of the Seven Sleepers—in which great erudition and great confusion are inextricably mixed together. The guilds were, however, not lost sight of—only that they had to accommodate themselves to the new preoccupations. It is no more the Qarmaṭians who created the guilds: according to the new dispensation "il faut donc admettre que la structure initiatique des corporations musulmanes est née à Madaïn, entre 636, date de sa conquête, et 733". How do we know this? Salmān al-Fārisī plays a great role in the later traditions of the *futuwwa*, that ideal moral and social code, which also provided ideals and ceremonies to the associations of the craftsmen. These traditions about Salmān al-Fārisī as one of the authorities of *futuwwa* appear in the texts late in the day, but according to Massignon "significant allusions to them are made by the historians from the ninth century on". It will cause no surprise to observe that no references are given. Massignon presumably means the initiation of the Ismā'īlīs, which has as we have seen nothing to do with the guilds nor has it to do with the *futuwwa* or Salmān. Now "the Ismā'īlī conspiracy goes back at least to the year 733–749, a time when it was already split into two rival initiations". He refers to the early sects connected with Ismā'īl, son of the Iman Ja'far al-Ṣādiq, in the second/eighth century, which in my opinion can in any case not be equated with the Ismā'īlī movement as it emerged in the middle of the third/ninth century. Secondly, we have seen that there is in any case no evidence that the Ismā'īlīs had anything to do with the rise of the guilds. Thirdly, that curious *terminus ad quem* for the rise of the guilds deserve a few words. Salmān plays a role (or rather, it is asserted that he plays a role) in Ismā'īlī and the Khaṭṭābī sects, which came into being round A.D. 740. Salmān is honoured (centuries later) as the patron of the guilds. Ergo: the guilds came into being before 733–749. From all this false reasoning one point ought to be singled out: the supposed rule, that if something is common to two movements, it can be dated before the separation of the movements—an argument used by Massignon with predilection for dating phenomena. Rejection of Marxism is common to Catholics and Protestants: therefore the terminus ante quem of Marxism is the Reformation. Some Jewish philosophers of the later Middle Ages are aware of Thomistic philosophy: therefore the terminus ante quem of Thomas of Aquino is the first century A.D. Some Shī'ite Ṣūfīs, as some Sunnite ones, follow the doctrine of Ibn 'Arabī: therefore the terminus ante quem of Ibn 'Arabī is the first century A.H. But let us put an end to the discussion of this tissue of fallacies: it is distressing to find that the later theories of Massignon about the guilds, no less than the earlier ones, have found believers.[25]

I consider it necessary to give a detailed criticism of Massignon's theories, which were generally accepted. When I originally wrote my refutation, I could not trace any contradictor excepting Nallino who has published his brief *caveat* in an out-of-the-way article of the Italian Encyclopaedia. But while I was writing my piece, two others scholars expressed their disagreement. S. D. Goitein,[26] in his study of the life of the artisans in Islam as they appear in the papers preserved in the Geniza (tenth to thirteenth centuries), points out that while it is fashionable to talk about Muslim guilds, "it has yet to be shown that they were in existence during the eleventh and twelfth centuries. While reading the relevant article about the subject (Ṣinf) in the Encyclopaedia of Islam, one realizes that it does not provide a single real proof of their activities prior to the thirteenth century." What he says about the evidence of the Geniza is of particular value:

Scrutinizing the records of the Cairo Geniza or the Muslim handbooks of market supervision contemporary with them, one looks in vain for an Arabic equivalent of the term "guild". There was no such word, because there was no such institution. The supervision of the quality of the artisans' work was in the hands of the state police, which availed itself of the services of trustworthy and expert assistants. In the case of professions which either required highly specialized knowledge such as that of the physicians, or were particularly exposed to fraud or other transgressions of the law, the appointment of a "reliable, trustworthy man from their own profession" is recommended in order to secure proper service. The whole tenor of the books on market supervision, as well as the very recommendation just mentioned, prove that the artisans were not organized in corporations of their own which fulfilled the task of upholding professional standards. It is noteworthy that the most detailed work on market supervision from this period recommends the appointment of special supervisors or heads for only a very small fraction of the many professions treated. In the Geniza, too, the ʿarīf, as such a chief was called, appears only very rarely and then, unfortunately, without an indication of the group headed by him.... Regarding apprenticeship and admission to a profession, no formalities and rigid rules are to be discovered in our sources.... Had there existed rigid grades of initiation into a profession, as was the case in the European guilds, the police handbooks referred to could not have failed to treat such an important subject. Their silence proves that there was no fixed system in this matter at all.... The protection of the local industries from competition by new-comers and outsiders is richly documented by the Geniza records, but nowhere do we hear about a professional corporation fulfilling this task.... The fourteenth century was the heyday of Muslim corporations, especially in Anatolia ..., which adopted the doctrines and ceremonies of Muslim mystic

[25] L. Gardet, *La cité musulmane*, Paris 1954, pp. 259–60.

[26] *Studies in Islamic History and Institutions*, Leiden 1966, pp. 267 ff.

brotherhoods. One looks in vain for similar combinations of artisanship and religious cult in the period and the countries discussed in this paper.

Secondly, though originally he intended to speak on a different subject, Professor Cahen finally decided to deal in his communication to the colloquium with the problem of guilds in the early Islamic period. Thus unexpectedly we discussed the same subject, and if we came to similar negative conclusions about the existence of guilds, both of us, moreover, coinciding with the views of Goitein, this convergence of the results reached by three people who thought about the same subject independently from each other, is in itself of some value. I have decided to retain in my paper the section on the guilds for this reason, but also because a dissection of the historical argumentation employed by Massignon (which was not undertaken by Goitein, and only briefly by Cahen) is needed, also as a caution against succumbing to similar reasoning elsewhere—by Massignon or others. I have concentrated on the criticism of certain aspects of Massignon's method, and the reader may find it interesting to compare Cahen's discussion with mine—the two are complementary.

We must then make *tabula rasa* of the theories of Massignon and start again. The earliest texts—as far as known at present—about the organization of craftsmen are the references in twelfth-century treatises of the *ḥisba* both in the East and in Spain to foremen of trades (the Arabic terms are *'arīf, amīn, muqaddam*) responsible to the *muḥtasib* for the carrying out by the tradesmen under him of the *muḥtasib's* orders.[27] Similar evidence is also forthcoming from the Mamlūk period, and in fact the role of the foremen (by whichever names they go) as assistants of the various

---

[27] For Spain see al-Saqaṭī, *Un Manuel hispanique de ḥisba*, ed. G.-S. Colin and E. Lévi-Provençal, p. 9 ll. 8–11, p. 43 l. 5, p. 45 l. 21, p. 48 l. 3, p. 56 l. 8, p. 59 ll. 18 and 21, p. 61 l. 13; Ibn 'Abdūn, *Journal asiatique*, 1934, p. 233; for the East, al-Shayzarī, *Nihāyat al-Rutba*, pp. 12, 72 (cf. Ashtor, *Rivista degli Studi Orientali*, 1958, p. 186), and the passages from various historians quoted by Ashtor, *RSO*, 1956, p. 86. *'Arīfs* of some professions are mentioned, though rarely, also in the original documents preserved in the Geniza; see Goitein, *Studies in Islamic History and Institutions*, p. 268: " It is noteworthy that the most detailed work on market supervision from this period recommends the appointment of special supervisors or heads for only a very small fraction of the many professions treated. In the Geniza, too, the *'arīf*, as such a chief was called, appears only very rarely and then, unfortunately, without an indication of the group headed by him. A Geniza document mentioning a contribution by the *'arīf al-naqqādīn*, or chief of the money assayers, is from the thirteenth century ". (For evidence Goitein refers to his forthcoming book *A Mediterranean Society*, ch. ii(2), notes 13–15.) I wonder, however, whether we may conclude with certainty that only select crafts had *'arīfs*. Ibn Abdūn demands that each craft should have an *amīn*—though this may be, as Goitein says, a " pious wish ".

delegates of the government (such as the *muḥtasib*) is a constant factor in the history of the organization of the crafts and trades in Islam. There is no reason to doubt that such government supervision of craftsmen through representatives appointed to the leadership of the various crafts goes back to times before traces of the practice first appear in the texts. It is also natural to assume that members of the same craft, especially as they tended to congregate in the same part of the market,[28] were led by their common interests to associate however loosely in some or other form. Nor is it giving too free a rein to one's fancy to assume that the traditions of the crafts go back to the earliest Islamic epoch and beyond. The practices of a given craft—say of the coppersmiths or the weavers—in an old city were hardly changed overnight by its passing from Roman to Muslim domination, nor even by the conversion of the craftsmen to Islam. In the Roman Empire the crafts and trades were organized into associations (called *collegia* and other names), the chief purpose of which was to allow the government as close a control of the working population as possible. There were ups and downs in the history of this system: at times it weighed heavily on those subjected to it, who and whose children were not allowed to leave their trade—such a compulsory and hereditary adherence to the associations facilitating government supervision and taxation. But whether tightly or more loosely organized, the guilds existed for the sake and the purpose of the government. It must be admitted that our knowledge of the state of affairs at the moment of the Arab conquest is very scanty. We have a study which purports to show the survival of the guilds in Egypt up to the time of the Arab invasion. (Our documentation for Egypt is, of course, thanks to the survival of papyri, more extensive than that for other provinces.) The evidence

[28] For the antecedents of this system in Antiquity see Monneret de Villard, *Introduzione allo studio dell' archeologia islamica*, pp. 147–56. In addition, we may recall the theory of A. Boëthius, according to whom the Hellenistic practice, which survived in Islam, was to have a central market area, while in contrast the western Roman practice, inherited by medieval Europe, was to have shops all over the city; see his *Roman and Greek Town Architecture*, Göteborg 1948, especially p. 17; " Urbanism in Italy ", *Acta Congressus Madvigiani*, Copenhagen 1958, iv, 92. An early 'Abbāsid governor of Ifrīqiya assigned to the various crafts separate parts of the market of Kairouan, Ibn 'Idhārī, i, 78. Ibn 'Abdūn strongly recommends that each craft should be concentrated in a separate place (*Journal asiatique*, 1934, p. 233, transl. Lévi-Provençal, p. 94). The topographical description " Street of such-and-such Craftsmen " is of course well known from all parts of the Islamic world in all periods. Goitein, however, shows that the topographical concentration of the crafts, though it facilitated the supervision of the craftsmen by the authorities, was by no means strictly imposed and gives many examples of shops of craftsmen situated in the " wrong " place (*Studies in Islamic History and Institutions*, pp. 258–60).

mainly consists of references to various trades, or groups of various kinds of tradesmen. There is not much said about their organization, but significantly there are references to chiefs of various crafts.[29] (From Byzantium we possess the tenth-century *Book of Prefect* with regulations for the crafts and professions of Constantinople, regulations the aim of which is to ensure government control which is exercised by the prefect of the city.) There is, therefore, a strong presumption that the state of affairs found by the Muslim conquerors in the provinces of the Byzantine empire was similar—only that it is likely that the disruption of Byzantine administration caused by the Persian war in the course of which Syria and Egypt were occupied by the Persians, relaxed the efficiency of government control. A hypothesis, which, bridging the gap between late Antiquity and the twelfth century, postulates the continuation of the ancient traditions, is attractive, but it would be much more satisfactory if, instead of being reduced to mere speculation, we were in possession of textual evidence for the ways in which the crafts and trades were organized in the early Islamic centuries. Finally, it seems to me that this form of organization of which we catch a glimpse in the later Middle Ages—the organization of crafts for the sake of government supervision—remains valid also subsequently, till modern times; this is the impression given by the numerous studies devoted to the guilds in more modern times. It is true, however, that in the later Middle Ages the organization of the crafts seem to become more articulate, especially by adopting the ideology of the *futuwwa*.[30] There is a large and valuable literature on the subject, though there is still place for comparative and historical treatment, since the development of the internal arrangements within the guild and other questions of a historical nature (for example the role of the Ottomans in the spreading of particular phenomena) are still obscure. These details are, however, not of immediate relevance for our problem.

If we take a quick look at the guilds of Western Europe, which appear from the eleventh century on, we notice that in a way there is a similarity between them and the Islamic (and Roman) associations. It is true that

[29] A. Stöckle, *Spätrömische und byzantinische Zünfte*, Leipzig 1911, pp. 136–7, cf. also the references to chiefs of crafts on pp. 88–9. A. E. R. Boak, " The Organization of Gilds in Greco-Roman Egypt ", *Transactions of the American Philological Association*, 1937, pp. 212 ff., discusses the rare references (in earlier documents) to *nomoi*, or laws which regulated the organization of guild associations; it is characteristic of the loose organization of the Islamic crafts that no such laws existed in the Islamic period—just as no city laws did.

[30] It is emphasized by Cahen (below, pp. 52, 62) that the state of affairs seems to change the later period and that they should not be simply projected back into the earlier one.

they seem to have come into being as voluntary associations, distinguished by economic, religious and charitable aims.

> But, important as it was, association alone was not sufficient to bring about the formation of the crafts. A large part was also played by the public authority or authorities. The regulative character which had dominated the whole economic legislation of the Roman Empire did not disappear with the fall of the latter. It is still clearly recognisable, even in the agricultural period of the Middle Ages, in the control exercised by the kings and feudal powers over weights and measures, coinages, tolls, and markets. When the artisans began to move into the nascent towns the castellans or the mayors who were established there naturally required them to submit to their authority. . . . It was inevitable that this early industrial regulation should be increasingly absorbed and then perfected by communal authority, at the time of the formation of the urban constitutions. . . . Now, it was obviously impossible to enact laws relating to products without including the producers, since the only means of ensuring the good quality of the former was to supervise the latter. The most efficaceous way of doing this was to form them into groups according to professions and subject them to the control of the municipal authority. Thus the spontaneous tendency which drove the artisans into corporations was reinforced by the interests of administrative control.[31]

The religious and social functions of the European guilds have their parallels in the Islamic world, where the crafts gradually come under the influence of religious ideals and adopt elements of the *futuwwa*; just as in Europe the guilds have their patron saints, so do the Islamic crafts tend to chose for themselves saintly patrons. Also the internal divisions between masters, apprentices and journeymen have parallels in the Islamic crafts, though one would like to know more about the history of this system, mainly observed in modern times. There are, however great differences. The economic policy of monopolism, so closely connected with the guild system in Europe, seems to be less prominent in the Islamic guilds—although a more reasoned assessment must wait for a closer study of the economic history of Islam. What is more relevant to our subject—the Islamic crafts show a much less institutional organization than that developed by the European guilds. While in a number of cities the guilds have never thrown off the supervision of municipal control, in the cities of the Netherlands, Northern France, the Rhineland, Italy, the " artisan associations claimed an autonomy which often involved them in disputes, not only with authority but also with one another. From the first half of the thirteenth century, they demanded the right of self-government, of meeting to discuss their concerns, of possessing a bell and a seal, and even of sharing the government of the town with the rich

---

[31] H. Pirenne, *Histoire économique de l'Occident médiéval*, 1951, pp. 321–2; see the whole discussion, from p. 318 on, with bibliography. The quotation after the English translation, *Economic and Social History of Medieval Europe*, London 1958, pp. 181–2.

merchants in whose hand it was centralized. In the course of the fourteenth century, they were successful in obtaining, although not everywhere, the right to nominate their own *doyens* and *jurés*, to be recognized as a political body and to share authority with the *haute bourgoisie.*"[32] Nothing like this happened in Islam: whatever picture we make of their history, the craft organizations never assumed a proper corporative form, any more than did civic organizations. Here again, one can summarize the development by saying that in the later Islamic period there was a groping towards the evolution of guilds, but that the process never reached the final stage as it did in medieval Europe.[33]

THE ABSENCE IN ISLAM OF CORPORATIONS IN GENERAL

I should like to put forward the idea that one of the striking differences between the society of medieval western Christendom and Islamic society was this: that whereas in the former all sorts of corporate institutions proliferated, in the latter they were entirely absent. The propensity to organize institutions in the form of corporations was not in the West something primeval, but arose, if I am not mistaken, sometime about the eleventh century. I am not competent to give a reasoned account of this development or to try to determine its causes, but shall perhaps not stray too far from the mark if I suggest that the example of the religious orders with their highly developed constitutions had a great deal to do with this; a secondary factor may be the existence in Roman law of the idea of legal associations and juridical persons. At any rate, wherever we turn in the Middle Ages after the eleventh century, we find new institutions organizing themselves in the form of corporations. In the cathedrals the chapters are organized, in order to elect their bishops. In the cities there arise the guilds, and the communes, with their corporate existence and elected officers. In the twelfth century a number of the more important schools begin to constitute themselves into corporations or *universitates*, and thus we have the universities—again with their elected officers. The contrast with the state of affairs in Islamic civilization is striking. Let us take the last example, that of the schools. Also in the Islamic world, the period

---

[32] Pirenne, English transl. p. 185.

[33] This makes abundantly clear why it was utterly wrong to toy with the idea (Massignon, " Les corps de métier ", pp. 487–9 = *Opera Minora*, i, 381–4) that the Islamic " guilds " gave rise to the European guilds.

from the eleventh century on was one in which the schools thrived and the new institution of the *madrasa* conquered one province after the other. The novelty in the *madrasa* was precisely that it substituted for the teaching by individual, private, masters an organized college with endowed chairs. If there were in Islamic civilization a trend towards corporations, the time would have been ripe for something like the contemporary university in the Latin West. However, no such development took place and the *madrasa* remained an institution which is typologically akin to the state-endowed schools of Antiquity and Byzantium rather than to the Western universities. By the way, I think this makes it quite clear how absurd is the attempt made by Julián Ribera to ascribe the rise of the western university to the Muslim *madrasa*,[34] an attempt which received the short shrift it deserved from the hands of the historians of the medieval universities.

Or again, let us take the mystical orders in Islam, the Ṣūfī *ṭarīqas*, which developed in the later Middle Ages. It would be obviously false for many reasons to assimilate them to the religious orders of Christianity. Nevertheless, it seems to me instructive to reflect on the contrast between the organization of the two types of orders. How different is the position of the shaykh of a *zāwiya* from that of an abbot, the government—or rather the absence of government—of a *ṭarīqa* from the governments of a western religious order!

This lack of all attempt at organizing the old or the new institutions in corporate forms also applies to the life of the cities. I have dealt with the organization of the market and tried to show that there is no evidence for the existence of anything resembling the western guilds. In the light of my suggestion about the absence in Islam of the idea of corporation in general, I think it becomes clearer why it should have become difficult for guilds to arise: there was no tradition of corporate life for the tradesmen to imitate. In the same way the rudiments of civic autonomy which existed also in the Islamic world could not develop into real municipal corporate institutions.

If we turn to the best textbook which we have on Islamic law to find out what it has to say on the legal status of corporations, we do find a chapter on juridical persons, namely the estate of a deceased person, the pious endowment (*waqf*), the public treasury—but these were all the legal persons known to Islamic law. In fact, the author after enumerating the

---

[34] Again, just the most characteristic specific property of the University is missing in Islam—just as in the case of the guilds. Massignon (loc. cit. above p. 47 note 33) parallels the influence of the Islamic guilds in Europe with that of the Islamic " universities ".

juridical persons as known to Roman law: municipalities and corporations of craftsmen, patrimonies temporarily without owner (such as the estates of deceased persons), charitable foundations—says expressly: " Muslim jurists do not know—and that is easy to understand if we think of the political and social differences between the Islamic state and those of the Roman type—neither the juridical personality of municipalities, nor of that of collectives of persons such a guilds ".[35]

It seems that this prolification of corporations is a particular characteristic of medieval western civilization, so that the lack of it cannot be used as a specific characterization of Islamic civilization, since this lack it shares with most other civilizations. (Ancient Greco-Roman civilization also knew corporate institutions, though not quite to the same degree as western European civilization.) Nevertheless I think it is useful to point out this contrast. Western European and Islamic civilizations were limitrophous, and it is important to realize that the frontier between them divided areas with sharply divided forms of social organization. It was due to not realizing the contrast that led scholars to assume influences of Islamic institutions on European institutions in which the corporate organization was the really characteristic feature. Such theories had to be rejected also for other reasons—but now we realize that Islam knew no corporations, it becomes obvious in any case that it could not have given birth to European corporate institutions.

Thus it is not entirely unwarranted that—apart from the city life of Antiquity, to which Islam succeeded—I have chosen for comparison Western Europe. To be sure, it would be also instructive to compare the Islamic institutions also with those of yet other civilizations. (J. Gernet's description of the Chinese city can lead to interesting meditations.) But I hope that even my more limited comparisons will have served the purpose of clearing the air. I may have used too much the *via negationis* and tried to establish what is absent in the Islamic city, rather than seeking out what there is and describe positively its characteristic. I left this task to the specialists who spoke after me. It may perhaps be said that it was not entirely superfluous to delimit at the beginning the scope of our discussions. We had in our midst students of various civilizations in addition to us Islamists, and they—especially the students of classical Antiquity or of the European Middle Ages—might have expected us to discuss such topics which they are accustomed to discuss in connection with the cities which they study: the magistrates of the cities; the city laws; the

[35] D. Santillana, *Istituzioni di diritto musulmano malichita*, i, 170–1.

various forms of privileges bestowed upon cities and so on and so forth. For them—but also for ourselves—it might have been instructive to realize with full consciousness that there is nothing really to discuss under such headings when we talk of the cities of the Islamic world.

Y A-T-IL EU DES CORPORATIONS PROFESSIONNELLES DANS LE MONDE MUSULMAN CLASSIQUE?

Quelques notes et réflexions

par

C. Cahen

Existe-t-il des corporations professionelles dans le monde musulman classique, aux quatre ou cinq premiers siècles de l'Hégire? Deci-delà on trouve des propositions sommaires qui donnent l'impression qu'on répond en général à cette question plus ou moins implicitement comme si l'affirmative allait de soi; mais jamais elle n'a fait l'objet d'une véritable étude. Le seul exposé d'ensemble sérieux qui ait été consacré aux corporations professionnelles musulmanes en général est celui d'un collègue jeune qui à l'époque était encore de 28 ans plus jeune, Bernard Lewis; il y dégage, avec la clarté que nous lui avons toujours connue depuis, l'état de la science en 1937;[1] mais je ne crois pas me tromper en disant que, pour les premiers siècles, il se réfugie avec une nuance de réserve derrière l'autorité de quelques grands maîtres, en particulier Massignon, sans avoir pu, et, nous le verrons, pour cause, leur emprunter des indications documentaires comme la suite de l'article en contient. A vrai dire, c'est surtout Massignon en effet qui a parlé de corporations professionnelles dès cette époque;[2] mais le respect dû à la mémoire d'un homme qui fut grand n'oblige pas à considérer qu'il ait eu sur toutes choses un jugement également sûr ni bien informé.

Pour reprendre la question, il est, je crois, d'abord indispensable de la bien préciser, car peut-être l'insuffisance de la réponse jusqu'ici donnée provient-elle pour une part d'une relative confusion dans la manière de la poser. Les précisions nécessaires portent, je crois, sur les points essentiels suivants:

---

[1] Bernard Lewis, " Islamic Guilds ", dans *Economic History Review*, viii (1937).

[2] Louis Massignon a exposé allusivement ses idées dans de nombreux articles consacrés à des sujets divers, parmi lesquels nous détacherons spécialement: " Guilds (Mohammedan) ", dans *Encyclopaedia of Social Sciences*, éd. Séligman, 1931. " Ṣinf ", dans *Encyclopédie de l'Islam*, lère éd., iv, 1935. " La futuwwa ou pacte d'honneur artisanal entre les travailleurs musulmans du Moyen Age ", dans *La Nouvelle Clio* 1952. Voir aussi la note suivante.

1. Nous traitons des premiers siècles; à la fin de la période que nous appelons Moyen Age, et aux temps modernes, il existe dans la plupart des pays musulmans une certaine organisation professionnelle corporative: bien des traits en restent à discuter et interpréter, mais la tendance n'est pas contestable.[3] La question que nous avons à nous poser est donc de savoir si ce qu'on trouve alors existait auparavant, ou si nous sommes devant le résultat d'une évolution qu'il faudrait alors déterminer et comprendre.

2. Nous parlons d'organisations professionnelles, c'est-à-dire dont la profession forme le cadre. Personne ne conteste qu'il existe dans la période que nous considérons des organisations corporatives, et nous en reparlerons tout-à-l'heure à propos de la *futuwwa*; la question est de savoir si, quels qu'en soient les membres, et même si individuellement la plupart exercent des professions, c'est la profession qui définit et constitue les cadres de certaines d'entre elles, ou si elles sont bâties sur d'autres bases.

3. Nous parlons de corporations. Personne ne conteste que le monde musulman, dès l'époque que nous envisageons, a connu quelque forme d'organisation professionnelle. La question est de savoir jusqu'à quel point, et surtout s'il s'agit d'organisation corporative, c'est-à-dire consistant en associations spontanées encadrant plus ou moins largement la vie de leurs adhérents, ou si nous avons affaire à des organismes émanant de l'appareil administratif étatique.

Je résume donc: existe-t-il dans les ages dits classiques de l'Islam des associations privées à base et à rôle professionnels, ou, réciproquement, l'organisation professionnelle est-elle à base d'associations privées spontanées?

La question, historiquement, n'est pas arbitraire. On sait que le Bas-Empire Romain avait développé sous le nom de "collèges" des organismes professionnels à caractère intensément étatique.[4] Bien qu'une certaine évolution en ait libéralisé la rigueur, ce sont toujours des organismes d'Etat que nous présente l'Empire Byzantin, héritier de Rome, au

---

[3] Il n'est évidemment pas question de donner ici de bibliographie. On la trouvera, jusqu'en 1923, dans L. Massignon, *Enquête sur les Corporations musulmanes . . . au Maroc*, dans *Revue du Monde Musulman*, lviii (1924), 256 pp., et on pourra la compléter par la bibliographie méthodique des *Abstracta Islamica*, dirigée par le même, dans la *Revue des Etudes Islamiques*. Voir infra p. 54 note 9.

[4] Bibliographie et exposé de base dans *Histoire Générale du Travail*, éd. L. H. Parias, i, v chap. 3–4 et p. 381. La documentation non-papyrologique reste encore à peu près celle qu'a rassemblée J. P. Waltzing, *Etude historique sur les corporations professionnelles chez les Romains*, 5 vols. 1885–1900.

Xe siècle où, grâce au document connu sous le nom de Livre du Préfet, nous pouvons le mieux les connaître: c'est-à-dire que, sans parler de quelques métiers directement constitués dans le cadre de l'Etat, les autres, bien que composés de particuliers libres, sont réglementés et contrôlés par l'Etat.[5] Il semble bien qu'en Europe occidentale aussi, en tous cas en Italie, jusqu'au XIe siècle, dans la mesure où existaient par endroits quelques métiers groupant un nombre suffisant de membres, c'est encore cette forme d'organisation qui ait prévalu en général.[6] On sait par contre que dans la deuxième moitié du Moyen Age il s'y est développé des corporations privées puissantes. Il n'est pas sans intérêt pour l'histoire comparée de préciser en passant que, contrairement à l'opinion ancienne qui voyait dans ces corporations la source des communes, on constate maintenant que c'est au sein des communes, formées en dehors de toute base professionnelle, que se sont ensuite constituées et délimitées des corporations professionnelles.[7] Commune et corporation sont l'une et l'autre issues de l'insuffisance de l'organisation étatique, et ont décliné à mesure du développement des Etats modernes. Telles qu'on a pris l'habitude de se les représenter d'après cette expérience de l'histoire, les corporations professionnelles sont donc des associations privées groupant tous les maîtres d'un métier, en réglant elles-mêmes l'exercice, et encadrant, même en dehors de la vie professionnelle stricto sensu, un certain nombre d'activités de leurs membres, surtout de l'ordre de la religion et de l'entraide. Pour Massignon, il y aurait eu dans l'Islam, depuis le Xe siècle, des corporations plus ou moins réductibles à ce type, et elles auraient même exercé une influence sur celles de la Chrétienté, qu'elles précèdent dans le temps. Laissant de côté cette dernière hypo-

---

[5] Le meilleur exposé me parait rester encore celui que donne Gunnar Mickwitz aux chapitre vii et viii de son livre *Die Kartellfunktionen der Zünfte* . . . , Helsingfors 1936. Bibliographie à jour p. 293 de Speros Vryonis, " Byzantine Dèmokratia and the Guilds in the XIth Century", dans *Dumbarton Oaks Papers*, xvii/1963 note 13 (cf. infra p. 61 note 30).

[6] C'est sur l'Italie, en raison des continuités institutionnelles et de son appartenance au même monde méditerranéen qu'une partie du monde musulman et que Byzance, qu'il faut avant tout porter les yeux; dans celle du sud, restée byzantine, la continuité est naturelle, mais elle apparait même dans la bonne documentation que nous avons par exemple, pour la capitale impériale de Pavie dans le nord, dans les *Honorantiæ civitatis Papiæ* (XIe s.), éd. dans *Monumenta Germaniæ Historica*, xxx/2, pp. 1450–7.

[7] Cela est particulièrement visible aux origines des communes italiennes, encore une fois, mais parait vrai aussi de la grande majorité des communes de l'Europe Occidentale septentrionale.

thèse,[8] c'est le bienfondé de la première que nous devons maintenant éprouver.

Malheureusement, Massignon n'a nullepart explicitement développé tout son raisonnement, et la reconstitution que j'en propose est elle-même peut-être hypothétique. Je crois qu'on peut le résumer ainsi: aux temps modernes, il existe un certain type de corporations professionnelles qu'attestent en particulier pour la Constantinople ottomane Evliyā Tchelebi dès le XVIIe siècle, et divers documents damasquins, marocains etc. pour le XIXe et le début du XXe, jusqu'à l'avènement du syndicalisme.[9] Ces corporations, if faut bien qu'elles soient venues de quelque part—cette formule, je la tiens personnellement de sa bouche même. Ce quelque part, c'est le milieu musulman proche-oriental des alentours de l'an 300 de l'hégire, 900 de l'ère chrétienne. Pourquoi? Parce qu'à l'époque moderne, il y a souvent des liens entre corporation professionnelle et *futuwwa*, et que le mouvement connu sous ce dernier nom apparait en pleine lumière vers ce temps-là; parce que cette *futuwwa*, telle qu'on la connait avec plus de détail un peu plus tard, présente, dans ses rites d'association, des parentés avec l'ismā'īlisme, la doctrine politico-religieuse qui était justement en plein essor au début du IV/Xe siècle; et qu'on constate un particulier intérêt de l'ismā'īlisme pour le travail manuel et les artisans. En somme Massignon tire parti de convergences elles-mêmes d'ailleurs à la fois larges et partielles, entre trois catégories d'organisations qu'il considère sub specie aeternitalis, combinant des caractères qu'il leur connait en des temps récents avec le fait établi de leurs débuts éloignés. Je ferai, sur cet ensemble de raisonnement, les remarques suivantes:

1. S'il est évident qu'en matière d'histoire économique et sociale on ne peut s'enfermer dans des limites chronologiques aussi étroites et précises qu'en matière d'histoire évènementielle, il est cependant d'une

[8] Massignon la formule dans son article " Les corps de métiers et la cité islamique ", dans *Revue internationale de Sociologie*, xxviii (1920), 473–88, mais ne l'a pas reformulée depuis lors. Elle est, sauf cas très spécial, insoutenable.

[9] Voir n. 2 et 3 supra. Pour Damas, voir spécialement la *Notice sur les corporations de Damas*, d'Elias Qudsi, publiée par Carlo Landberg dans les Actes du Vie Congrès des Orientalistes, Leiden 1885, vol. ii; le précieux et encore trop peu connu *Dictionnaire des Métiers Damasquins* d'al-Qāsimī (même période, mais publié seulement en 1960, La Haye-Mouton, 2 vols.), important pour les techniques, l'est beaucoup mois pour l'organisation sociale.—Pour l'Empire Ottoman, consulter le livre important de R. Mantran, *Istanbul dans la seconde moitié du XVIIe siècle*, Paris 1962, ii, chap. 4, et H. A. R. Gibb et Harold Bowen, *Islamic Society and the West*, i, chap. 6, 1950.—Pour le Maroc, après l'*Enquête* . . . de Massignon, la belle monographie de R. Le Tourneau sur *Fès*, 1949.—Pour l'Egypte, le beau livre récent de Gabriel Baer, *Egyptian Guilds in Modern Times*, Jerusalem 1964.

mauvaise méthode d'enjamber les siècles comme si rien ne s'y transformait. L'expérience de certains peut aider à dresser le questionnaire que l'on applique à l'enquête sur d'autres, mais non conduire à leur affecter a priori des caractères qu'il s'agit précisément de découvrir. La notion qu'un certain type d'organisation doit nécessairement dériver d'un précédent est elle-même fallacieuse et n'explique rien; chaque société se forme les organisations qui lui conviennent et ne conserve celles de son passé, compte tenu de la durée de certaines routines, qu'autant qu'elles s'attachent encore à des besoins présents. On peut tirer un enseignement de la pérennité de certains traits, mais non poser en hypothèse que pour exister un jour, ils ont besoin d'être nés l'avant-veille.

2. Cela dit, il est bien certain que l'on ne peut maintenir à peu près aucun des éléments du schéma général de Massignon. Il est vrai qu'à partir de la fin du Moyen Age il se produit un certain recouvrement de la structure professionnelle par la *futuwwa*, du moins dans le domaine irano-turc;[10] mais rien n'indique que ce recouvrement soit ancien, et non le résultat d'une évolution: quelle que soit la place qu'occupent dans des organisations populaires anciennes de *futuwwa* des gens exerçant diverses professions, tout donne l'impression au contraire qu'à cette époque ils y sont groupés indépendamment de leurs métiers particuliers et que la *futuwwa* n'interfère en rien avec l'activité propre de leur travail.[11] Cela n'a d'ailleurs rien pour surprendre un occidental: il est bien établi maintenant que les groupements qui dans les villes du Moyen Age naissant s'occupaient de religion et d'entraide[12] étaient en général constitués en dehors de toute base professionnelle. Il y a, pour l'Islam, un problème du rapprochement entre *futuwwa* et profession à partir d'un certain moment (et en Orient seulement), mais il n'y a pas interconnexion originelle.

3. L'idée d'un intérêt spécifique des ismā'īliens pour les artisans tombe également, semble-t-il, assez à faux. Massignon l'étaie sur la constatation plus générale du caractère socialement revendicateur de certaines branches du mouvement ismā'īlien, sur l'idée plus vague d'une parenté entre certaines de leurs formes d'organisation et celles de la *futuwwa*, sur quelques passages consacrés aux métiers manuels dans les *Rasā'il Ikhwān*

---

[10] Voir l'état actuel des questions dans la 2e partie de l'article " Futuwwa " dans l'*Encyclopédie de l'Islam*, 2e éd., par Taeschner (résumant et mettant au point en particulier les nombreux travaux antérieurs du même sur ce sujet, dont il est le principal spécialiste).

[11] J'ai insisté sur cet aspect des choses dans la première partie signée de moi, de l'article " Futuwwa " ci-dessus signalé, ainsi que dans mes " Mouvements populaires et autonomie urbaine dans l'Asie Musulmane au Moyen Age ", dans *Arabica* 1958–1959 (tiré à part, Leiden 1959).

[12] Et même, en un sens, jusqu'aux compagnonnages des temps modernes.

al-Ṣafā' et ailleurs, enfin sur un épisode de XIe siècle à Bagdad où l'on voit un émissaire ismā'īlien essayer de nouer des intelligences auprès d'un groupe de *futuwwa*;[13] et d'autre part, plus généralement, sur l'essor économique de l'Egypte fāṭimide. Mais rien de tout cela ne tient. L'intérêt de l'ismā'īlisme pour les métiers reste limité, théorique, et largement déduit de la littérature antique; les analogies d'organisation entre groupes plus ou moins paralégaux en une société donnée sont naturelles et, tant que rien n'en établit de particulière précision, n'autorisent aucune conclusion; l'épisode bagdadien, qui se situe dans le cadre momentané de la lutte entre Fāṭimides et Seldjūqides, ne prouve rien que pour lui même, et ce qui est au contraire frappant est, étant donné le détail avec lequel nous connaissons les manifestations de la *futuwwa* bagdadienne du Xe au XIIe siècle, combien il apparait comme exceptionnel et isolé. On ne peut déduire non plus aucune politique spécifiquement proartisanale de l'essor économique dans l'Egypte fāṭimide, dû à un ensemble de facteurs autrement larges et complexes.[14] A vrai dire, il n'y a aucun témoignage d'une particulière pénétration de l'ismā'īlisme dans les milieux artisanaux du Proche Orient. Les évènements connus nous le montrent influent dans certains milieux ruraux, voire parfois bédouins, en Iraq et en Iran, plus que dans la petit peuple urbain, qui à Bagdad était ḥanbalite; milieux ruraux dont Ibn Waḥshiyya, derrière lequel Massignon veut voir un " shī'ite extrêmiste ", avait dressé le bilan de civilisation traditionnelle face à la montée de l'islam urbain.

De toute façon, le raisonnement général ne peut suffire, et il nous faut pour progresser essayer de trouver une documentation directe. L'ennui est que, pour l'époque classique, elle parait extrêmement difficile à trouver.

Une parenthèse d'abord sur les Traités de *ḥisba*. La notion générale de *ḥisba* remonte assez haut dans l'Islam, mais il n'à été conservé et, selon toute apparence, composé de précis spécifique de *ḥisba*, j'entends: expliquant les devoirs techniques du *muḥtasib* et non seulement des principes généraux, qu'à partir de l'extrême fin du XIe siècle en Occident, de celle du XIIe en Orient (et encore en quelques pays seulement): répartition qui n'est peut-être pas fortuite, et peut correspondre à un renforcement d'organisation chez les Almoravides d'une part, les Ayyūbides de l'autre. Il existe depuis les débuts de l'Islam un *ṣāḥib al-sūq*, où l'on a voulu voir, ce qui est douteux à mon avis, un héritier de

---

[13] Ibn al-Djawzī *al-Muntaẓam*, éd. Hyderabad, viii 326; Sibt b. al-Djawzī, *Mir'āt az-Zamān*, an 473 (inédit); *Mouvements* pp. 44–5 (=*Arabica* 1959, pp. 42–3).

[14] Entièrement gratuite est l'affirmation parfois reproduite d'une destruction par les Ayyūbides de privilèges aux métiers donnés par les Fāṭimides.

l'agoranome antique, et qui, modifié dans sa signification religieuse, devient sous les 'Abbāsides le préposé à la *ḥisba*, le *muḥtasib*. Mais nous savons mal, concrètement, ce qu'étaient alors les activités du *muḥtasib*. Cependant, encore dans les Traités de *ḥisba*, il nous apparait fondamentalement comme un représentant de l'Autorité ou de la Justice, qui n'est nullepart confronté à une organisation corporative ni a fortiori n'en émane.[15] Ces Traités, même pour leur époque, ne peuvent donc nous servir à rien pour notre objet présent, sinon pour cette impression négative.

En dehors des Traités de *ḥisba*, nous sommes réduits au hasard des allusions rencontrées dans des œuvres de toute nature, et qu'aucun de nous ne peut évidemment prétendre de loin connaître toutes. Dans de telles conditions, ce que je peux apporter aujourd'hui n'a aucun caractère même provisoirement ferme, et ce que je peux seulement faire est de souhaiter que, sur la base d'un questionnaire établi dans la clarté, chacun au cours de ses lectures puisse noter les renseignements susceptibles d'élaborer peu à peu des réponses. Voici, à cette tâche, quelques contributions:

Nous connaissons très bien pour certaines villes, en particulier Bagdad, l'histoire au moins épisodique des troubles populaires. Or il est extrêmement rare—et pour Bagdad je n'en connais aucun cas—de rencontrer dans le récit de tels troubles l'intervention d'un quelconque groupement que l'on puisse qualifier de professionnel, même si certains participants se trouvent désignés par le nom de leur profession. Ce qui intervient, quand ce n'est pas la soldatesque, c'est la foule informe ou, quand il y a une organisation relative, la *futuwwa*; tout au plus nous dit-on que tel souq a été assailli, ou que les marchands ont, par peur, fermé boutique. Particulièrement remarquable est, à Bagdad dans la seconde moitié du IV/Xe siècle, le récit de deux émeutes suscitées à quelques années d'intervale par la prétention du gouvernement būyide d'introduire de nouveaux impôts sur l'industrie textile, plus spécialement la soierie, qui faisait vivre tant de Bagdadiens:[16] aucun mot dans le récit de ces émeutes ne fait allusion à l'intervention de quelque sorte que ce soit d'organisation des " soyeux " ni autres artisans du textile.

Les seuls exemples peut-être différents que je connaisse sont les suivants, très exceptionnels et peu clairs: en Arabie, selon al-Ṭabarī et

---

[15] Voir le résumé de ces questions dans l'article " *ḥisba* " de *l'Encyclopédie de l'Islam* 2e édition, par M. Talbi et moi-même.

[16] Abū Shudjā' al-Rudhrāwārī, continuation de Miskawayh, *Tadjārib al-Umam*, dans Margoliouth, *The Eclipse of the Abbasid Caliphate*, iii 71, et Hilāl al-Ṣābi, *Histoire*, ibid. 386.

al-Maqdisī, il y a des luttes entre factions diverses dont une entre tailleurs (ou marchands de blé) et bouchers, à La Mecque entre tenanciers de *ḥammāms* et marchands de sel, si le texte est valable, et à Zabīd au Yémen entre bouchers et Bédouins, sous la même réserve.[17] Mais jusqu'à quel point s'agit-il d'affaires professionnelles? Al-Maqdisī nous dit que les tailleurs sont shī'ites et les bouchers sunnites, et nous énumère sur la même lancée d'autres *'aṣabiyyāt* définies en termes tantôt religieux, tantôt ethniques etc. Bien entendu certaines oppositions de caractère apparemment idéologique peuvent en recouvrir d'autres, qui pourraient être professionnelles; mais les textes n'en disent rien, et nous sommes donc hors d'état de le préciser. Nous ne sommes guère plus avancés pour comprendre en quoi ont pu consister les combats dramatiques qui par deux fois, en 307/919 et 317/929 de l'hégire, à Mossoul opposèrent les marchands d'alimentation et les marchands d'étoffe flanqués des cordonniers,[18] ou, à Hérat en 6021/205—mais ici nous sommes déjà à plus basse époque—les artisans du fer et ceux du cuivre.[19] Je ne doute pas qu'on puisse relever quelques autres cas de ce genre—suggérant au moins un certain esprit de corps—mais il est impossible pour le moment d'aller plus loin à l'aide de cette catégorie de documents.

La littérature juridique nous apporte peut-être quelques autres enseignements utiles. Je ne pense pas qu'on puisse y relever nulle part aucun exposé consacré pour elle-même à aucune organisation corporative:[20] le Droit musulman ne veut connaître que des individus. Il y a néanmoins un chapitre du *fiqh*—particulièrement dans les recueils de *fatwās*—où l'on trouve une allusion intéressante, et, assez étrangement, c'est celui du Droit pénal, comme l'avait déjà vu il y près d'un siècle A. v. Kremer.[21] En cas de crime, le dédommagement dû met en jeu des solidarités de groupes qui sont normalement ceux de la famille (au sens large) ou de la tribu, dans la tradition arabe, et, pour ceux qui n'ont pas de tribu, le *dīwān* où ils sont inscrits, pour les soldats et les fonctionnaires, le groupe professionnel pour ceux qui en ont, et, quand il n'y a rien, l'Etat: ce

[17] Al-Maqdisī, p. 102; al-Ṭabarī, éd. De Goeje etc., p. 1909, au 262; cf. al-Fāsī dans Wüstenfeld, *Die Chroniken der Stadt Mekka*, ii, 198–9.

[18] Ibn al-Athīr, *Al-Kāmil*, éd. Tornberg, viii, 89 et 157.

[19] Ibn al-Athīr, xii, 136.

[20] Le *fiqh* interdit toute fondation *waqf* au bénéfice d'une catégorie professionnelle, celle-ci ne devant être constituée qu'au bénéfice des pauvres de cette catégorie (cela même se fait rarement); par le biais des fondations au bénéfice d'une mosquée, d'une madrasa, d'un hopital etc., on peut constituer un *waqf* au bénéfice de tous ceux qui y sont inclus professionnellement, mais non pas de la profession plus largement.

[21] *Kulturgeschichte des Islams*, ii, 187.

dernier cas, en fait, le plus couramment réalisé dans l'Etat ʿabbāside et ses héritiers. La mention du groupe professionnel implique évidemment pour lui la reconnaissance d'une certaine " personne morale "; la difficulté est, comme toujours avec le *fiqh*, de savoir dans quelle mesure le principe ainsi admis se trouve en fait appliqué. Schacht estime qu'il a en tous cas assez vite cessé de l'être.[22] Il se peut que certaines *fatwās* d'Asie Centrale à la veille de l'invasion mongole suggèrent une évolution contraire. Certains recueils de ce genre, en effet, à côté du cas général où la solidarité de profession ne joue pas, envisagent quelques exemples particuliers où elle peut jouer: les foulons et chaudronniers à Samarqand, les cordonniers à Isfīdjāb, les artisans du bois à Merv (on nous dit là incidemment qu'il en va de même pour eux en Adherbaydjan): dans ces métiers, nous dit-on, il existe une *nuṣra, yatanāṣarūna,* ce qui signifie sinon forcément une organisation professionnelle complète, du moins, dans le cadre de la profession, un système de secours mutuel et d'entraide, une solidarité de quelque forme.[23] Les précisions données ont l'intérêt de nous montrer à la fois que ce système n'est pas général, puisqu'on cite des cas où il existe, et de nous faire toucher avec ces cas peut-être l'amorce d'une évolution; à moins qu'il ne s'agisse, dans cette région, d'une survivance spécifique: je ne peux absolument rien dire pour en décider en ce moment.

Que peut-on chercher d'autres? J'avais placé des espoirs dans la littérature d'*adab*, la littérature religieuse, etc. et les dictionnaires: mon enquête est trop limitée pour que je puisse tirer argument du fait que je n'ai jusqu'ici rien trouvé. Les descriptions de fêtes, s'il y avait des corporations professionnelles tant soit peu reconnues, devraient, comme il arrive parfois à plus basse époque, leur faire quelque place; je n'en ai pas encore relevé de cas.[24] De quelques références fournies par Massignon résulte seulement l'existence assez ancienne d'une vénération pour Salmān, sans qu'on puisse préciser ni à quel titre ni en quel milieu.[25] On ne peut rien déduire du fait que certaines mosquées portent le nom d'un

---

[22] *Introduction to Islamic Law*, p. 186.

[23] *Fatwās* d'al-Walwalīdjī, Bibl. Nat. Paris arabe 4813, f° 169 v°; Qāḍī-Khān, *Fatwās*, Caire 1282, vol. iii (en marge des *Fatāwī ʿĀlamgīriyya*).

[24] La présence de marchands parmi les catégories de notables qui assistent à des réceptions de souverains ou d'ambassadeurs ou prêtent le serment de *bayʿa* prouve la considération sociale dont ils jouissent, mais ne nous apprend rien sur l'éventuelle existence d'une organisation corporative.

[25] Al-Samʿānī, *Ansāb*, 467a (sur Abū Aḥmad al-Qalānisī, un religieux qui, avec un grand marchand, va visiter le tombeau de Salmān); Ibn al-Fuwaṭī (le Calife en 643/1240 va sur la tombe de Mūsā b. Djaʿfar et sur celle de Salmān); encore Abū Nuʿaym al-Iṣfahānī, *Ḥulya*, x, 311.

métier, puisque c'est normalement aussi celui d'un quartier ou d'un souq. Rien non plus de ce que dans les relevés budgétaires apparaissent dans certaines provinces des prestations dûes par certains métiers, puisqu'on ne sait comment s'en faisait la levée.[26]

A vrai dire, les textes mentionnent parfois des *shaykhs* ou *ra'īs* des marchands d'étoffes, des grands marchands surtout voyageurs *tudjdjār*, des médecins, peut-être quelques autres cas. Mais ils ne nous apportent pas de précision sur les points qui nous importeraient le plus.[27] A l'époque des Traités de *ḥisba*, le *muḥtasib* a sous ses ordres, pour le seconder auprès de chaque métier, un spécialiste appelé en général *'arīf* en Orient et *amīn* en Occident.[28] Ce personnage est choisi, semble-t-il, dans la profession, et il est difficile qu'il ne jouisse pas d'une certaine confiance des membres de cette dernière, mais il n'en est pas moins présenté par les Traités comme l'agent du *muḥtasib* auprès d'eux plus que l'inverse. Nous voudrions savoir ce qu'il en était des personnages mentionnés à de plus hautes époques sous un nom de fonction ou un autre: c'est, pour le moment, un voeu pieux.

La seule chose qui apparaisse sûre est l'existence d'un certain esprit de corps, ou tout au moins d'un certain prix attaché à la profession, en ce sens que, pour tous les non-Arabes et plus largement pour tous ceux qui ne soulignent pas une appartenance tribale, le nom est en général accompanné d'un surnom qui désigne l'appartenance professionnelle. Le relevé des professions que l'on peut faire dans les innombrables dictionnaires de savants et lettrés[29] est peut être un peu trompeur, parce que les professions distinguées sont mieux avouées que les autres, et que les savants ne doivent pas se recruter également dans toutes; il n'en signifie pas moins qu'un grand nombre d'homme se définissent volentairement par la profession.

On a bien compris que nous ne doutons pas, bien entendu, de la

---

[26] Ni les papyrus égyptiens, ni les documents judéo-arabes de la Geniza du Caire n'apportent, à ma connaissance, de précision permettant de conclure à une organisation corporative où que ce soit.

[27] Il s'agit de toute manière de professions de type spécial, dont on ne pourrait rien conclure pour les autres. Mais il n'y a pas de doute que le chef des médecins est nommé par le Gouvernement et contrôlé par le *muḥtasib*, comme le sont les instituteurs etc. Les gros marchands d'étoffe *bazzāzūn* sont à certains égards différents des autres métiers, car il s'agit uniquement de commerçants en gros, qui ne sont pas artisans; l'étoffe est fabriquée pour eux par d'autres, comme dans toutes les sociétés médiévales du même niveau technico-social.

[28] Voir l'*Encyclopédie de l'Islam*, 2e éd., sous ces deux mots.

[29] Une thèse a été faite en ce sens à l'Université de Jérusalem, dont un résumé est sous presse pour le *Journal of the Social and Economic History of the Orient*.

réalité d'une certaine forme d'organisation professionnelle. Il y a une répartition topographique des métiers, il y a des règles qu'ils doivent respecter, il y a un usage qui concerne la condition des apprentis, des esclaves employés, etc. par rapport aux maîtres, et il y a le *muḥtasib* avec ses agents qui contrôle plus ou moins tout cela. Mais tout cela ne fait pas une corporation, et, si l'on ne peut rien conclure de ferme du silence peut-être provisoire des textes, on ne peut se défendre de l'impression que, tout de même, si l'on rencontre si peu la corporation, c'est qu'en effet elle existe fort peu, jusqu'à une époque plus basse que celle communément admise.

Historiquement cela signifierait que, grosso modo, le Proche Orient a vécu, à cet égard aussi, sur la lancée de la basse Antiquité, sans que la conquête arabe y ait changé grand'chose. L'ennui, pour la vérification de cette idée, est que nous savons fort mal où en était vraiment la condition des collèges professionnels dans les provinces asiatiques de l'Empire Byzantin ainsi qu'en Egypte, et dans l'Empire Perse Sāsānide; certains n'excluaient pas quelques formes d'organisation corporative combinée à une stricte règlementation étatique, et on ne peut juger exactement d'Antioche, par exemple, ou de Ctésiphon, a fortiori, d'après Constantinople.[30] On peut supposer que, dans les villes conquises par les Arabes, la chute de l'ancien Etat, que le nouveau n'a pu immédiatement remplacer tout à fait, a desserré le contrôle: mais en est-il résulté simplement une émancipation des particuliers, ou une tendance à la substitution de l'association privée au collège d'Etat? Tout ce que je peux dire est que la réorganisation rapide d'un régime étatisé a vraisemblablement freiné ce qui a pu momentanément se faire jour de telles tendances.

Quoi qu'il en soit, il parait évident qu'une corporation professionnelle musulmane, même si on en admet l'existence, ne peut correspondre pleinement à ce qu'ont été les corporations de l'Europe chrétienne à leur belle époque. Non seulement parce que l'emprise de l'Etat s'est toujours maintenue plus forte, et que par conséquent c'est lui qui exerce ou contrôle une bonne part des attributions réglementaires qu'elle monopolise ailleurs, mais plus profondément encore parce que l'étendue des pouvoirs que le Droit et l'usage reconnaissent à l'un comme à l'autre est beaucoup

[30] Pour l'Iran sāsānide, voir maintenant N. Pigulevskaya, *Les villes de l'Etat iranien*, trad. française 1963, 2e partie, chap. iv. Dans l'Empire Byzantin, ce qui était vivant était le régime des " dèmes ", qui ne sont pas à base professionnelle. Bibliographie au début de l'article de Sp. Vryonis, " Byzantine Dèmokratia and the Guilds in the XIth Cent. ", dans *Dumbarton Oaks Papers*, xvii/1963, article important mais où le mot " guilds " reste employé trop élastiquement.

plus limitée qu'en Occident. Sans parler même d'un éventuel rôle politique ou religieux, il parait difficile que ce soit la corporation, si elle existe, qui définisse les conditions d'adhésion (l'inscription sur les régistres de l'Etat est obligatoire), ni les modalités techniques d'exercice du métier, que contrôle le *muḥtasib*. A l'exception peut-être de conjurations tacites pour les prix alimentaires en cas de disette, ce n'est pas non plus la corporation, sous quelque forme que ce soit, qui fixe les prix; l'Etat n'y intervient de son côté que pour combattre l'accaparement dans ces conditions exceptionelles.

Par conséquent, quelle que soit la solution à laquelle nous aboutirons lorsque les enquêtes auront pu être conduites sur une documentation plus étendue, il restera toujours vrai que, comme l'a déjà noté le Professeur Gibb, il vaudrait mieux éviter de traduire par corporation le mot arabe *ṣinf* ou ses équivalents, qui désignent certes une catégorie professionnelle, mais sans toutes les implications que notre histoire à nous nous fait mettre dans le mot corporation.[31]

Cela dit, il est certain que, en partie, en Orient, par l'entremise de la *futuwwa* elle-même évoluée, il se produit une évolution des métiers dans le sens de nos corporations, bien qu'arrêtée à mi-chemin.[32] Il faut donc en comprendre les raisons et modalités. C'est un autre problème, que je ne traite pas ici, mais qui devait, pour finir, être évoqué. Une fois de plus, il faut éviter la vieille idée d'un Orient immobile. S'il a l'air de l'avoir été à côté de l'Occident devenu galopant, il ne l'a pas plus été, à son rythme, qu'aucune autre société médiévale.

On m'a dit une fois, dans un autre cénacle, que j'étais décourageant. Ce n'est certes pas mon intention. Si je l'étais, c'est que je serais découragé, ce que j'espère ne jamais être. Mais, si l'on veut avancer, il faut prendre conscience de l'urgence indispensables d'enquêtes nouvelles, établies sur la base d'un questionnaire plus précis et exact que cela n'a été souvent le cas jadis. Je n'ai pas d'autre ambition que d'y avoir légèrement aidé.

---

[31] Gibb et Bowen, *Islamic Society and the West*, i, 281, note 4.

[32] Il est curieux de constater qu'Ibn Baṭṭūṭa est déjà frappé par le caractère corporatif des métiers iraniens (sans *futuwwa* inhérente à leur organisation, bien que la *futuwwa* fût développée en Iran)—ce qui laisse supposer qu'ils l'avaient moins ailleurs— et que cependant Chardin sera lui frappé par leur caractère non-corporatif: chacun juge à partir d'une expérience contraire.

POST-SCRIPTUM

Dans la communication qu'on vient de lire, mais qui a été présenté en 1965, je n'ai naturellement pas pu tenir compte de certains travaux parus depuis lors, en particulier de la belle *Mediterranean Society* de Goitein, qui cependant n'en modifient pas les conclusions. D'autre part je n'avais pas pris conscience, en préparant mon travail, que M. Stern en préparait un parallèle, qu'on peut lire dans le présent volume. Il est évident que ces deux efforts se recouvrent partiellement, et chacun de nous par conséquent doit renvoyer à l'autre. Cependant, bien entendu, chacun de nous a sa manière propre, et les deux communications ne sont pas identiques. Leur convergence n'en a que plus de poids.

Signalons aussi que Gabriel Baer, qui avait l'intention, non réalisée de présenter une communication sur la même thème au Congrès des Orientalistes de 1967, aboutissait également de son côté aux mêmes résultats, à partir de considérations quelquefois différentes (j'ignore sous quelle forme l'article paraitra).

ELEMENTS POUR L'ETUDE DES AGGLOMERATIONS URBAINES DANS L'IRAN MEDIEVAL

par

Jean Aubin

I. COUP D'ŒIL SUR L'ETAT DE LA QUESTION

L'histoire des villes de l'Iran islamique n'a pas encore été considérée en discipline particulière. Excepté les notices écrites par Minorsky, en partie sur la base des compilations de l'érudition qadjare, pour la première édition de l'*Encyclopédie de l'Islam*, et qui décrivent dans ses péripéties externes, de façon linéaire, l'évolution d'une localité donnée, la bibliographie du sujet serait bien peu substantielle si on en retirait les titres de contenu insignifiant ou désuet et les ouvrages généraux où figurent des digressions relevant plus souvent de l'histoire sociale que de celle du fait urbain. La publication de la deuxième édition de l'*Encyclopédie de l'Islam* n'a pas créé l'occasion espérée d'une mise au point (la plupart des rubriques de géographie iranienne y semblent imitées de la *Géographie* de Malte-Brun). L'apport le plus positif des années récentes est certainement représenté par quelques monographies de géographes non orientalistes sur des cités d'aujourd'hui.

Les difficultés, il est vrai, sont fortes. L'indifférence des pouvoirs publics, aussi bien que des milieux cultivés, au bouleversement des sites et à la disparition des restes anciens qu'entraîne la croissance actuelle des villes iraniennes, ne sont pas sans précédents ni parallèles. En Iran, toutefois, ces destructions irrémédiables sont moins qu'ailleurs compensées par l'activité des curieux du passé. Encore que depuis une douzaine d'années livres et brochures témoignent du regain d'intérêt dont jouit l'histoire locale, le manque de préparation des érudits amateurs fait leur zèle trop constamment infructueux. Ils rendraient d'infinis services à relever les vestiges monumentaux et épigraphiques, à recueillir les toponymes en voie de disparition, les traditions, les souvenirs, qu'ils ne rendent pas en mettant bout à bout platement des citations de textes édités et notoires. Parente pauvre des sciences islamologiques, l'archéologie islamique n'a, en pays iraniens, été orientée vers l'étude de l'histoire urbaine que dans les régions dépendant de l'Union Soviétique. Singulièrement plus active, l'archéologie préislamique a surtout exploré, en Mésopotamie et en Asie centrale, des zones marginales: les résultats obtenus ne sauraient être étendus a priori au monde iranien dans son ensemble. L'obscurité en laquelle demeure, en dépit des fouilles, la vie urbaine de l'Iran sasanide—reflétée dans des textes arabes postérieurs—constitue une gêne considérable pour aborder l'examen du fait urbain à l'époque islamique: nous le saisissons à un temps de son évolution dont les phases précédentes nous échappent.

En regard de ces conditions défavorables s'inscrit la quantité et la valeur des sources textuelles islamiques, grossies dans les derniers siècles d'une volumineuse documentation en langues européennes. A côté des chroniques dynastiques, des traités de jurisprudence ou de controverse religieuse, etc., en arabe et en persan, littérature passablement riche en matériaux d'histoire urbaine, il faut souligner le prix des histoires de villes. L'Orient médiéval, au contraire de l'Occident, possède une historiographie urbaine fournie, où domine sans doute, au début, le genre décevant des répertoires biographiques de théologiens, mais qui s'est prolongée, en Iran, en une série d'œuvres descriptives et narratives, d'abord en arabe, plus tard traduites ou directement écrites en persan.

C'est sur cette documentation textuelle, importante en nombre et en qualité, que repose presque exclusivement, dans les circonstances présentes, la possibilité de connaître l'histoire urbaine. Si le recours aux sciences auxiliaires classiques n'est que par exception autorisé, la nature des textes ne favorise pas davantage l'emploi des techniques auxiliaires nouvellement élaborées; vides de contenu statistique, démographique ou économique, ils ne sont complétés qu'à partir du XVIe siècle par des collections d'archives, persanes et européennes, pour l'heure inaccessibles ou inédites; il est peu probable qu'on obtienne des suites chiffrées satisfaisantes avant la seconde moitié du XIXe siècle. D'autre part, le niveau rudimentaire de la cartographie iranienne interdit, à petite échelle, d'exploiter les données topographiques et, à grande échelle, de mesurer la densité des points d'agglomération par rapport à la superficie réelle des terres cultivables et de l'habitat. L'insuffisance des études de géographie humaine condamne la géographie historique à s'exercer dans l'abstrait.

Il serait naturel qu'on songeât à pallier le retard des recherches d'histoire urbaine de l'Iran médiéval en prenant modèle sur les travaux consacrés aux villes islamiques, c'est-à-dire en fait, jusqu'ici, à des villes du monde arabisé. Je ne crois pas que l'étude du phénomène urbain gagne à être d'ores et déjà entreprise à la lumière de ce qu'enseignerait une confrontation sur la " cité islamique ". Non que nous contestions que, s'il y a des villes en Iran, elles ne soient musulmanes. Comme les villes italiennes ou flamandes sont chrétiennes. Caractère manifestement second (mis à part le cas des villes de pélerinages), qu'aucun historien n'acceptera en guise d'explication du phénomène urbain. Certains des traits qui opposent la ville telle qu'elle se forme dans l'Ouest de l'Europe, et la ville orientale telle que l'Islam la connaît, peuvent bien ressortir au mode religieux, le contraste n'en relève pas moins, pour aller à l'essentiel, de la typologie comparée de la ville occidentale, au sens étroit, et de la ville orientale, au sens large. Ce serait bloquer les perspectives de la recherche que d'estimer qu'on définit la vie urbaine dans l'Islam en disant de la ville qu'elle est islamique. Comme si l'Islam était un, comme si le prototype théorique de la cité idéale correspondait aux formes diversifiées de ville orientale qu'il a connues et connaît toujours.

Dans le seul domaine iranien, à l'époque qu'on nomme par convention " médiévale ", le milieu géographique, les circonstances historiques, l'association fonctionnelle font apparaître plusieurs types de ville. Marché agricole, centre artisanal, place marchande, point stratégique, lieu de pélerinage, foyer intellectuel, autant de fonctions qui, simples ou combinées, modèlent la physionomie et le sort de la ville. Mais pas seules. Les ports du littoral maritime diffèrent des ports du littoral désertique, les villes des terres chaudes de celles des terres froides, celles du plateau intérieur de celles de la région caspienne ou de l'Asie centrale. La personnalité des villes est nourrie de beaucoup plus que des attributs caractériels décernés à leurs habitants par les auteurs médiévaux. Peuplement, usages, mode de vie, font qu'une ville du Fārs est dissemblable d'une ville du Khurāsān ou de l'Azerbaydjān, dans son aspect et dans son atmosphère.

Plutôt que de traiter la ville iranienne en exemple ou en variante de la " cité islamique ", dans une finalité justificative, il paraît plus urgent de chercher par quelle voie obtenir le meilleur rendement d'une documentation uniforme et peu explicite, et comment on peut passer de l'inventaire descriptif au classement dynamique et à la formulation des problèmes complexes.

Les notations qui suivent contribueront à faciliter l'établissement d'un questionnaire d'enquête sur l'évolution historique des villes iranennes. On ne mentionnera que quelques-unes des questions liées au sujet, choisies parmi celles qui, solubles à l'aide du médiocre outillage méthodologique pour le présent disponible, peuvent servir au perfectionnement des procédés de recherche.

II. LE CADRE DU PHÉNOMÈNE URBAIN

On n'a pas prêté l'attention convenable à la notion d'espace qu'impliquent les vocables géographiques iraniens. A ne retenir que ceux qui sont intelligibles, ils traduisent une vision et un effort d'organisation du milieu naturel par les hommes. On est immédiatement frappé, par exemple, de l'ambivalence du nom désignant un district et son chef-lieu. Tantôt le chef-lieu prend le nom de son territoire. Ainsi Kirman, qui s'est jadis appelée Bardasīr, a été appelée *shahr-i Kirmān,* " la ville (chef-lieu de la province) du Kirman ", puis est devenue simplement Kirman. La forme *shahr-i Ray,* " la ville du (district de) Ray ", est toujours employée à propos d'une petite bourgade de la banlieue Sud de Téhéran. Tantôt, ce qu'on croirait être un nom de ville n'en est pas un: sans être obligatoirement précédé d'un terme spécifiant la division administrative, le nom du chef-lieu qualifie le territoire de sa juridiction. Chiraz signifiera, souvent, non point la ville de Chiraz, mais " le (territoire qui dépend de) Chiraz ", la province de Fārs; aussi bien, dans le contexte d'un récit sur le Fārs, le mot *shahr,* " la ville ", pris en valeur absolue, désignera Chiraz. Les textes médiévaux contiennent maints exemples de ce double usage, qui est général (cf. *shahr-i Ṭūs, shahr-i Sīstān,* etc.; mais *Ṭūs,* " le Ṭūs ", *Iṣfahān,* " l'Ispahan ", etc.). L'évolution sémantique des mots qui signifient " ville " et " district ", *shahr* et *shahristān,* montre que cette ambiguité au niveau des noms propres a existé au niveau des noms communs.

Cette tendance du persan à ne pas distinguer entre le territoire, étroit ou vaste, et sa localité principale, invite à replacer l'étude du fait urbain dans le cadre des divisions territoriales historiques. L'unité de surface à observer n'est pas celle que délimitent les murs de ville ou leur ceinture de faubourgs: l'agglomération est indissociable de son territoire. L'implantation des groupes nomades allogènes a brisé l'armature historico-géographique ancienne, favorisant en cela la politique centralisatrice des dynasties modernes, de sorte que, l'usure des mécanismes économiques aidant, nous ne pouvons sans un laborieux travail de reconstitution (jusque dans la nuit des âges préislamiques), reconnaître l'importance fondamentale de ces cellules vivantes de l'organisation sociale des pays iraniens qu'étaient les " cantons " (*rustāq, rab', nāḥiyat*) ou " pays ", dont beaucoup ont désormais perdu leur vieux nom.

Chacun de ces " pays " groupe plusieurs villages; il a pour chef-lieu une petite agglomération au caractère urbain embryonnaire, siège de l'administration locale, de la vie intellectuelle, d'un artisanat spécialisé, d'un marché permanent. Le petit noyau, ou même, parfois, momentanément, les deux noyaux (cf. Nūqān et Ṭābarān dans le Ṭūs) que comporte chaque cellule territoriale, représente une virtualité urbaine aux chances inégales. Dans l'assemblage de cantons qui forme un district ou une province, quelques-uns seulement exerceront une attraction sur les cantons limitrophes, et un seul s'élevera au rang de métropole régionale. Devons-nous pour autant gratifier du titre de ville tous ces points de congestion démographique, dont certains restent de grands villages, sans réussir à se constituer en petites villes? Une description objective y verra simplement, sises dans un paysage campagnard qui les enserre de ses jardins et de ses champs, des agglomérations. Dans quelles conditions se produit ce phénomène d'agglomération, et dans quelles conditions disparaît-il? Tel est le premier sujet de l'étude du fait urbain. Ensuite seulement on considèrera l'organisation des communautés humaines.

III. FACTEURS ET TYPES D'AGGLOMÉRATION

Comment, dans l'environnement rural de la civilisation iranienne, naissent et meurent les villes? La courbe d'évolution des villes de la période islamique montre quels sont les facteurs favorables à la vie urbaine et comment ils la transforment.

a. Facteurs géographiques. Les grandes villes sont, en Iran, situées au bord d'un haut relief qui pourvoit aux besoins en eau de l'agglomération et de sa zone de cultures. Illustration la plus nette, Ray/Téhéran, au pied de l'Alborz. Ou encore Tabriz et Marāgha, sur le périmètre du mont Sahand; Nīshāpūr et Ṭūs/Mashhad, de part et d'autre du Kūh-i Bīnālūd. Mais Ispahan est aussi une ville de piedmont; et de même Yazd, bâtie à distance du massif montagneux auquel la relient des chaînes de canaux souterrains. Il est exceptionnel que le réseau hydrographique de montagne alimente un cours d'eau puissant; lorsque tel est le cas, la ville peut naître très loin des sommets qui lui assurent la vie: exemple extrême, l'oasis de Marv, nourrie par le long pédoncule d'une rivière descendue de l'Hindoukouch.

Il n'est pas de métropole qui ne jouxte de vastes terroirs agricoles et maraîchers, aptes à produire la majorité des produits alimentaires à proximité des lieux de consommation: Ray entre la plaine du Shahryār et celle de Varāmīn, Ispahan sur la basse vallée du Zanda-rūd, Istakhr en bordure de la plaine du Kurbāl, qui a été ensuite le grenier de Chiraz. Quel que soit l'appoint du ravitaillement caravanier (cf. Nīshāpūr reçevant les produits de l'Ustuvā), il y a corrélation entre le volume des villes et l'étendue de la superficie arable avoisinante. Les grands ports marchands du Golfe Persique ne font pas exception. Il est vrai que la plaine côtière de Sīrāf est exigüe, qu'Ormuz est rigoureusement stérile. Néanmoins ces deux cités, qui recevaient de l'extérieur par bateau des denrées non périssables (riz, dattes), faisaient venir des vivres frais l'une de son arrière-pays, l'autre de l'île de Qishm.

b. L'essor des villes marchandes grandies dans un milieu naturel défavorable est dû à un autre facteur du développement urbain, le facteur économique. Toute ville en extension est immanquablement greffée sur une artère commerciale active. Que le courant caravanier tarisse, et les villes meurent. C'est ainsi que nous découvrons en Iran méridional des constellations de cités disparues. Chaque grand axe de circulation traine après lui un chapelet de ces centres morts. Au niveau de l'enquête, la viographie est un bon instrument de détection de l'histoire économique.

c. Le facteur politique intervient soit au titre de l'opportunité stratégique, soit par la pression des groupes d'intérêts. L'expansion des principautés est déterminée par le quadrillage du tissu routier et urbain Quand l'agglomération ne se trouve pas sur le parcours d'une piste de grande fréquentation, ses notables s'efforcent d'en infléchir le tracé pour le faire passer par leur ville (cf. Faryumad, Khunj). Il y a concommittance entre l'essor d'une cité et l'accession de son aristocratie aux charges du gouvernement central.

Dans le déclin de la vie urbaine les mêmes facteurs jouent inversement. Il y a interaction, souvent rapide, de la rupture naturelle ou provoquée de l'équilibre géographique, du marasme économique, du désordre politique. On l'observe bien lors de la période d'extension du pastoralisme, qui a transformé la vie urbaine. Les terrains de parcours des éleveurs étant situés à l'écart du réseau traditionnel des routes et des villes, de multiples fondations ont surgi, durant l'époque mongole, dans des lieux géographiquement peu favorables. Ces fondations ont promptement périclité, parce que, hormis la volonté éphémère des princes, bientôt attirés par les sites traditionnels, rien n'assurait leur durée: ni la permanence des parcours, ni la vocation artisanale et agricole. Seul subsista la plus célèbre de ces créations, Sulṭāniyya, qui est le meilleur exemple du type d'association ville-pâturage, déjà bien connu en Asie centrale, mais alors nouveau en Iran, où les villes appartenaient au type d'association ville-oasis. Bientôt déchue, après la mort de son fondateur, Sulṭāniyya ne devait disparaître qu'au XVIIe siècle; sa survie s'explique par son triple rôle de marché d'une région de peuplement tribal, de place stratégique et d'étape sur la grande route commerciale Est–Ouest.

En s'acculturant, l'aristocratie nomade permit aux villes anciennes de s'embellir d'édifices publics; elle leur juxtaposa ses propres fondations (Shanb-i Ghāzān) et des résidences d'apparat, entourées de vastes parcs où elle continuait à mener la vie des camps (Samarqand, Hérat). La substitution du régime pastoral au régime traditionnel n'en provoqua pas moins une dégradation sensible de la vie urbaine, par endroits soudaine, ailleurs continue, avec une chute accélérée au XVe siècle, causée par les invasions turkmènes. En dehors de quelques métropoles régionales (Hérat, Chiraz, Tabriz), la plupart des villes déchurent au rang de bourgs ruraux, les plus favorisées survivant comme marchés desservant les zones de pâturage (Ṭūs, Varāmīn) ou comme gîtes d'étape. Les collectivités urbaines étaient traitées par les pouvoirs nomades en groupes dangereux (représailles, massacres collectifs), en réservoir de main d'œuvre (déportation) et de richesse (péages, mise à rançon, mise à sac). Les accomodements consentis aux villes qui maintenaient une activité industrielle (Kāshān, Yazd) indiquent bien que l'attitude de l'aristocratie nomade à l'égard du fait urbain n'était en rien aveugle ou inconséquente. La substitution du système d'économie pastorale s'est marquée également, après l'échec des tentatives de fondations nouvelles, par le développement des *ordōbāzār*, villes de tentes des commerçants, qui se déplaçaient à la suite des camps (*ordo*) princiers ou militaires, et qui doublaient, et souvent concurrençaient, les bazars urbains.

De manière paradoxale, la période safavide et post-safavide, sur laquelle existe la documentation la plus dense, est aussi la plus négligée. Quels furent les effets de l'arrêt des grandes vagues d'invasion, de l'expansion coloniale iranienne vers l'Inde, de l'expansion coloniale européenne? Entre les dépressions du XVe siècle et du XVIIIe siècle, quel fut le rythme de la restauration de la vie urbaine, encore assez florissante pour exciter l'admiration des voyageurs européens? Quand et comment placer le décalage entre l'urbanisme européen et l'urbanisme oriental? Quelle fut la part des minorités religieuses (arméniens, zoroastriens, banians) dans la prospérité urbaine? Comment s'établit à la période safavide le rapport ville-campagne? Et quelle est la hiérarchie réelle des classes urbaines? Autant de questions capitales auxquelles on ne saurait actuellement répondre.

IV. LA TOPOGRAPHIE URBAINE

Il convient d'étudier par eux-mêmes les principaux éléments de l'espace délimité et construit qui contient, qui répartit et qui mélange la population citadine: défenses, quartiers, lieux publics.

a. On sait déjà que, dans les villes iraniennes du haut Moyen Age, un faubourg (*rabaḍ*; pers. *bīrūn*, " l'extérieur ") flanque la cité ancienne (*madīna/shahristān*), dans laquelle se dresse, le plus souvent au centre, la citadelle (*kuhandiz*). En général, l'enceinte du *shahristān* est du type préislamique modifié. Qu'il s'agisse d'une enceinte circulaire ou quadrangulaire, l'enceinte archaïque est percée de quatre portes dont l'emplacement est imposé par des calculs astronomiques. C'est le cas de Samarqand, de Hérat, de Nishāpūr, de Bardasīr, de Jīruft, de Jay, de Hamadān, de Jūr, de Dārābjird. D'autres villes semblent avoir eu, dès avant l'Islam, un nombre de portes plus élevé, telle Balkh; de petites cités n'auraient eu que deux ou trois portes. Un classement s'impose, et la recherche d'une explication. L'islamisation apporte un changement: une cinquième porte est percée si le besoin s'en fait sentir, là où la commodité des habitants commande qu'elle le soit; c'est la " porte nouvelle " (*bāb al-jadīd*), à Zaranj, à Ispahan, etc. L'âge de la signification cosmogonique de la ville est révolu.

A partir des années troubles du XIe siècle, les agglomérations s'entourent de remparts. Il y a bien des imprécisions dans les textes, certains donnant comme ouvertes des villes que d'autres disent fermées. On distingue mal s'ils font état des vieilles murailles de *shahristān* ou des défenses élevées autour de la zone peu à peu urbanisée hors les murs, jusqu'alors imparfaitement protégée, et qui de zone suburbaine est devenue le nouveau cœur de l'agglomération. La confusion des sources entre clôtures *shahrband* et clôtures *kuchaband* est parfois à l'origine de ces apparentes contradictions. Destinée à protéger contre la menace extérieure, l'enceinte, complétée par les défenses des quartiers et par la citadelle (qui dans certaines villes n'est plus centrale mais latérale), sert en outre à isoler et à fractionner la masse turbulente et fluide des citadins. Elle est enfin une barrière fiscale. Il n'est donc pas contradictoire qu'une source mentionne la construction d'un rempart défensif là où selon d'autres sources existe déjà un mur, qui peut n'être qu'un modeste moyen délimitatif. (Cf. à l'inverse le maintien d'un mur d'octroi dans les villes dont Tamerlan fit démanteler les fortifications.)

b. La ville iranienne est en réalité un agglomérat de quartiers autonomes, ou du moins antagonistes. On s'efforcera donc de suivre le destin de chaque quartier, et les relations des quartiers entre eux. A l'origine, il y aurait parfois, selon les traditions locales, la formation de la ville par soudure de plusieurs villages. En d'autres cas la division est perpétuée par la persistance de collectivités hétérogènes. Il importerait de savoir si ont varié les limites, les noms et le nombre des quartiers. Certains sont formés d'une seule rue (*kūy*, *kūcha*, *maḥalla* sont parfois synonymes). L'étude des rues, la localisation des édifices, sont nécessaires à une définition sociale et économique du quartier et de la structure urbaine dans laquelle il s'insère. (Les travaux de Belenickiy et de Masson sur Hérat ont montré combien on pouvait tirer des données topographiques des sources.) L'étude des quartiers serait à compléter par celle de la frange demi-urbanisée qui s'étend entre ville et campagne: les caravansérails extérieurs, le " quartier des jardins " (*kūcha-bāghāt*), les terrains de course (anciennement *asfrīs*, attesté par des noms de portes de ville, plus tard *maydān*, localement *lard*), etc.

c. On a mis en exergue le rayonnement de la mosquée sur la vie de la cité islamique. Mais on ne l'a mesuré, ou affirmé, que sur une courte période. Il faudra nuancer. Elément permanent de l'horizon urbain, objet favori du faste monumental, la mosquée est concurrencée, comme lieu de dévotion, par d'innombrables mausolées et surtout par les *khānaqāh*. Au cours des siècles, elle tend à devenir une partie annexe dans le complexe architectural qui se développe autour d'elle, et qui comprend, à côté de la *madrasa* et du *khānaqāh*, des lieux publics: bains, dispensaires, foyers d'accueil, bazars, qui sont les centres vivants de la vie communautaire. C'est autour de ces lieux profanes que gravite l'ensemble des activités qui font qu'il existe une ville. A ce propos, il faut bien toucher à une question toujours dissimulée: quoi de plus proprement urbain que la commercialisation de la débauche? Les quartiers mal famés, ces *kharābāt* dont le nom revient si souvent dans les œuvres poétiques, lieux de rencontre de tous les asociaux, ont exercé une influence trop méconnue sur les comportements psychologiques et sur la vie sociale.

V. L'HISTOIRE SOCIALE DES VILLES

L'histoire urbaine est au cœur de l'histoire sociale iranienne. Mais il s'en faut de beaucoup qu'elle la recouvre. La place privilégiée que lui fait notre documentation, par rapport à l'histoire agraire et à l'histoire des sociétés nomades, est-elle méritée? La ville a-t-elle été toujours le foyer, ou le refuge, du dynamisme social? La question est, bien entendu, si générale qu'elle devra être préparée par l'examen de points particuliers, qui touchent moins à la sociologie de groupes au caractère urbain peu affirmé, qu'à l'explication des mécanismes du phénomène d'agglomération.

a. Entre l'agglomération et son environnement rural, les liens sont étroits. M. Bosworth les a déjà définis en parlant de Nīshāpūr. Il attribue toutefois à un préjugé islamique la répulsion envers la vie à la campagne. Ne faut-il pas y voir plus simplement l'attitude courante du citadin à l'égard du *rūstā'ī*, le " rustaud "? S'agissant de l'Iran, le thème de " l'Islam religion de citadins " est à adoucir. Le type idéal de l'homme iranien, à haute époque, est celui du *dihqān*, propriétaire campagnard; ce que seront, ultérieurement, tant de cheykhs de derviches, qui éleveront leur *khānaqāh* dans de petits bourgs ruraux, à l'écart des grosses villes. Il faudra rechercher quel est le degré de la concentration de l'artisanat au centre urbain; s'il existe des relations particulières de quartier à canton; si le recrutement des bandes populaires urbaines est toujours à composante de *'ayyār* ruraux; si les migrations saisonnières de main-d'œuvre sont de règle; quel est le rayon d'attraction de la ville; par quel apport extérieur se reconstitue la population après les guerres, les famines, les épidémies. Ainsi l'histoire des sociétés villageoises, à peine reflétée dans nos sources, s'éclairera par la connaissance des rapports entre ville et campagne.

b. Parmi les troubles populaires, sur lesquels une enquête méthodique est indispensable, il faudrait distinguer ceux qui sont des luttes de factions, endémiques, et ceux qui, à certaines périodes, ont le caractère de luttes de classes.

c. Les classes dirigeantes investissent une partie de leurs revenus, de provenance variée (domaines ruraux, ferme du fisc, monopole des grains, participation aux entreprises commerciales) en achat de possessions immobilières urbaines. Comment la propriété immobilière urbaine se répartit-elle entre les familles de notables? Quelle est leur emprise sur les lieux publics, sur les abords des villes, sur les routes qui y donnent accès? En quelle proportion s'agit-il de fondations d'intérêt social? L'aristocratie militaire a-t-elle des assises urbaines? A défaut d'actes notariés et de cadastres, les *vaqf-nāma* donnent à cet égard des renseignements précis, suppléant aux indications générales des chroniques.

d. Le corps politique n'est pas structuré par des institutions (il n'y a pas de régime des ordres). Les classes ne sont pas organisées comme telles (il n'y a pas, en ce sens, de noblesse). Il n'existe pas de lien juridique entre les groupes sociaux organisés (sayyids, marchands, gens de métier) et le pouvoir. On ne peut donc s'attendre que la ville ait un statut administratif propre, avec corps de ville, institutions consulaires, etc. Un notable qui, entre quelques autres, s'impose au choix du prince par sa richesse, son entregent, sa clientèle, y gouverne en intermédiaire de l'autorité centrale, qui souvent le contrôle par ses officiers délégués. Les tentatives d'autogouvernement, qui se produisent en cas de péril ou de crise, ne sont jamais durables. Même lorsque la situation géographique et économique semble propice à la transformation d'une oligarchie en corps de gouvernement, il ne se crée aucun organe de vie municipale. Ormuz, par exemple, ville-état et ville marchande, est régie comme les autres seigneuries. On se gardera d'en conclure que les villes sont dépourvues de toute existence politique. Ces constatations négatives laissent entier le problème de l'administration urbaine.

Si nous prenions le mot " ville " dans l'acception qu'il a acquise dans l'histoire occidentale, on serait conduit, au terme d'un enchaînement de fausses analogies, à conclure qu'il n'y a pas de villes en Orient parce qu'on n'y retrouve pas les traits qui font les villes en Occident. Mais il devient clair que, loin d'être la norme, ce qui se passe dans la partie occidentale de l'Europe a représenté l'exception. Les enquêtes récentes sur les agglomérations " pré-urbaines " d'Europe ouvrent d'ailleurs au comparatisme des perspectives familières à l'historien des villes orientales, qui étudie des agglomérations demeurées au stade fonctionnel.

NOTE SUR LES VILLES CHINOISES AU MOMENT DE L'APOGEE ISLAMIQUE

par

J. Gernet

I

La Chine diffère profondément des pays d'Islam : milieu géographique, société, économie, formes politiques, structures mentales, expérience historique collective, rien de comparable dans les deux civilisations. Mais c'est justement cette différence si radicale qui peut rendre leur rapprochement révélateur.

Alors que la plupart des villes du Moyen Orient ont les nomades à leurs portes et que, dans cette partie du monde, s'imbriquent bien souvent les genres de vie opposés du citadin, de l'agriculteur et du nomade—particularité qui est sans doute pour une part dans le sentiment de supériorité qu'éprouve l'habitant des villes—l'Extrême-Orient semble être la région de l'Eurasie où steppes des pasteurs et déserts à caravanes d'une part, terres aménagées et cultivées d'autre part soient aussi nettement séparées. Assurément, cette distinctiôn n'est vraie que dans son ensemble, car il existe, sur les confins septentrionaux du monde chinois, toute une zone mouvante où se mêlent sédentaires et nomades. Mais, face aux espaces habités par les tribus d'éleveurs, le domaine des agriculteurs sédentaires, constructeurs de murailles, est tout entier celui de la civilisation, de la culture et des techniques. Un même mot désigne les remparts qui protègent le monde chinois contre les incursions de la steppe et ceux qui entourent les villes. Aussi bien la ville n'a-t-elle pas, dans la tradition chinoise, de place prééminente. Elle est définie concrètement comme enceinte de murailles et on s'y réfère généralement comme au siège d'une circonscription administrative, sans qu'on puisse distinguer le plus souvent entre la ville et le territoire qui en dépend. L'opposition entre ville et campagne reste très imprécise et ne commencera à être ressentie qu'au moment où apparaîtront, sous les Song (960–1279), de grosses agglomérations marchandes. Assurément, il semble que les hautes classes habitent de préférence dans les villes, mais il est vrai aussi que familles aristocratiques et familles lettrées n'ont pas toujours d'attache urbaine et qu'à l'inverse les villes chinoises ont longtemps abrité une population en partie paysanne.

En vérité, la construction des villes fait en Chine partie intégrante de cet ensemble de grands travaux qui permettent à l'Etat d'assurer le transport, le stockage et la répartition des principaux produits, de favoriser la production et de se protéger contre ses ennemis (routes, canaux, greniers, entrepôts, digues, réservoirs, fortifications . . .). L'espace chinois est ainsi aménagé dans son ensemble et l'Etat fournit à la population le cadre général de son habitat. Pourquoi, dans cet ensemble, la ville serait-elle particulièrement privilégiée?

Géré par un corps de fonctionnaires civils, l'empire dispose de l'essentiel des richesses. Il s'approprie le surplus des céréales, des tissus, de la force de travail, contrôle la monnaie, la production de denrées de base comme le sel et celle des métaux, fixe les prix sur les marchés qu'il contrôle et ne laisse au commerce privé qu'une partie des transactions. Il faut ajouter qu'une des principales richesses commerciales de la Chine n'est pas un produit d'origine urbaine, mais rurale: c'est dans les campagnes que sont tissées les soieries. En outre, l'administration a ses propres fabriques et ateliers. Ces conditions ne favorisent guère la croissance d'une classe urbaine de marchands et d'artisans libres.

Voilà qui explique sans doute une contradiction d'abord surprenante: malgré une grande activité économique et un volume d'échanges considérable, malgré sa richesse et son avance technique dans bien des domaines, la Chine n'a connu qu'assez tardivement la ville comme réalité spécifique, distincte de la campagne par sa forte densité, la nature de ses activités, son genre de vie et ses types humains.

La conscience d'être un citadin et d'appartenir à une même communauté urbaine ne se fera jour que chez l'habitant des grandes villes de l'époque des Song. Mais ce ne sera que de façon confuse: historiquement, c'est sur d'autres formes de groupement humain, de dimensions plus modestes, que la société chinoise a été bâtie. Cette morphologie sociale particulière, qui est en rapport étroit avec les cadres politiques généraux du monde chinois et qui forme avec eux un ensemble de caractère systématique, voilà peut-être l'élément le plus décisif. Mais l'étude concrète des villes chinoises nous permettra sans doute de l'entrevoir plus clairement.

II

Nous ne connaissons bien que certaines des villes de l'époque des

Tang et de celle des Song. Ce sont les grandes capitales et par conséquent des villes d'exception. Mais c'est tout avantage, car les grandes métropoles sont villes par excellence. Nulle part ailleurs, le fait urbain ne peut être plus manifeste.

La construction de Chang'an (l'actuel Xi'an, capitale du Shenxi) et de Loyang, au Henan, aux environs de l'an 600, se situe dans le contexte général de la restauration d'un empire centralisé qui impliquait une réorganisation administrative, des réformes agraires et fiscales, une refonte du droit pénal, de grands travaux enfin tels que villes, canaux et greniers. Ce sont des villes immenses, tracées au cordeau par des armées de travailleurs. Composées d'enceintes de remparts qui abritaient une cité et des palais impériaux, une ville administrative et une ville résidentielle, elles correspondent, à quelques détails près, à un type de ville traditionnel depuis les débuts de l'empire.

La ville de Chang'an, pour nous limiter à son cas, couvre une superficie de plus de 70 km2 (soit à peu près celle de Paris intra muros) et tient dans

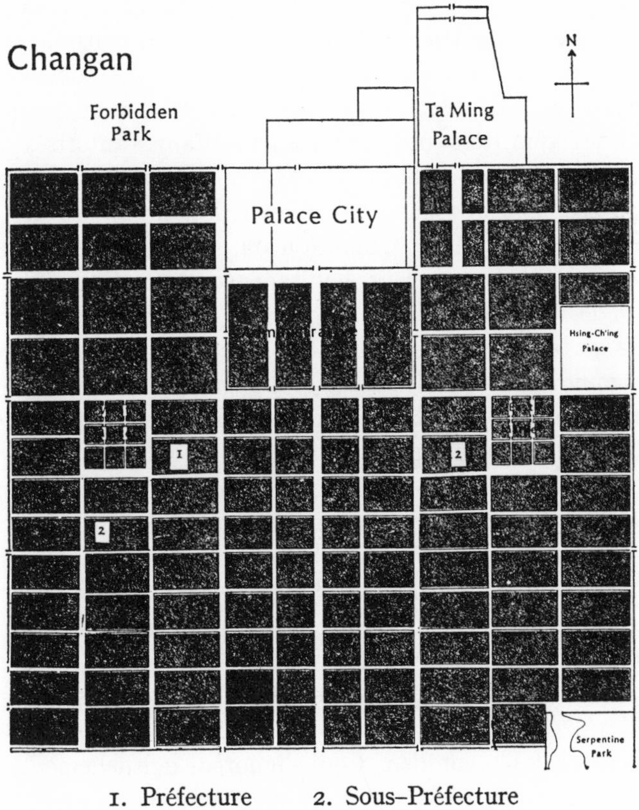

1. Préfecture 2. Sous-Préfecture

un rectangle dont les côtés Nord–Sud mesurent près de 8 km et les côtés Est–Ouest près de 10. L'espace réservé à l'habitation, plus de 50 km2, est divisé par de très larges avenues qui se coupent à angle droit et délimitent plus de cent quartiers, divisés eux-mêmes, intérieurement, en ilôts plus petits. Cette disposition en damier se retrouve dans les champs, les villages et aussi dans les marchés que l'administration a établis à l'intérieur de la ville. Elle est évoquée par un caractère d'écriture formé par deux parallèles horizontales et verticales qui se croisent à angle droit, et ce caractère se rencontre dans des expressions qui s'appliquent aux champs cultivés, aux marchés et aux espaces urbains. Elle implique l'existence d'un pouvoir politique qui répartit les emplacements, procède à des allotissements et recourt au besoin à des transferts de population. Et en effet, comme les métropoles des Han ou de l'époque des invasions barbares entre IVe et VIe siècle, Chang'an, Loyang et les régions avoisinantes ont été peuplées de façon systématique.

Les quartiers de ville ont longtemps porté le nom de *li* qui s'applique également aux quartiers de village et qui est en même temps une mesure de longueur et de superficie (indice qu'il s'agit bien à l'origine d'allotissements). Comme les quartiers villageois, les quartiers urbains sont entourés de murs sans autre ouverture que quelques portes. Au-delà de ces murs, l'intervention de l'Etat est déjà moins sensible, plus indirecte. Les habitants des quartiers ont leurs représentants autorisés auprès de l'administration. Fait notable, la législation en matière de règlements urbains ne se préoccupe pas de l'organisation intérieure des quartiers. C'est seulement dans ces quartiers (ou dans les ilôts de quartiers) qu'il existe une vie collective, car leurs habitants sont souvent unis par des liens de parenté, des liens de caractère religieux et parfois de nature professionnelle. Ces sortes de villages, isolés les uns des autres, fermés la nuit à partir du couvre-feu, sont les seuls groupements humains que connaisse l'administration impériale et leur cohésion tend à les rendre collectivement responsables au regard des pouvoirs publics.

Ces réalités de la morphologie sociale se traduisent dans la topographie de la ville: la ville n'a pas de centre, mais seulement un axe principal, la voie Nord–Sud qui aboutit à la cité administrative séparée par ses remparts des quartiers résidentiels. Il n'existe ni place publique, ni centre religieux commun à l'ensemble des habitants et symbole de leur cohésion. La ville, œuvre temporaire comme toutes les créations de l'empire (les constructions chinoises ne sont pas faites pour durer, les canaux s'envasent rapidement, les murailles de terre se dégradent . . .), groupe de petites unités sociales qui n'ont entre elles aucun lien et qui s'ignorent mutuellement. L'espace chinois est original: ce n'est pas par rapport à un centre que l'on s'oriente dans la ville ou dans les campagnes, mais par rapport aux directions cardinales.

Cet espace est de nature abstraite et cosmique comme le pouvoir qui en est le créateur. En effet, parce que ce ne sont jamais les agglomérations humaines, mais les territoires qui importent, l'Etat semble être partout et nulle part. Du point de vue administratif, la ville n'a aucune réalité. Elle ne forme pas un tout à l'intérieur de ses murailles, car la grande voie Nord–Sud qui constitue son axe principal marque aussi la limite de deux sous-préfectures dont les territoires couvrent à la fois une moitié de la ville résidentielle et les campagnes environnantes. Et ces territoires eux-mêmes font à leur tour partie de cette circonscription beaucoup plus vaste qu'est la préfecture métropolitaine, elle-même enfin sous la dépendance de la cité administrative centrale. Le réseau hiérarchisé des organes administratifs apparaît comme indépendant des petites communautés humaines dont sont parsemés les territoires à l'intérieur des remparts de la ville et au dehors. De même, dans une large mesure, la vie de ces petites communautés apparaît comme indépendante de ce système. Le niveau du politique a un caractère de transcendance par rapport aux groupes humains et à la vie concrète de ces groupes.

III

En construisant Chang'an, l'Etat a fourni le cadre de son existence à une partie de la population de l'empire. Il s'est efforcé de peupler l'intérieur de la ville, mais aussi toute la région de la capitale. Nous ne savons malheureusement pas quelle était la population de Chang'an ni d'aucune ville chinoise, car les recensements portent seulement sur les habitants des territoires, préfectures et sous-préfectures. Mais deux faits certains peuvent être retenus: d'une part, la ville résidentielle est très inégalement peuplée, de l'autre, la densité des habitants en dehors de la capitale est relativement plus élevée que dans les autres régions de la Chine aux VIIe et VIIIe siècles. Un grand nombre des quartiers du Sud de Chang'an sont occupés par des champs, des parcs, des vergers, des terrains de manœuvre, des aires pour le jeu de polo, des hôtels particuliers ou des monastères qui occupent de très grandes surfaces. Dans cette partie de la capitale, la densité des habitants est probablement inférieure à celle des campagnes voisines: on comprend pourquoi l'administration chinoise ne distingue pas entre les territoires qui se trouvent à l'intérieur et à l'extérieur des remparts. Les remparts ne délimitent pas une agglomération qui serait dans son ensemble beaucoup plus peuplée que les campagnes et distincte d'elles.

Ils constituent seulement un abri en cas d'incursions étrangères et de troubles intérieurs, abri d'autant plus vaste que le territoire métropolitain est un des plus peuplés et que la capitale, siège du pouvoir central et de la cour, doit manifester, par ses dimensions, le prestige et la puissance impériales.

La partie la plus peuplée et la plus vivante de Chang'an est formée par les quartiers voisins de la cité administrative, le long de la voie Est–Ouest que prolonge à l'intérieur de la ville les grandes routes menant, à l'Ouest, vers le Gansu et le Sichuan, à l'Est vers le Henan et la vallée de la Huai. Cette agglomération semble même déborder en dehors des remparts. Des faubourgs se sont sans doute formés assez tôt le long de ces deux grandes routes. Mais le caractère marchand de cette agglomération ne s'est affirmé que difficilement, contre la volonté des pouvoirs publics.

Pour satisfaire aux besoins de l'administration et du Palais impérial, pour rendre plus aisé aussi le contrôle des activités commerciales et artisanales ainsi que la perception des taxes, les bâtisseurs de Chang'an ont prévu, comme il était de tradition, de grouper tous les corps de métier et tous les commerces dans deux vastes enceintes qui couvrent, dans chacune des deux parties de la ville, une superficie de près d'un km2. Boutiques et ateliers ne pouvaient être installés librement en dehors de ces " marchés ", ni à l'intérieur des quartiers, ni dans des bâtiments qui auraient eu leur façade sur les avenues de la ville. C'est un privilège réservé aux membres de la noblesse impériale et aux grands fonctionnaires que d'avoir une ouverture donnant directement sur ces avenues. Ainsi, la rue n'a pas encore, au VIIe siècle, cette fonction d'artère marchande si familière au monde islamique et aux cités de l'Europe médiévale, ou plutôt la rue commerçante n'existe que dans les emplacements prévus pour les marchands et artisans. Ce sont des allées, consacrées chacune à l'exercice d'un métier étroitement défini. Ces allées, dont on compte 220 au marché de l'Est, portent le nom de *hang* qui s'appliquera par la suite aux corporations. Les deux marchés de Chang'an sont surveillés par des commissaires impériaux qui établissent les prix, contrôlent les poids et les mesures, veillent au respect des normes de fabrication, font régner l'ordre et perçoivent les taxes sur les ventes et sur la location des boutiques. Marchands et artisans, qui occupent une place inférieure dans la société, sont en outre l'objet de réquisitions: livraisons de marchandises et tours de corvée dans les ateliers impériaux. Les marchés officiels paraissent donc avoir entravé le développement du commerce et de l'artisanat urbain, ou du moins leur institution témoigne d'une orientation durable de ces activités en Chine: c'est de l'administration impériale que marchands et artisans obtiennent leurs plus grosses commandes.

IV

Dans la Chine des VIIe et VIIIe siècles—Chine en expansion vers l'Asie centrale jusqu'à la Transoxiane et dont le centre de gravité se situe dans la vallée de la Wei et du bas fleuve Jaune—l'activité marchande est en partie le fait d'étrangers: commerçants arabes et persans à Canton, dans les ports du Fujian, à Yangzhou et dans le bassin du Yangzi, sogdiens et ouigours surtout dans le Nord. C'est une activité marginale qui ne paraît pas avoir eu de répercussions sensibles sur la société de l'époque. Au contraire, à partir de la fermeture des routes d'Asie centrale, le centre de gravité de l'économie chinoise se déplace vers le bas Yangzi. Le monde chinois se tourne pour la première fois vers la mer et on assiste à un essor remarquable du commerce fluvial dans tout le bassin du Yangzi et sur les canaux qui y sont reliés, ainsi que du commerce maritime sur les côtes du Zhejiang, du Fujian et du Guangdong. Les premières grandes villes chinoises apparaissent à ce moment et se développent rapidement à partir du XIe siècle. Les causes de cette étonnante expansion économique sont sans doute multiples: accroissement des rendements agricoles par l'introduction de nouvelles variétés de riz, facilités des communications dans la Chine du Sud–Est, progrès des techniques maritimes (emploi de la boussole marine) et des techniques commerciales (effets de commerce, papier-monnaie), accroissement général des moyens de paiement, emploi de la houille dans les fonderies de fer. . . . Mais elles n'intéressent que de façon indirecte l'histoire des villes et on n'en retiendra ici que leurs effets sur le développement urbain. L'expansion économique a fait éclaté les cadres anciens que l'Etat avait voulu jusqu'alors imposer aux activités marchandes et artisanales, elle l'a amené à modifier dans ses formes le contrôle qu'il exerçait sur l'économie, elle a transformé peu à peu la physionomie des villes et permis à leur fonction commerciale de s'affirmer.

Tout d'abord, des boutiques et des ateliers s'établissent en dehors des enceintes qui avaient été prévues à leur intention. On en trouve dans les quartiers populaires et dans les faubourgs qui se forment en dehors des remparts (désignés par le terme *xiang* qui prend ainsi une acception toute nouvelle). Des marchés qui ne sont plus étroitement surveillés par les pouvoirs publics apparaissent aux portes des villes ou se constituent à des nœuds de routes importants, donnant ainsi naissance, parfois, à de nouveaux centres urbains. Dès la fin du XIe siècle, une grande ville comme Kaifeng présente déjà un aspect très différent de celui qu'avait Chang'an au VIIe siècle. On n'y trouve plus de quartiers clos—au moins sans doute dans les parties les plus actives de la ville. La rue est devenue une artère marchande. Au groupement de fait des commerçants et artisans dans des allées consacrées à des métiers nettement définis se sont substituées des corporations, toujours étroitement spécialisées mais dont les membres n'occupent plus dans la ville d'emplacement déterminé. L'Etat a de plus en plus largement recours à ces intermédiaires que sont les grands marchands pour l'approvisionnement des gros centres urbains et pour celui de ses armées. Les revenus qu'il tire des douanes, des taxes commerciales, des régies deviennent plus importants que ceux qui proviennent des impôts en nature, céréales et tissus prélevés sur la paysannerie. Les livraisons exigées des marchands et les tours de corvée imposés aux artisans tendent à être remplacés par des impôts en monnaie.

En résumé, les progrès de l'économie monétaire ont un double effet: ils libèrent, dans une large mesure, le commerce et l'artisanat de la tutelle qu'avait fait peser sur eux l'administration impériale; ils obligent l'Etat à un effort d'adaptation qui rend son fonctionnement plus complexe. Les organismes économiques se multiplient dans l'administration des Song et le nombre des fonctionnaires s'accroît rapidement.

Les deux plus grandes villes de l'époque des Song ont un caractère urbain très accusé dont témoignent la prolifération des commerces de luxe, le développement des distractions, la présence d'un sous-prolétariat d'origine rurale, la répartition topographique des métiers et des classes sociales, la multiplicité des associations religieuses, sportives, artistiques, régionales. . . . Les problèmes difficiles que pose la vie d'une très grosse agglomération obligent l'Etat à étendre ses fonctions: ce ne sont plus seulement la défense de la ville, sa police et la bonne marche de l'économie d'Etat qui l'occupent, mais la lutte contre le feu, l'hygiène, l'organisation de services sociaux (hôpitaux, dispensaires, cimetières publics, secours aux indigents . . .), et toutes les questions d'urbanisme que rendent plus complexes la concentration des habitants sur un petit espace. De nouveaux organismes urbains apparaissent donc à l'époque des Song.

Mais toutes ces nouveautés ne modifient pas le caractère étatique de l'empire chinois. Bien au contraire, elles l'accentuent. Aucun groupe social ou professionnel n'est assez puissant pour s'opposer à l'Etat ou se substituer à lui, parce que les anciens cloisonnements subsistent: le groupement par quartier et voisinage, les liens que conservent les émigrés de la même province ou du même village, la spécialisation extrême des métiers. Les corporations ne visent à rien d'autre, en dehors de leurs activités d'entraide, qu'à contrôler le recrutement de leurs membres et à s'assurer une sorte de monopole. La ville reste une agglomération de familles et de gens de métier. Elle n'a point de personnalité.

V

L'histoire des villes chinoises laisse entrevoir pourquoi la croissance urbaine n'a pas abouti à des changements sensibles du régime politique. bien que la Chine ait connu à l'époque des Song une extraordinaire expansion économique. Sans doute existe-t-il de très riches marchands et des corporations puissantes, mais leurs préoccupations restent purement professionnelles et ne débouchent jamais sur le politique. Le gouvernement apparaît comme une activité indépendante de tout groupement particulier, analogue à une activité naturelle. Comme dit un proverbe révélateur: " le ciel est haut, l'empereur est loin ". Ce pouvoir lointain et qui s'étend partout ne peut être accaparé par aucun groupement local. Il ne peut y avoir de politique au sens étymologique du mot, c'est à dire d'autonomie locale, parce que, d'une part, les seules unités humaines cohérentes sont de petites dimensions (habitants d'un même quartier, membres d'une même corporation spécialisée) et que, d'autre part, la hiérarchie administrative superpose à chaque territoire un territoire plus vaste qui l'englobe. La complexité de la machine administrative s'est accrue avec l'essor économique, rendant ainsi plus difficile encore un bouleversement du régime politique. Nul doute que c'est un développement historique particulier qui a engagé sans retour possible le monde chinois dans cette voie: celle d'un pouvoir abstrait et impersonnel qui domine de très haut une vie locale où chacun ne connaît que son canton, son village, ses voisins et sa famille.

THE FOUNDATION OF BAGHDAD

by

Saleh Ahmad El-Ali

I

Arab rulers, unlike the Greek, Roman and Sāsānian Emperors, were reluctant to stamp their names on the cities they founded. But this does not imply that they were ignorant of city life or lacking in appreciation of its importance in the development of human history. Mohammed was born and lived in the religio-commercial centre of Mecca, and spent the last decade of his life in Medina, where he established the nucleus of the Muslim state and laid down the foundation of its administration. His hostile attitude to the nomadic beduin life appears clearly in many Koranic verses and prophetic sayings, as well as in judicial clauses which deprive the nomads of many rights enjoyed by city dwellers.

On the eve of the rise of Islam, Arabia had many urban centres, on the coasts, and in scattered fertile areas. Its inhabitants were familiar with the administrative and legal organizations of other cities through their contacts with neighbouring countries. Such familiarity is reflected in the arabised vocabulary of administration; these penetrated even the Koran, which contains many such terms, as for example, *Umm-al qurā* (metropolis), *ḥāḍira* (emporium), *ḥaḍir* (apanage), *madīna* (city), and so on.

The rapid Islamic conquests enabled the Arabs to dominate lands extending from central Asia to the Atlantic. Their empire included countries of varied and ancient cultures and ways of life, as well as numerous urban centres differing in size and in social, political and administrative organization. By dominating all the Sāsānian Empire and most of the Byzantine provinces, they assumed control of the two differing systems prevalent in the Middle East. The Byzantine Empire had perpetuated the Greco-Roman tradition whereby cities had legal status and definite legal political organization, as well as privileges of local legislation. Each city was usually surrounded by a wall, and had a centre which included the main temple, or cathedral, government offices and the agora. The government was responsible for the numerous public buildings and monuments. The city was usually administered through one or more chosen or elected councils.

The Sāsānids, so far as the scanty and incomplete information indicates, did not grant cities *per se* any legal status or privileges. Their cities had neither popular councils nor special rights. They were urban centres which differed from other regions in economic and administrative importance rather than in legal status or organization.

The Sāsānian city usually had a walled citadel (*quhandiz*) which was the seat of the governor, the centre of government bureaus, and the camp of the army. The houses and the markets extended to the surrounding fields, forming a suburb usually unwalled and having few public buildings or recreation places. Administratively, the city was the capital of a province, or centre of an *astān* or *ṭassūj*. The city had a governor, a judge, a police prefect and fiscal officials and their bureaux; some cities were minting places. The capital of the Empire was the seat of the Emperor and his court officials, the imperial bureaux, and the leading religious officials.

The Arabs ruled by right of conquest with absolute authority to introduce, modify or abolish any practice or institution. But for practical reasons they seem to have left the conquered cities to follow their respective traditions, and so long as they did not interfere with the revenue or upset public security, did not interfere in ways which would bring about a drastic change in the existing organizations. Nevertheless the establishment of the new Arab Empire created conditions and circumstances which were bound to affect and modify the prevailing organizations and institutions.

The continuation of the conquests and the protection of the frontiers, as well as the preservation of order and peace inside the Empire, compelled the governors to establish military garrisons in some of the conquered cities. Foreseeing the need for these garrisons, the Arabs included the right to settle Arab garrisons in the treaties with some of the conquered cities. The scanty information on the topography of these cities does not show whether the Arabs settled in one specific sector, or in scattered quarters, or whether they shared the houses of the local population. In Damascus and Marw, about which we are better informed, the governors and aristocracy dwelt in various quarters inside the city, while the majority of the Arabs settled outside the wall. But even here the Arabs preserved their own social and administrative organization without attempting to impose them on the natives.

As early as the time of the Caliph 'Umar the Arabs founded six *amṣār*, a basis for their warriors (*muqātila*) and families, and administrative centres of the provinces conquered by the Army of that *miṣr*. They were Jābiya, Jawwātha, Medina, Kūfa, Baṣra and Fusṭāṭ. The first two were soon abandoned, while Qayrawān was founded in the time of the Caliph Mu'āwiya, when the term *amṣār* was also applied to other administrative Centres in which Arab garrisons were stationed permanently, such as Qazwīn, Ardabīl, Rayy and Marw.

Medina enjoyed a distinctive position; it was the capital of the Muslim state at the time of Mohammed and the first four caliphs. Mohammed in the state founded by him laid emphasis on the sovereignty of God and the authority of the prophet. He cared greatly for judicial authority and public security. The government was simple, with no permanent officials or intricate bureaucracy. The tribal organization was the basis of inheritance and blood money, as well as of the topography of the settlement. The old practices and traditions were left untouched so far as they did not affect the principles of Islam.

This organization of Medina was retained, despite the great political, economic and enthnographic developments which resulted from the conquests. Medina was the seat of the prophet's companions, and was later considered the norm of Islamic society. Undoubtedly Medina had intimate and direct relations with the surrounding Ḥijāzī Arab tribes who had embraced Islam since the time of Mohammed. Many of the Medinese were farmers and owned estates in the surrounding fertile spots. The prominent role of the Medinese in early Islam gave the city a distinct position even when it ceased to be the capital of the Empire.

Kūfa and Baṣra, the two *miṣrs* in 'Irāq, were founded by the order of 'Umar on the borders between the arid desert and the cultivated plains without any water barrier to separate them from the desert or hinder the movement of the army and peoples. Their streets had to be wide enough for the use of camel and horses. This fitted the simplicity of Islam; also the temperament of the Arabs was then inclined either to fighting or indulging in literary and political discussions rather than caring for huge buildings or lavish dress. Thus the camel market (Mirbad) in Baṣra, and the sheep market (Kunūsa (literally: garbage)) in Kūfa were the centres of social and literary activities, beside the mosques which gradually assumed the same function. In the centre was the cathedral mosque, the governors' residence, and the bureaux. They were the chief main public buildings, built of dry mud, and after more than twenty years rebuilt in brick. They were in harmony with the simple nomadic, military life and serious outlook of the Arabs.

Tribal organization was the basis of the topographic and administrative organization. Each clan lived together in a quarter (*khiṭṭa*) called after it; and each member of the clan had a preferential right to buy his neighbours' allotment (*shuf'a*). Members of the clan shared equally in paying the blood money of the unpremeditated murder committed by any one of them. They also inherited the property of any heirless member. They shared a common responsibility in preserving peace, security and order inside the clan. Each clan had an appointed warden who was responsible for the register of the members, the distribution of stipends, and communicating official orders.

Yet the Arab population of the *miṣr* constituted the body of the army whose duty was to defend the Empire and maintain peace. They were controlled by their governors who represented the caliph and were in charge of the public interests of the *miṣr* and its province. Being Muslims, they gradually assimilated the main principles of Islam which were based on individual rather than collective responsibility in matters of ethics as well as law. The governors gradually established the authority of the state. The peaceful common life, and the penetration of Islamic principles encroached upon tribal solidarity and deprived it of its *raison d'être*, but did not obliterate it completely. The tribal division of the quarters, the tribal appellation, and the estimation of the nomadic ideals of life lingered on for many decades.

The stipend is one of the distinct characteristics of the *miṣr*. The state distributed most of the revenue of the provinces conquered by the army of the *miṣr* amongst the Arabs in the *miṣr*. Each of the *muqātila* received an annual allowance of 200–2500 *dirhams*, with an additional monthly ration. The stipend was confined to the *amṣār*, distinguishing them from other Arab and Non-Arab cities. It led to a flourishing economic life and attracted more Arab and Non-Arab immigrants, until the new-comers were so numerous that the state was unable to include them in the registers of stipend.

Since the Islamic state was expected always to remain on the offensive, the *amṣār* were left without a ditch or wall up to the time of Abū Ja'far. Nor did the governors care for digging canals or aqueducts for drinking water.

The *amṣār* became centres of active political, economic and cultural life during the first century of Islam. It is no exaggeration to say that Islamic history in the first century is the history of the *amṣār*, which played the leading role in political events and produced the chief narrators and historians. They also produced the great Muslim jurists who discussed the problems facing their society and formed their opinions by theorizing the actualities of life and the practices of the community, so that most of the material of Muslim jurisprudence, which is considered as representing the ideal of Muslim life, was derived from the conditions prevailing in these *amṣār*. The legal and administrative institutions of the *miṣr* were based on the practice of everyday life. The administration was simple, consisting of guards, judges, and army bureaux, responsible for the payment of the stipends. Their jurisdiction was limited to the settlement of the Arabs, who differed culturally and administratively from the rest of the population.

II

Despite the glorious position and the great role of Baghdad in the history of Islamic civilization, very few books were written on its foundation and development. Ibn al-Nadīm who wrote his comprehensive index of Arabic books more than two centuries after its foundation, mentions only three books: *Faḍā'il Baghdād* by Yazdajard b. Mihmandār; *Faḍā'il Baghdād wa-Akhbāruhā* by Aḥmad b. al-Ṭayyib al-Sarakhsī, and *Kitāb Baghdād* by Ṭayfūr. Of these we have only a few excerpts from the first, and the sixth part of the third, which deals with the political events in Baghdad at the time of al-Ma'mūn. The *Ta'rīkh Baghdād* by al-Khaṭīb al-Baghdādī (450 A.H.) is the first book on Baghdad preserved in its entirety.

The foundation and early condition of Baghdad did not receive a full treatment in the general histories e.g. of Khalīfa b. Khayyāṭ, al-Ya'qūbī, Ibn Qutayba, Abū Ḥanīfa al-Dīnawarī, or al-Mas'ūdī (who dealt however with Baghdad in detail in his lost book *al-Awsaṭ*). Arab geographers gave mostly brief descriptions of the Baghdad in their time (the third and fourth century A.H.). Ibn al-Faqīh is the only exception, but the complete Mashhad manuscript of his book had not yet been published. Apart from its first 100 pages, the voluminous *Ta'rīkh Baghdād* of al-Khaṭīb is devoted to the scholars and prominent personalities rather than to the city itself, and so are its continuations by later authors.

Our chief sources for the study of the early foundation of Baghdad are al-Ya'qūbī's *al-Buldān*, al-Ṭabarī's *History*, and the *Ta'rīkh Baghdād* by al-Khaṭīb. Al-Ya'qūbī describes in detail the foundation of the Round City and its surroundings, without referring to his sources, and as he was far away from Baghdad when he wrote his book a century after its foundation, we can not be sure as to how far its chapter on Baghdad is complete. Al-Ṭabarī deals with the foundation of Baghdad in two separate places of his book. He describes the characteristic features, villages and settlements in the area on which Baghdad was founded. He also discusses the costs of building, the gates and the wall. His information is incoherent, incomprehensive and incomplete. Al-Khaṭīb devoted about a hundred pages of the first volume of his book to the foundation and early topography of Baghdad, mentioning some of his sources. He has a long chapter on the canals of Baghdad that seems to be derived from Suhrāb's *'Ajā'ib al-Aqālīm*. Some of his material on the streets and lanes, and on some of the gates is derived from Wakī'. There are quotations from Muḥammad b. Khalaf Wakī', Nafṭawayh, Hilāl b. al-Muḥassin and 'Alī b. al-Muḥassin al-Tanūkhī. The long and fully detailed quotations from the first two authorities deal with the topography of early Baghdad.

III

In founding Baghdad, al-Manṣūr aimed at securing a basis for his imperial army and a centre for administration. Therefore he searched for a fertile place conveniently situated on the main routes of communications with the various parts of the Empire. The locality of Baghdad was suggested after careful study; it was not far from the ancient capitals, Opis of the Akkadians, Seleucia of the Seleucids and Parthians, and Ctesiphon of the Sāsānians. It was situated on the Tigris, in a fertile and thickly cultivated area with many canals piercing the land to serve for irrigation, communications and defence. There were many Christian monasteries and settlements. The land was cheap and flat with no natural or legal restrictions to its expansion

The caliph al-Manṣūr can be said to have continued in a sense the simple and unpretentious Arab tradition. He did not call the new city or any of its buildings by his name. Instead he chose names derived from the Koran for his city (Dār al-Salām) and his second great palace (al-Khuld)—both names alluding to Paradise. He did not object to the general use of the ancient Aramaic names of the city and its main quarters (Baghdād, Karkh and Ruṣāfa).

Al-Manṣūr moved to his new capital only after quelling three menacing uprisings: those of his uncle 'Abd Allāh b. 'Alī (the 'Abbāsid), Abū Muslim (the Khurāsānian), and Muḥammad and Ibrāhīm, sons of al-Ḥasan (the 'Alid), each of whom aimed at deposing him from the caliphate. The quelling of these rebellions relieved him from suspect elements, and enabled him to have in his capital only sincere supporters; the population did not raise any revolution against the 'Abbāsid caliphs. The 'Abbāsid family sided with him against the rebellion of 'Abd Allāh b. 'Alī; he in turn chose from amongst his family the governors of the provinces. Nevertheless he neither granted them an allotment of land nor allowed any of them to build a dwelling-place in his Round City. Their register (*dīwān*) remained in Syria up to the time of al-Mahdī who transferred it to Medina and not to Baghdad. There is also no evidence as to the residence of any 'Alids in Baghdad during the early times of al-Manṣūr.

The Round City of al-Manṣūr lacked any luxury establishments or recreation places such as theatres, gymnasiums, gardens, statues, or public monuments. Horse-racing grounds did not exist before the time of al-Hādī, 30 years after its foundation. Even the Khuld palace of al-Manṣūr and the great palaces of his sons were built outside the Round City. Water canals and aqueducts did not exist in his early plans and were added after several years of its occupation. Thus the city of al-Manṣūr shows features that make it similar to the early Arab *amṣār*.

Al-Manṣūr realized that firm rule should create a capital well established according to a carefully thought-out plan. The engineers and architects were mere executors of his ideas. Having the limited purpose of establishing a well protected seat of government, the caliph planned to have it well fortified, not only by the already existing network of canals, but also by a wide and deep ditch, and a massive double wall. It is worth noting that he also fortified the old *amṣār*, Baṣra, Kūfa and Medina, by ditches and walls for the first time. The City, round in shape, was about 1000 cubits, i.e. 600 metres in diameter; this makes it more a citadel (*quhandiz*) of the Persian type. The round shape was the most convenient form for defence purposes.

In the centre of the City was the caliph's residence, the cathedral mosque, and the bureaux, just as was the case in the early *amṣār*. This expresses the intimate relationship between religion and state, and gave the state an additional dignity. The palace and the mosque were the most distinguished buildings in the Round City, which had no other famous building all throughout 'Abbāsid history.

The army was the effective instrument which enabled the 'Abbāsid dynasty to replace the Umayyads in the caliphate. It was also the principal power upon which al-Manṣūr relied to establish his authority and defeat his enemies. Sources referred to the number of 'Abbāsid soldiers who fought in some of the battles. The largest was about 20,000. The most expressive text on the numerical strength of the army is a quotation in al-Ṭabarī from al-Manṣūr who, when Ibrāhim b. al-Ḥasan revolted, said " O God! my camp has only 2000 men. I have scattered my soldiers: thirty thousand are with al-Mahdī in Rayy, forty thousand are with Ibn al-Ash'ath in North Africa; and the rest are with 'Īsā b. Mūsā [in Medina]. O God if I emerge safely from this, my camp will never be less than 30,000 " (Ṭab., iii, 305). This text, if true, shows that his military forces in Baghdad were about 30,000.

Al-Ya'qūbī states that al-Manṣūr "granted his clients and commanders lands inside the [Round] City where roads were named after them. He granted others at the gates of [i.e. outside] the City. He granted the soldiers fields around the City, and to his family the outskirts, he granted a plot of land to his son al-Mahdī and a group of his family, clients and commanders" (*History*, iii, 109). Al-Ya'qūbī says elsewhere that "in every one of these roads most of his commanders who are worthy of being trusted to reside with him, and most of his clients and of those whom he needs in the menacing events. The two ends of each road have a firm gate" (*Buldān*, p. 241). This shows that the residents in the Round City were the trustworthy clients and commanders. Al-Khaṭīb says that at each of the four Gates of the city was a commander with 1000 soldiers, i.e. the total number of the forces on the four gates was 4000 soldiers. Probably this was the total number of families residing in the Round City.

Al-Khaṭīb claims that the "roads of the city were called afte. the names of the clients of Al-Manṣūr (i, 89). Al-Ya'qūbī gives the names of these roads. Twenty-nine of them were called after persons who were probably adherents [clients] of the caliph. He mentions also four roads called after their occupants i.e. the Guard, the police, water carriers prayer callers; two other roads called the narrow, and one called after a group of people, the Marw al-Rūdhī.

The people of Marw al-Rūdh are the only group mentioned as having a settlement in the Round City. This may be due to the extent of al-Manṣūr's reliance on them. Indeed al-Ṭabarī refers to their military role in the early 'Abbāsid period: they took part in defeating the Umayyads, they fought against the pirates of Ibn Kawan (iii, 79), against the Khārijite al-Mulabbad (iii, 124), 'Abd al-Jabbār al-Azdī (iii, 136), and Ustādhsīs (iii, 355), and took part in quelling some of the revolutions after the time of al-Manṣūr (iii, 493, 979); one of the leaders of the Rāwandiyya, Abū Khalid, was from Marw al-Rūdh.

After finishing the establishment of the Round City, al-Manṣūr moved the treasury and the bureaux there. The Round City now contained the Royal Palace, the cathedral Mosque, the houses of the Caliph's young sons, the bodyguard, and the bureaux; it has therefore become more of a Royal Residence or Dār al-Khilāfa. The extent of its growth was limited by the ditch and the walls. The caliph endeavoured to keep its formal, administrative, and military character, and therefore he expelled the merchants at an early date and did not allow them to settle therein.

IV

The Round City, being limited in area, was insufficient for the needs of the caliph or for the expected growth of population: his followers and entourage, and the immigrants to the new capital, were so numerous that the city was bound to expand beyond its walls.

The earliest settlers were undoubtedly the followers and supporters of the caliph; they were the 'Abbāsid family, the companions, the clients, the commanders, the army, and the masses. The 'Abbāsid family was, by now, clearly distinguished from the 'Alids, and preserved its solidarity during the rebellion of 'Abd Allāh b. 'Alī and the clash between al-Amīn and al-Ma'mūn. Al-Manṣūr cared for his family, and advised his son al-Mahdī " to respect them, push them forward, bestow grants on them, promote them over the rest; their glory and prominence is yours " (Ṭab., iii, 445). " He granted each of his uncles one million *dirhams*, and distributed among his family in one day ten millions *dirhams*. He was the first caliph to distribute such a large sum of money " (Ṭab., iii, 421), and he appointed many of them commanders and governors of provinces.

Al-Mahdī went further in his care of his family; in 160 A.H. he " gave back his family their confiscated properties " (Ṭab., iii, 485). Eight years later he " transferred his family's register from Syria to Medina. He also devoted the incomes from the estates on al-Ṣilāh Canal to his family " (Ṭab., iii, 523). The first census of the 'Abbāsid family occurred in the year 200 A.H. when they were thirty-three thousand (Ṭab., iii, 1000).

Al Manṣūr planned that the houses of his younger children and of his own slave servants should be around the Raḥba (*Buldān*, p. 240). But the impressive and large land grants and palaces of the members of 'Abbāsid family were outside the Round City. To the south of it and on Ṣarāt canal were the grants of 'Abd al-Wahhāb b. Ibrāhīm, al-'Abbās, Isḥāq b. 'Īsā b. 'Alī, the original gate-keepers, of the Sharawī family; Ja'far, his son, and most important of all, the grant to al-Mahdī, his elder son and heir apparent. This grant, called al-Sharqiyya, had one of the three cathedral mosques, and was the seat of one of the three judges in Baghdad for many centuries.

East of the Round City were the grants of his sons Sulayman, Ṣāliḥ and Ja'far, as well as the Caliph's palace al-Khuld (*Buldān*, ii, 17). When Ruṣāfa was founded on the eastern bank of the Tigris, it contained some of the grants of the 'Abbāsid personalities, Ismā'īl b. 'Alī, al-'Abbās b. Muḥammad, and al-Sarī b. 'Abd Allāh (*Buldān*, p. 252). Probably there were other unmentioned 'Abbāsid grants near the above mentioned ones which were outside the Round City to the south and east of it.

The Companions, the Anṣār and the Arabs

Our sources repeatedly mention the Companions (*ṣaḥāba*) who are distinguished from, and rival to, the clients (*al-mawālī*) (Ṭab., iii, 488). They were the prototype of the " elite " (*khāṣṣa*) who replaced them from the time of al-Rashīd onwards (Ṭab., iii, 488, 567, 770).

The companions came second in rank to the 'Abbāsid family (Ṭab., iii, 430, 567). They numbered 700 at the time of al-Manṣūr (Ṭab., iii, 495) and were from various Arab tribes. They were quartered on the Ṣarāt, near the 'Abbāsid grants, and had their own mosque (al-Khaṭīb, vii, 430, xii, 205). Each of them received 500 *dirhams* a month (Ṭab., iii, 365).

In 160 A.H. al-Mahdī transferred from Medina to Baghdad some 500 Anṣārīs, chiefly from the Zurayq clan and granted them settlements near the palaces of the Barmakids where they had their own *rabaḍ*, street, and mosque. Later on they had a provost (*naqīb*).

The other Arabs in Baghdad were Khuza'a, al-'Arāb, the Kūfites, the Baṣrīs, the Wāsiṭīs, and the Yamanīs. No other quarter was called after an Arab tribe; most of the quarters were called after cities rather than tribes.

The Clients (al-mawālī)

The clients were one of the groups upon which the early 'Abbāsid, relied. They were ranked below the 'Abbāsids and the Companions (Ṭab., iii, 477, 558, 1027, 1030, 430) and above the Commanders (Ṭab., iii, 430, 558, 546, 775, 1027, 1130). They were used by al-Manṣūr at home to run his own affairs (Ṭab., ii, 440; *Murūj*, iii, 315) and were given a highly favourable position by al-Mahdī (Ṭab., iii, 532, 488).

The term " clients " was used for the individuals, groups, or army directly connected with the caliph. In Baghdad they had a street (al-Khaṭīb, iii, 105, iv, 325) and a stable (al-Ya'qūbī, p. 243).

The Army

The chief aim of establishing Baghdad was to find a base for the imperial army which seem to have numbered 30,000 men (Ṭab., iii, 305). 4000 of these were quartered inside the Round City, and the rest around it. The structure and organization of this army was the basis of the topographical organization of early Baghdad.

The Khurāsānīs were the back-bone of the army of al-Manṣūr, who describes them as " our followers, supporters and the mainstay of our dynasty " (Ṭab., iii, 431, 445; cf. also 454, 473, 475). They were the most important part of the armies which defeated the Umayyads, quelled the menacing revolutions and fought the Byzantines. Coming originally from Khurāsān, they spoke Persian. The names and appellations of most of their prominent personalities were purely Arabic, which suggests that they were not all of Persian stock. Many of their commanders were called after various districts of the eastern provinces, e.g. Jurjān (Ṭab., iii, 54, 92, 94) Khuwārizm (Ṭab., iii, 399, 801) Bukhārā (Ṭab., iii, 802) Abīward (Ṭab., iii, 290, 300) Khuttal (Ṭab., iii, 307) and Sijistān (Ṭab., iii, 355).

Al-Ya'qūbī describes in detail the outer surroundings of the Round City. He says that the outskirts were divided into four sectors (*arbā'*). The southern sector was the largest; in it were the settlements of the Fārsīs, the Kirmānīs as well as the 'Abbāsids and their Sharawite clients. In the west were the settlements of the Khuwārizmīs, the Bukhārīs and the Marw al-Rūdhīs. In the north west were the settlements of the people of Balkh, Marw Khuttal, Bukhārā, Isbījāb, Ishtakhunj, Kābul and Khuwārizm. Each group, he adds, had a commander and a chief. In the north were the settlements of al-Manṣūr's slaves, the Kirmānīs, the Sughdīs, the Ṣamaghans and the Faryābīs. In the east, i.e. on the Tigris banks, were his sons' palaces, as well as the settlements of the Jurjānīs, Farghānīs, Baghawīs, and the Africans.

Al-Ya'qūbī mentions the commander of each of these groups (*Buldān*, 241–6). Al-Khaṭīb mentions the quarters of some of them e.g. the Bughawīs (i, 410, iii, 394), the Fārsīs (i, 85, vii, 15, iii, 38), the Khuwārizmīs (i, 85, v, 357, x, 110), the Rāzīs (vii, 366), the Marwīs (vi, 296, 28) and the Kābulīs (vi, 28).

The latest census of the Arab army in Khurāsān refers back to the time of the insurgence of Qutayba (96 A.H.) when it numbered fifty thousands, divided into six major parts. One of them was the Kūfites, and the rest were called after the major Baṣrī tribes, Tamīm, Bakr, Azd, 'Abd al-Qays, and Ahl al-'Āliya. The army was subdivided into many groups each of which garrisoned a city. Probably each of these subdivisions was called, in course of time, by the name of the district or the city in which it was quartered. It must be borne in mind that Qutayba introduced the policy of levying on each of the conquered cities a certain number of men to fight with the Arab army. Therefore we may safely assume that the Muslim army in Khurāsān and Central Asia was grouped on a city basis; the army of each city consisted of both Arabs and non-Arabs, and the commander of each group had a special importance. It is worth noting that in the later Umayyad régime, even in Syria, there were some army groups called after their commanders. The 'Abbāsids took over the army of Khurāsān without revising its organization and quartered it in Baghdad. The above mentioned quarters of Baghdad reveal the subdivisions of the later Umayyad army in Khurāsān. Each of the subdivisions consisted of both Arab and non-Arab groups.

The Abnā'

Among the military groups settled outside the Round City were the *Abnā'* (Ṭab., iii, 936). They were variously called "the sons of the ['Abbāsid] propaganda" (*abnā' al-da'wa*) (Ṭab., iii, 499), "the sons of efficiency" (*abnā' al-kifāya*) (Ṭab., iii, 849), "people of bracelets and diadems" (Ṭab., iii, 825) and "the sons of kings" (Ṭab., iii, 830). They were about 20,000 fighters (Ṭab., iii, 828, 840), who had fought in many battles, and sided with al-Amīn in his struggle with al-Ma'mūn.

The *Abnā'* spoke Arabic, some of them were poets (Ṭab., iii, 833, 936) and most of their commanders who are mentioned were Arabs. They were probably the descendants of the army levied by the Arabs on the local cities and provinces of Khurāsān and Central Asia.

The Africans and the Nomads

The Africans were quartered east of the Round City (al-Ya'qūbī, p. 249); they were part of the 'Abbāsid army at the time of al-Manṣūr (Ṭab., iii, 305), of al-Amīn (Ṭab., iii, 873, 907, 882) and of al-Ma'mūn (Ṭab., iii, 1005, 1018, 1073). The nomads (*al-a'rāb*) are mentioned as part of al-Amīn's army (Ṭab., iii, 827–40). They were quartered in al-Ruṣāfa.

Soldiers received an annual salary in money and were responsible for supplying themselves with equipment. The caliph laid down the plan of the city, paid the costs of the ditches, walls, arcades, palace, cathedral mosque and the bureaux. He also granted land to the people who themselves paid the cost of building their own houses.

The Officials

Baghdad, the new capital of the Empire, was the centre of the imperial and local bureaux and offices. Most of these were located in the Round City adjacent to the caliph's palace; while the offices of the police prefect and the commander of the guard and most other bureaux were around the central palace. The chiefs of bureaux were granted lands in the south, outside the Round City, near the quarters of the Companions. A number of other chiefs of bureaux were granted lands in al-Ruṣāfa, east of the Tigris.

The offices of the chiefs, who were Arabs, were not hereditary. The grants were personal and did not include the numerous other junior officials and employees. But there is no reference to their number or settlements in the city.

Employees seem to have been mostly recruited from the surrounding country. A large number of the clerks came from Anbār and were quartered near the Anṣār on the south-east borders outside the Round City. They appreciated Sāsānian culture and followed the old Persian traditions, but used the Arabic language, which was the most important common link amongst the inhabitants of the new cosmopolitan capital.

Arabic was the mother tongue of the Arabs, the religious language of the Muslims and the cultural instrument of the scholars who began to flock to the flourishing new imperial capital, enjoying the freedom of thought and non-interference of the state. Those scholars were scattered in the various quarters of the city. They did not have one academic centre, but preferred to teach in the mosques.

The early ʻAbbāsid caliphs endeavoured to encourage Arabic culture, and chose Arabic scholars to educate their sons. They encouraged the collecting of pre-Islamic poetry as well as the translation into Arabic of Greek and Indian works in medicine, astronomy, geometry and mathematics in general. Many commanders and notables shared with the caliphs in their interests and thereby aided in establishing Arabic firmly in the new city as well as in the Empire.

The earliest settlers in Baghdad were free people chosen for their allegiance to the caliph and for their common interest in the new régime. Baghdad had few immigrants from Kūfa where the first ʻAbbāsid caliph was enthroned; it had none of the Banū Musalliya who carried out the ʻAbbāsid propaganda. On the other hand, Ḥijāzīs, in spite of their lack of enthusiasm for the early propaganda, were settled in Baghdad. The Rāwandīs, the sect which stressed reverence of the ʻAbbāsids to the verge of divine incarnation, were allowed to express and propagate their views but were not granted that active support which al-Ma'mūn and his two successors gave to those who believed in the creation of the Koran, and did not win the active support of the citizens of Baghdad. It should be borne in mind that the most important element of the population were the Khurasānīs who were not inclined to dogmatic disputes and religious innovation: their common interest was to cling to the caliph.

The early settlers in Baghdad were of different origins and cultures, the heterodoxy of population was wider in Baghdad than in most of other cities. The new capital was a real metropolis, and better representative of the Islamic Empire than semi-nomadic Medina or quasi-Byzantine Damascus. Arabic, Aramaic, Persian and Turkish cultures were living together as early as its foundation; and the scantiness of the Greco-

Byzantine elements was compensated by the active translation of the Greek intellectual heritage into Arabic.

The population were nevertheless linked together by the common bonds of the Arabic language, the Islamic religion, and their allegiance to the caliph who stood above racial divisions. The army and the officials formed the majority among the population of early Baghdad as of the *amṣār*; but whereas the *amṣār* were dominated by a population of almost purely Arabic nomadic stock whose relations with the government were not always smooth, the population of early Baghdad had good relations with the ruling 'Abbāsid caliphs. The non-Arab elements were many, but the caliph's support of the nomadic culture and the Arabs created a healthy balance and a peaceful process of establishing a cosmopolitan civilization into which were integrated the numerous different cultures that already existed in the Middle East.

V

The majority of the early population depended for their living on government grants and salaries. The caliph's uncles were granted one million *dirhams* each, and his family was granted ten million *dirhams*. Each of the companions (*ṣaḥāba*) was granted 500 *dirhams* monthly. The highest monthly salary, paid to the chief officials was 300 *dirhams*, and the lowest was 30 *dirhams*. The senior army officers received 2000 *dirhams*, and the juniors received 80 *dirhams*.

The salaries of the army and officials was the largest item in government expenditure. They were met from the revenues of the provinces pouring into the new city, which became the chief centre of a vigorous economic activity. The salaries distributed amongst a large number of the population led to a general rise in the standard of living, without leading to the rise of a limited class of rich people. They gave Baghdad a similarity to the old *amṣār* whose Arab population received the stipend. They also widened the gap between the new capital and the countryside, which continued to pay taxes to the new capital.

Expenditure on other public enterprises was not as high as on salaries. The government followed the old tradition laid down by Mohammed, whereby its duties were confined to defence, internal security, establishment of justice, and the collection of taxes to meet the expenses of administration. Al-Manṣūr was a serious caliph, a militant ruler and an admirer of the nomadic tradition which appreciated politics and literature rather than painting and architecture. His plans did not include the embellishment of the city nor the establishment of buildings for recreation. Therefore the Round City had no public gardens, playgrounds, pools, or beautiful buildings. His palace was the only impressive building inside the Round City. The other palaces were outside the Round City, even the Cathedral Mosques did not exceed four at the height of its prosperity. The only racing ground in the Round City was established at the time of al-Mahdī. Al-Manṣūr paid the costs of the walls and ditches, the caliphs palace, the mosque, the bureaux and the Arcades; while the private houses of the inhabitants were built on the owner's account.

People felt the need for public buildings and considered the provision of them a religious duty. Many of the rich and well-to-do people built mosques which fulfilled many social purposes. These endowments were voluntary and personal, dependent on the individual's wealth and religious and social conscience. They were not always correlated to public needs nor were they well distributed. The numerous individual mosques in a quarter might indicate the existence of many generous pious men rather than a dense population. The government had no bureau of endowments.

In founding the new capital for his army, officials and followers, al-Manṣūr planned to have small shops on the major streets of the Round City and to have in each quarter (*rabaḍ*) a minor bazaar and shops to meet the needs of the dwellers in that quarter. These bazaars were presumably small and non-specialized. They were more like the army markets which accompanied Muslim military campaigns; they were run too by the people of that market. Al-Manṣūr did not plan to have a large central market with specialized bazaars in his Capital.

Nevertheless the increasing numbers of the population, the large amount of money distributed amongst them, the rise of purchasing power and the standard of living, and the great demand for labourers, artisans and craftsmen to meet the needs of the city dwellers, attracted large numbers of immigrants, who flocked in such a number and so quickly that they upset the caliph's plans, and distorted the harmonious peaceful life of the Round City. They lacked the discipline of his army and the allegiance of his followers. The appointment of a *muḥtasib* did not prevent the business men (*ahl al-sūq*) from creating troubles for the caliph, who decided in 157 A.H. to move them to al-Karkh southwest of his city. Al-Karkh became the chief business centre, and was gradually subdivided into many bazaars each of which was confined to one kind of trade. But the quick growth of the population and of economic activity out-stripped the capacity of al-Karkh, and led to the expansion of Baghdad as a whole, until it became the greatest city in the Empire and the largest in the world.

THE CALIPH'S PERSONAL DOMAIN[1]

The City Plan of Baghdad Re-Examined

by

J. Lassner

Islamic urbanists recognize the existence of two distinct places of major occupation by distinguishing between the created and spontaneous cities of the Islamic realm—between cities built according to a preconceived plan, and those such as the garrison towns of the *amṣār*, whose development was stimulated by response to the particular needs of the Islamic conquest.[2] The early pattern of growth which was characteristic of such military colonies as al-Baṣra and al-Kūfa was rapid and without real awareness of the formal elements of city planning. However, the original military camps soon gave way to permanent installations. Extended routes of supply were replaced by fixed markets and an incipient industrial organization, as an outer town of artisans and merchants grew around the original military settlement. The growth of the *amṣār* town was therefore directed from the centre out, giving the impression that these urban areas were not so much the execution of an orderly plan, but the product of several stages of spontaneous generation.

The historical growth of Baghdad beginning with the magnificent Round City constructed by al-Manṣūr in 145/762 suggests a rather different type of urban development. The Round City or Madīnat al-Salām as it was also called was not a prefabricated military camp given permanence by a growing sedentary environment, but rather the creation of that consummate planning and execution which caused the essayist, al-Jāḥiẓ, to remark: It is as though it was poured into a mould and cast—clearly a major undertaking based on a preconceived plan of the Caliph's own choosing.[3] What then was the design and function of the original

---

[1] This paper is part of a book which I am currently preparing on the topography of Baghdad.

[2] For a general survey of the Islamic city, see G. Marçais, " La conception des villes dans l'Islam "; *Revue D'Alger*, ii (1945), 517–33.

[3] Al-Khaṭīb, i, 70; al-Ṭabarī, iii, 277; Yāqūt, i, 682.

CHRONOLOGICAL MAP

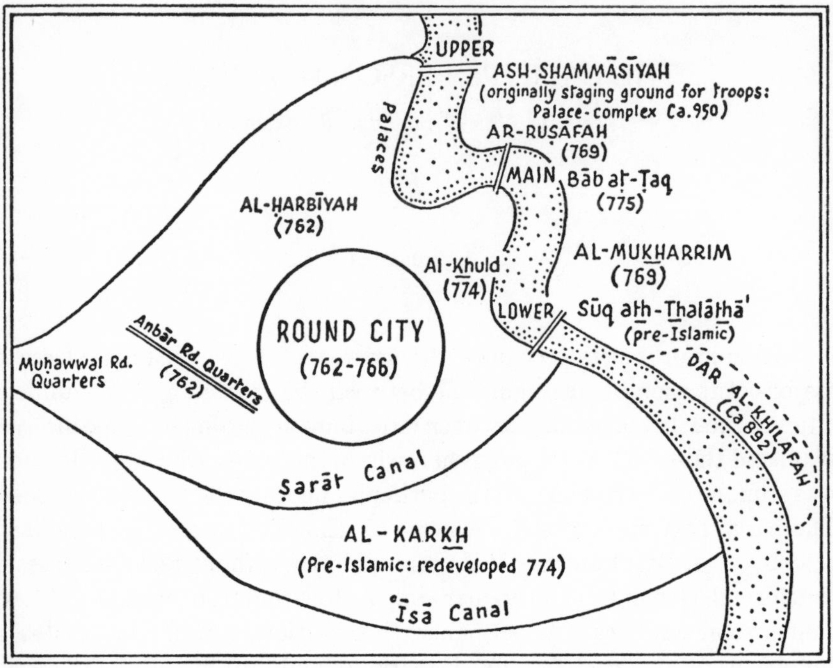

Islamic structure, and what was the pattern of its early development?

The successful completion of so vast a project presupposes not only a pre-determined architectural design, but a highly organized and efficient set of work procedures. It was not until a large labour force had been assembled that construction was actually begun, and it was not until four years later that all the major elements of the Round City were completed, allowing for the year in which construction was halted while the Caliph was busy with Shī'ite revolts in al-Baṣra and the Ḥijāz.[4] The essential feature of this public works programme was the recruiting of skilled and unskilled labour from the outlying regions of present-day Syria and Iraq, including such places as al-Mawṣil, al-Jabal, al-Kūfa, Wāsiṭ, and al-Baṣra. Salaries were fixed according to the division of labour and were apparently paid out at set intervals giving the impression of an emerging boom-town. The total number of workers is reported by al-Ya'qūbī to have exceeded 100,000, a figure which reflects the magnitude of construction, though perhaps exaggerated. Each quarter was under the general supervision of

---

[4] Construction began in 145/762. See al-Balādhurī, *Futūḥ*, p. 295; Ibn Qutayba, *al-Ma'ārif*, p. 192; al-Ṭabarī, iii, 277; al-Mas'ūdī, *Tanbīh*, p. 360; al-Muqaddasī, p. 121; al-Khaṭīb, p. 79; Yāqūt, pp. 680, 682.

a military commander whose troops provided for security, while technical affairs were entrusted to individuals who were experts in such matters.[5]

With thousands of workers assembling from the outlying districts, the skilled and unskilled labour, the artisans, and the military would have all required adequate housing and access to established markets for services, as well as an incipient industrial plant for the production of building materials. All these factors tend to indicate that Baghdad was assuming a quality of permanence even before the Round City was completed. In time the urban area grew around the original walls of Madīnat as-Salām and developed into a sprawling complex of interdependent elements, each containing its own markets, mosques, and cemeteries, and giving rise as well to its own autonomous institutions. Judging from the description of the fiefs situated there, the northwest suburb of al-Ḥarbiyya was heavily populated with al-Manṣūr's generals and military personnel.[6] From what has been said, it is likely that the earliest grants were issued concurrent with the growth of the original city and were situated in or adjacent to the various military colonies (*jund*) established in that sector according to tribal or ethnic grouping. The civilian labourers and artisans no doubt took up residence in the old inhabited market areas of al-Karkh to the south of the emerging city well before the completion of the original structure.[7] Therefore, contrary to popular belief, the growth of the suburbs on the West Side of the Tigris must have preceded rather than followed the construction of Madīnat as-Salām although there are statements which perhaps suggest otherwise. To be sure there was an expansion of the outlying areas, however, the textual evidence which indicates the subsequent development of these suburbs (157/774) after the completion of the Round City, presumably refers then to the needs created by a natural increase in the population of over a period of twelve years.[8] Such being the case, Baghdad, unlike the cities of the *amṣār*, did not at first develop from the inside-out, but rather from the outside-in.

This unique pattern of growth is to a large extent determined by the pre-Islamic character of the site, a factor which until now has been almost entirely neglected. Although the strategic situation of Baghdad was ideal for a major urban centre, the Sāsānid monarchs chose to establish their capital somewhat downstream at Ctesiphon (al-Madā'in). The major

---

[5] Al-Ṭabarī, pp. 272, 276–7, 278, 322; al-Ya'qūbī, *Buldān*, p. 238; al-Muqaddasī, p. 121; al-Khaṭīb, pp. 67, 70; Yāqūt, p. 681.

[6] *Ibid.*, p. 85; al-Ya'qūbī, *Buldān*, p. 248.

[7] G. Le Strange, *Baghdad During the Abbasid Caliphate*, London 1900, Map III.

[8] Al-Khaṭīb, pp. 79–82.

market areas servicing Ctesiphon as well as the hinterland, were apparently situated across the river at Seleucia, thereby resulting in the curious arrangement of a capital some short distance from its main commercial centre. It is this type of arrangement which the Caliph seems to have desired at Baghdad; but rather than move to Ctesiphon, he established an administrative centre at the confluence of the Tigris and the Ṣarāt. It was as we shall see not only the location but the architectural arrangement of the Round City which enabled the Caliph to emulate his Persian successors in withdrawing his administration from the immediate presence of the general population; for the affairs of government must be conducted at some distance from any source of possible subversion, but always close enough to basic services. It comes as no surprise, therefore, that al-Manṣūr's city was built adjacent to, but distinct from the old market areas of al-Karkh. The Round City was, in fact, the administrative centre of the realm which comprised together with its suburban districts, the greater urban complex—the imperial capital. As such Madīnat as-Salām was not an integrated city, but was more correctly a palace precinct, serviced by the commercial enterprises in the surrounding areas. This contention is fully supported by the available historical and architectural evidence.

As excavations have never been undertaken on the presumed site of the Round City, information on the architecture and physical layout is derived from literary sources, of which the two most significant accounts are the section on Baghdad in al-Ya'qūbī's *K. al-Buldān*, and those chapters in al-Khaṭīb's history which deal with the construction of Madīnat as-Salām and its mosques.[9] The Khaṭīb and al-Ya'qūbī appear to use independent authorities. Al-Ya'qūbī's source is not given, but it is indicated that the description is based on the city as it existed in the time of al-Manṣūr. The report of the Khaṭīb is derived essentially from an account of the jurist Wakī' (d. 918), which is in turn based on various older authorities. The two sources complement each other with regard to detail, the account of the Khaṭīb being the more extended description. Occasionally there are conflicting figures suggesting perhaps that the authors refer to different metrological systems.

Certain general characteristics of these works raise serious problems as to their value for any proposed reconstruction of the city. Al-Ya'qūbī's report is terse with little, if any, pretence at critical handling of the material. On the other hand, the Khaṭīb, whose forte was the religious

[9] See J. Lassner, "Notes on the Topography of Baghdad: The Systematic Descriptions of the City and the Khaṭīb al-Baghdādī", *Journal of the American Oriental Society*, lxxxiii, 458–69; esp. pp. 460, 461–2.

sciences, indicates perhaps by force of habit, several reports for various accounts, usually with a complete *isnād*. However, when taken as a whole, his account describing the plan of the Round City is quite fragmentary, and details are often lacking for certain major structures. Since numbers are easily confused in an Arabic text, the statistical evidence which is the basis of any architectural reconstruction is not above suspicion. In general, the Khaṭīb was probably a reliable transmitter of the information which he possessed; but lacking an inclination for technical problems, and without professional knowledge of architecture and topography, he seems to have been somewhat arbitrary in his choice of accounts, and not too concerned with the critical problems to be found in the original texts. The task of reconstructing the Round City is, therefore, highly theoretical and very speculative. The major architectural work on this subject is that of E. Herzfeld, whose reconstructions were subsequently accepted with some modification by K. A. C. Creswell in his monumental survey of *Early Muslim Architecture*.[10] It is clear that their efforts raise many questions which will only be solved if and when systematic diggings are undertaken on the suspected site of the Round City. However, on the basis of the literary evidence alone, it is possible to offer some divergent views which represent a new concept of the city plan, and a different thesis as to its architectural function and historical development in the earliest period.

When completed, the city of al-Manṣūr consisted of three architectural elements: the outer fortifications, an inner residential area of symmetrically arranged streets, and the vast inner courtyard where the Caliph's mosque and residence were situated. The outer fortifications took the shape of two concentric walls separated by an *intervallum* (*faṣīl*) and surrounded by a moat. The inner wall, since it was the protective wall of the city, was the larger of the two, and was flanked by roundels. Access to the residential area and the central court was gained through four elaborate gateways and arcades beginning at the outer wall and ending at the great circular courtyard. Situated equidistant from one another along the axis of the Caliph's residence, the four-gate complex framed the northeast, northwest, southeast and southwest quadrants of the residential area. A second *intervallum* separated the houses from the outer fortifications, and a third separated them from the enclosure wall of the great central court where the palace-mosque was situated.[11]

The sources conflict in reporting the total area which was circum-

---

[10] E. Herzfeld, *Archäologische Reise im Euphrat und Tigris Gebiet*, Berlin 1921, ii, 103 ff.; Creswell, ii, 4 ff.

[11] See fig. I.

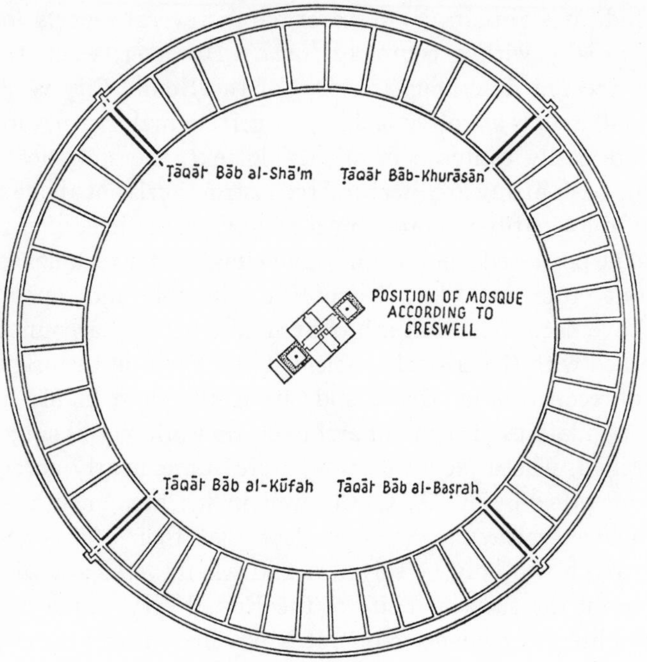

THE ROUND CITY
(Based on Herzfeld, p. 120)

Fig. I

scribed by the walls of the structure as there are no less than seven *isnāds*, giving figures ranging from 576,000 to 64,000,000 square cubits. Within this wide range, Herzfeld and Creswell were inclined to accept the report which is attributed to Rabāḥ, the architect of the city walls, and accordingly, obtained a figure of approximately 20,000,000 square cubits by calculating the distance between each of the symmetrically arranged gateways (1 *mīl*).[12] Allowing even for these larger measurements, the area circumscribed by the walls of al-Manṣūr's city was too small for the major urban centre of the ʿAbbāsid Empire. Moreover, certain architectural features of the Round City give the impression that it was constructed as a governmental complex that retained some of the outward features of an integrated city, but which was more correctly a palace precinct of which the Caliph's residence-mosque in the central court was the major element.

The Khaṭīb does not indicate whether any other structures occupied this court; however, al-Yaʿqūbī mentions two additional buildings. One adjacent to the Damascus Gate housed the chief of the guard (*ḥaras*) and

---

[12] See Lassner, *op. cit.*, pp. 461–2; Creswell, p. 8.

his troops; the other, the location of which is not indicated, was a large portico (*saqīfa*) raised on columns of burnt brick cemented with gypsum. This portico contained the apartment (*dār*) of the chief of police (*shurṭa*) and presumably room for his men, thereby providing maximum security for the Caliph's personal domain. These buildings were probably intended for those men who were actually on duty in the central courtyard.[13] The remainder of the contingent was no doubt quartered in those streets designated for the police and the guards, which were situated in the residential area flanking the arcades of the Baṣra Gate.[14] According to al-Ya'qūbī, these were the only buildings in the central court other than the palace and principal mosque. The text also indicates that surrounding the court[15] were the residences of al-Manṣūr's younger children, his servants in attendance, the slaves, and in addition, the treasury (*bayt al-māl*), the arsenal (*khizānat as-silāḥ*), *diwān* of the palace personnel (*al-aḥshām*), the public kitchen, and various other government agencies.

Despite these explicit statements in al-Ya'qūbī, and although it can be assumed that these buildings were an important element in the original city plan, there is no provision for these structures in the diagram of the Round City as reconstructed by Herzfeld and Creswell.[16] Le Strange, who is somewhat more faithful to the Arabic text, included these buildings in his plans, but lacking any clear picture as to their arrangements, he arbitrarily placed them at various points around the palace of the Caliph.[17] The text of al-Ya'qūbī is, however, explicit. Aside from the palace-mosque, there were only two buildings in the court itself: the structure designated for the guards, and the portico of the police. It is therefore clear that the various *diwāns* and the residences of al-Manṣūr's children and servants were not situated in the courtyard but surrounded it, thus forming a ring of buildings between the third *intervallum* which marked the limits of the residential area, and the central court itself. As for the city plan *in toto*, this ringed structure must be regarded as having originally been an integral element of the architecture of the central court, i.e., the

[13] *Buldān*, p. 240. Al-Ya'qūbī indicates that in his time this portico was used as a place for prayer (*muṣallā*), thereby suggesting that it was in fact the Dār al-Qaṭṭān which is mentioned by the Khaṭīb, pp. 108–9. That is to say, when there was no longer sufficient room in the principal mosque, the Dār al-Qaṭṭān was added to it in the year 260/873–4 or 261/874–5. The structure of a portico (surrounding a court) would have been ideally suited for conversion into a place of prayer.

[14] *Ibid.*

[15] *Ḥawla'r-raḥba kamā tadūrū.*

[16] However, Creswell does mention this account in his text (p. 17).

[17] See Maps II, III; text of Le Strange, pp. 30–1.

Caliph's personal domain, comprising the area, his residence and the governmental machinery.[18]

Incidental evidence from a historical source not only supports this contention, but also solves a number of difficulties arising from the text of the Khaṭīb. Among the statements which he preserves on the building of the city, al-Ṭabarī[19] mentions that the gates of the chambers (*maqāṣīr*) of a group of al-Manṣūr's generals and scribes opened on to the court (*raḥba*) of the mosque. Since the court is expressed here by the term *raḥba,* and not *ṣaḥn,* it is clear that the account refers not to the internal court of the mosque, but the great central yard which surrounded it and the adjoining

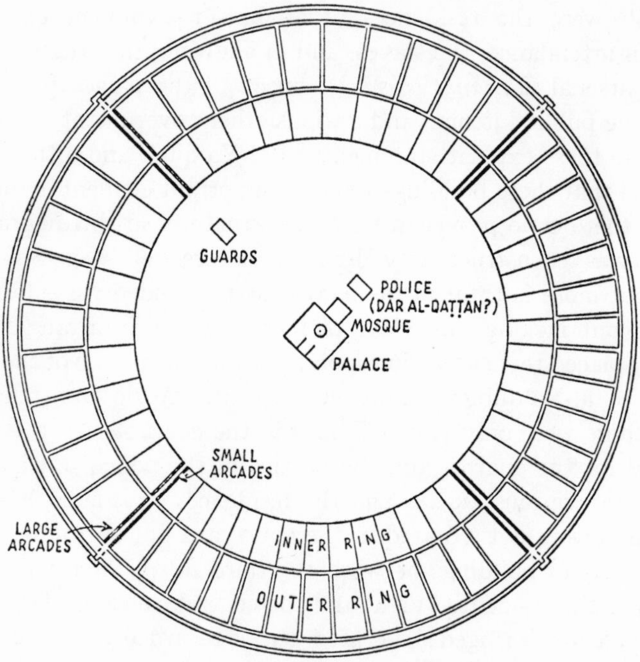

THE ROUND CITY

Fig. II

residence. These chambers cannot be accounted for in the plans of Herzfeld and Creswell; but the statement is consistent with the description of al-Ya'qūbī, as well as the reconstruction of the ringed area suggested above. Moreover, following this report, al-Ṭabarī continues with a discussion of the central courtyard. He cites an account, which is also

[18] See my reconstruction, figs. II, III, and V.

[19] iii, 322–3.

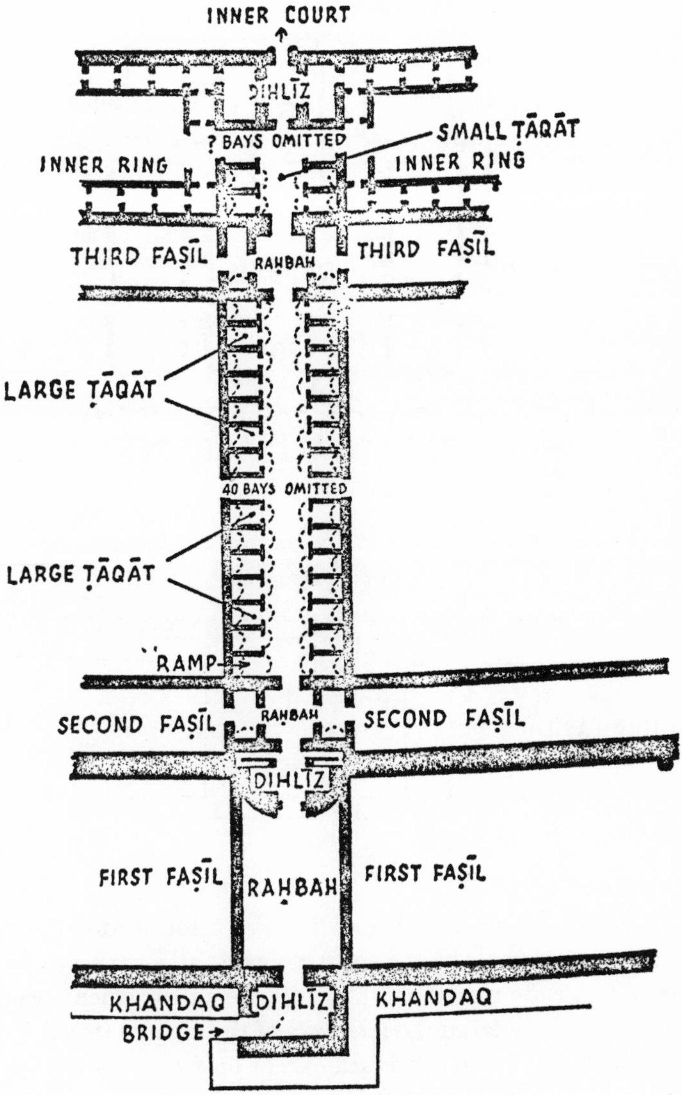

THE LARGE ṬĀQĀT

Fig. III

reported in the Khaṭīb, that ʿĪsā b. ʿAlī [the Caliph's uncle] complained about having to walk from the gate of the [central] court to the palace, and suggested that he might instead hitch a ride on one of the pack-animals

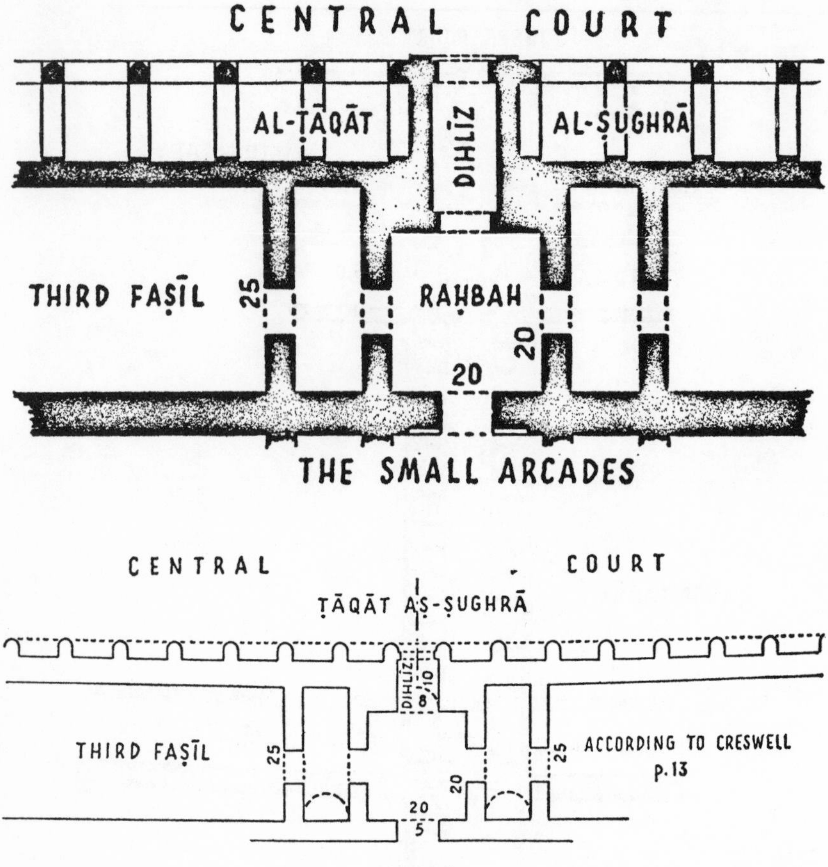

Fig. IV

that entered the courtyard.[20] The Caliph was astonished to find out that such traffic was entering his personal domain, and gave orders for the people [residing in the ringed area] to shift the gates [which opened on to the court] so that they faced the *intervalla* of the arcades (*ṭāqāt*).[21] No one was permitted to enter the courtyard except on foot. Markets were then transferred to each of the four arcades [previously occupied by guards] and remained there until the Caliph, fearful of the security problem which they

---

[20] *Ibid.*, p. 323; al-Khaṭīb, pp. 77 ff. The Khaṭīb apparently confuses two accounts: one concerning Dāwūd b. ʿAlī, the other ʿAbd al-Ṣamad. Note that Dāwūd b. ʿAlī is reported to have died in 133/750 before the city was built (al-Ṭabarī, iii, 73). The variant in al-Ṭabarī seems to clarify this confusion; the uncle was ʿĪsā b. ʿAlī who apparently suffered from the gout.

[21] That is to say, the third *intervallum* of the city marking the limit of the residential section. See figs. III and V.

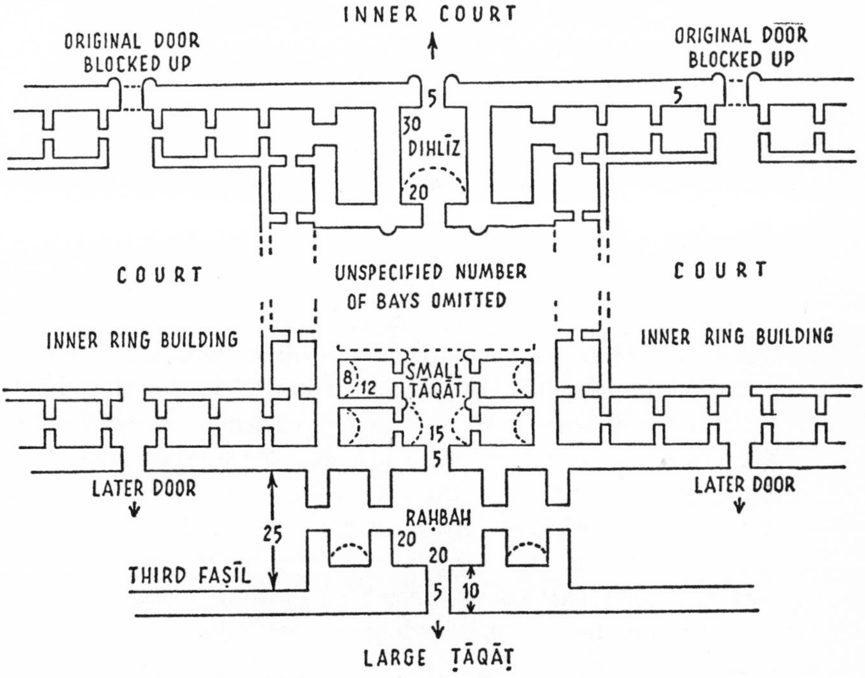

THE SMALL ṬĀQĀT (AṢ-ṢUGHRĀ) AND THE INNER RING

Fig. V

posed, removed them from the Round City when the matter was brought to his attention by a visiting Byzantine Ambassador.[22]

The story of ʿĪsā b. ʿAlī's attempt to ride into the court and thus overcome the pain of his gout not only confirms the existence of the presumed ringed area, but in doing so, provides a plausible explanation of the structure and function of the arcades which covered each gateway leading to the central court. These were flanked by rooms for the guards, who numbered 1,000 at each gate under the command of a hand-picked general; various ceremonial functionaries were also attached to the staff of the gate complex. The large arcades, which consisted of 54 arches, are reported to have been 15 cubits in width and 200 in length from the first arch to the court which separates these structures from the small arcades.[23]

---

[22] Variants of this account are found in the Khaṭīb, pp. 78–9, 80; al-Ṭabarī, iii, 323, 324; Yāqūt, *Muʿjam*, iv, 254.

[23] Al-Khaṭīb, pp. 76, 77. Herzfeld (followed by Creswell) is of the opinion that the length indicated by the Khaṭīb does not leave sufficient room for the guards (1000 men).

According to the Khaṭīb, the second series of arcades was adjacent to the corridor leading to the great central court; but there is no indication as to the number or arrangement of the arches.[24]

Because Herzfeld and Creswell made no provision for the ringed structure, they assumed that the great inner court was circumscribed by an enclosure wall only five cubits thick, which separated it from the third *intervallum* of the residential area.[25] Since the large arcades ended at this *intervallum*, the vagueness of the Arabic text left them with the problem of providing a suitable position for the small arcades. Herzfeld allowed for a series of free-standing arches which connected to the enclosure wall. The total width of the arcade was estimated at five cubits so as to correspond with the assumed projection of the corridor leading to the central court.[26] However, this reconstruction does not provide sufficient abutment for the thrust of the vaulting, assuming that analogous to the larger arcades, they supported a roof of burnt brick and not wood.[27] Moreover, Herzfeld's reconstruction is also marked by certain functional difficulties. If, one can assume a thickness of one cubit for each arch, then the total width of the passageway was only four cubits, thereby indicating a narrow walk, unconnected to any rooms, and leading nowhere along a very wide circumference.

Since Herzfeld's city plan just does not allow for an acceptable reconstruction of the small arcades, Creswell is forced to conclude that this structure was not a gallery, but a series of blind arches resting on half round piers along the enclosure wall, with the exception of the four entrances to the main court which were flanked by quarter round piers of the same projection. This plan which is based on the analogy of the Court of Honour at Ukhayḍir and the walls of the *ziyāda*'s at the great mosque in Sāmarrā gives the small arcades a decorative rather than structural function.[28] Creswell's reconstruction, although theoretically possible is

---

It is assumed that these guards were actually quartered in the flanking rooms. Consequently, a larger figure is arrived at by assuming that each room was eight cubits wide, with two cubits allowed for the partition walls. Cf. Herzfeld, p. 129; Creswell, p. 16; also fig. III.

[24] Al-Khaṭīb, p. 78. Al-Ya'qūbī does not mention this second series of arches.

[25] Herzfeld, p. 129, Creswell, pp. 16 ff. See fig. IV.

[26] According to al-Ya'qūbī, it was a vaulted structure of burnt brick cemented by gypsum, and was protected by two iron doors (*Buldān*, p. 240). Wiet (*Les Pays*, p. 15) incorrectly translates *wa-'alayhi bābā ḥadīdin* as *fermé par un porte en fer a deux battants.* This is presumably based on the analogy of the outer gateways; cf. al-Khaṭīb, p. 75. No dimensions are given for the corridor in the Arabic text. I have chosen the dimensions 30×20 on the analogy of the first corridor of the city (fig. III), and have reconstructed the buildings of the inner ring as a series of courts flanked by chambers. See fig. V.

[27] Al-Ya'qūbī, *Buldān*, p. 239.

[28] Creswell, p. 17. See fig. IV.

not convincing. The textual evidence of a sizeable ringed structure between the *intervallum* of the residential area and the central court, is obviously more plausible than the enclosure wall invented by Herzfeld. Moreover, the existence of a ringed structure provides for a lengthening of the main gateways leading to the Caliph's palace, thereby leaving sufficient space for the second series of arcades. The small arcades which framed the inner ring are presumably identical in structure with the larger unit that framed the residential quadrants; both are situated along the same access leading to the great central court. The distinction between the two arcades is then in the number of arches, rather than the position or function.[29]

Assuming the existence of this inner ring and its components, the architectural evidence tends to indicate that the Round City was, in fact, an administrative centre, and not at all a city in the conventional sense of the term. What is more, this view is consistent with the historical evidence and points to the need of re-evaluating the historical development of Madīnat al-Manṣūr in the formative period. The relocation of the gates in the inner ring, and the subsequent shift of certain markets to the four arcades is apparently an indication of the changing function of the Round City. The inner ring, as originally conceived, housed the machinery of government and certain elements of the Caliph's household, and comprised along with al-Manṣūr's residence and mosque, a single unit representing his personal domain. In order to insure maximum security, and no doubt avoid a repetition of the riotous events which took place in the palace of his former capital at al-Hāshimiyya, access to the central area was limited to four main passages, each at the termination of an elaborate gateway protected by military personnel. The gate-complex must be considered as an extension of the palace area to which it led, thereby explaining the required presence of various ceremonial functionaries, and more particularly, the existence of a royal audience-hall (*majlis*) surmounting each of the city's outer gates.[30] Thus the visiting dignitary, from the moment he stepped into the outer gateway, was made to feel as if he were in the presence of the Caliph's palace.

When al-Manṣūr shifted the entrances of the inner ring so that they opened on to the third *intervallum*, he connected the administrative agencies that were formerly part of the Caliph's domain with the residential area of the quadrants, thus limiting his personal domain to the structures actually situated in the great central court: his residence, mosque, and the security buildings. It was now possible to move various markets into the rooms flanking the arcades since the gate-complex was no longer an

---

[29] See figs. II and V.

[30] Al-Ya'qūbī, *Buldān*, p. 239; al-Khaṭīb, pp. 74–5.

integral element of the palace precinct, and therefore did not require the presence of the guard, whose duties were no doubt ceremonial as well as military. The new markets made it possible for the residents of the Round City to receive their provisions without leaving the walled area.[31] However, the limited space in the arcades for these markets is an indication that the great commercial centre of the city still remained in the suburb of al-Karkh where it had been situated since pre-Islamic times.[32] When the Caliph later decided to redevelop the suburbs and, for security reasons, to remove the markets from the arcades, he understandably chose to relocate them in the general area of al-Karkh, and provided for improved transportation in the commercial districts, and in the city itself.[33]

As previously reported, the Caliph's decision to relocate the markets and return the guard to the arcades, was determined by security problems which were brought to his attention by a visiting Byzantine ambassador. As no one was denied access to the markets, the Patrikios pointed out that the enemy may enter the city under the guise of carrying out trade, and that the merchants in turn could pass on vital information concerning the Caliph's activities. Al-Manṣūr then transferred the markets to al-Karkh, and ordered the general redevelopment of the area between the Ṣarāt and the 'Īsā Canal, according to a plan which he himself conceived. This intensive development of the suburban districts in 157/774 was probably due, in part, to the natural growth of Baghdad since the time the foundations of the Round City were laid twelve years earlier. With the presumed increase in population, it was also necessary to build a second principal mosque for the inhabitants of al-Karkh, who had previously recited their Friday prayers in the Round City. The existence of a second building would not only have relieved the congestion at the mosque of the

---

[31] Even after the markets were removed, al-Manṣūr, following the advice of Abān b. Ṣadaqa, left a grocer (*baqqāl*) in each of the city's quandrants. He was permitted to sell only vinegar and greens (cf. al-Ṭabarī, iii, 324–5).

[32] The old market of the West Side (Sūq Baghdād) was situated in al-Karkh (al-Ṭabarī, ii, 910, 914). The position of this market is fixed by al-Balādhurī as somewhere near Qarn al-Ṣarāt, the point at which the Ṣarāt Canal empties into the Tigris (*Futūḥ*, p. 246). For al-Karkh, see note 33.

[33] That is to say, the area comprised by al-Karkh, the southern suburb of the city; cf. Le Strange, Map I. The Caliph reportedly called for a wide garment and traced the plan of the markets on it. The butchers market (Sūq al-Qaṣṣābīn) was placed at the end for security reasons (al-Khaṭīb, p. 80). The development of al-Karkh is discussed in the Khaṭīb, pp. 79 ff. A less convincing explanation is found in Yāqūt. He indicates that the Caliph moved the markets from the city because smoke from them caused the walls to blacken (*Mu'jam*, iv, 255). Note a similar explanation is found for the Caliph al-Mu'taḍid's decision to abandon the construction of the Tāj Palace; cf. Ibn al-Jawzī, *Muntaẓam*, v/2, 144.

central court, but would have made it unnecessary for the people of the markets to enter the walled city for their prayers, thereby further tightening the security of the Caliph's domain.

In later times al-Karkh, which was heavily populated by Shī'ites, was the scene of frequent religious disturbances.[34] The historian al-Wāqidī (d. 207), a Shī'ite of modest persuasion is credited with having said that it is infested with the lowest rabble, to which the Khaṭīb added by way of clarification: al-Wāqidī meant by this statement certain sections of al-Karkh inhabited only by the Rāfiḍites (i.e., Shī'ites).[35] Whatever historicity there may be to the account of the Byzantine ambassador, there is still further reason to believe that the Caliph was troubled by the presence of a seditious element in the arcades of the Round City, if we are to believe a second explanation for the transfer of the markets as preserved by al-Ṭabarī and the Khaṭīb.[36] It is reported that in the year 157/774, Abū Zakariyyā' Yaḥyā b. 'Abd Allāh, who had been appointed supervisor (*muḥtasib*) of the city's markets, made cause with Shī'ite followers of Muḥammad and Ibrāhīm b. 'Abd Allāh[37] by inducing the rabble to revolt; the implication being that he used his position as market supervisor to carry on subversive activities against the state. The abortive revolt ended when the seditious *muḥtasib* was executed and his body was hung for all to see in the great central court, a public demonstration of the authority of the government and its swift justice. The subsequent transfer of the arcade markets to redeveloped districts outside the walled city, and the return of the guard to the flanking rooms seems therefore to have served two purposes: it relieved the increasing pressures of urban growth, while at the same time providing for increased security in the governmental machinery of the state.

In the wake of these developments, the original concept of the palace precinct was temporarily abandoned. Although the Round City continued to function as an administrative centre, the Caliph now moved to a newly built residence (al-Khuld), which was situated along the Tigris above the Khurāsān Gate,[38] and which became the first of a series of royal estates extending along the shore road.[39] The idea of combining the administrative agencies and the Caliphal residence within a self-contained unit, neverthe-

---

[34] This was particularly true of the Būyid period in the tenth and eleventh centuries.

[35] Al-Khaṭīb, p. 81.

[36] *Ibid.*, pp. 79 ff.; al-Ṭabarī, iii, 324.

[37] That is to say, the two brothers who led revolts in al-Baṣra and the Ḥijāz in 145/762; cf. al-Ṭabarī, iii, 278, 281.

[38] Al-Khaṭīb, pp. 75, 80, 92–3; al-Ya'qūbī, *Buldān*, p. 249.

[39] Al-Khaṭīb, p. 87; *Buldān*, p. 249.

less remained a desideratum of various 'Abbāsid rulers. Implicit in the notion was the desire to direct all the affairs of government from a central location, at some distance from the general populace.[40]

---

[40] See J. Lassner, " Why Did the Caliph al-Manṣūr Build ar-Ruṣāfah—A Historical Note ", *Journal of Near Eastern Studies*, xxiv, 95 ff.

SĀMARRA

A Study in Medieval Town-Planning

by

J. M. Rogers

I. INTRODUCTION

This paper is the result of an attempt to deal in general terms with a very characteristic phenomenon in medieval Islam, namely the establishment, often only a few years after conquests, of new inhabited areas, very often, so far as we can see, at the fiat of the ruler. Many of them have utterly disappeared and may, indeed, have lasted no more than a few years; others, among them Sāmarrā and Sulṭāniyya, remain in colossal ruins, apparent monuments to the failure of their founders to impose on an area life which would survive their death. And although it is obvious that one cannot press comparison too far between ninth-century Mesopotamia and thirteenth-century Iran, it seemed that illuminating conclusions might result from a comparison of these two cities, each of which came into being at a time when a dynasty after an initial period of military expansion was beginning to settle down and beginning also, perhaps, to acquire rather grand ideas of what was expected of it.

The comparison had to be abandoned, however, because of the lack of comparative material. For each we have the evidence of the Muslim geographers, but in Iran the archaeological evidence, always a vital complement to the literary sources, is defective to an unbelievable degree. There is, for example, no town-plan of Sulṭāniyya in existence, the best that we have for Tabrīz is the few monuments published by F. Sarre in his *Denkmäler Persischer Baukunst*, and the only plan of an Īl-Khānid palace that we possess is due to Naumann's recent excavations at Takht-i Sulaymān.[1] And the literary evidence is not sufficiently circumstantial to repair the deficiency.

It seemed more suitable, therefore, to leave a systematic account of

[1] R. Naumann in *Archäologischer Anzeiger*, 1961, 1963, 1964, 1966.

what is known of Mongol towns to a separate article,[2] and to deal with Sāmarrā alone, since it, even in isolation, presents interesting possibilities for initiating a study of town-planning in medieval Islam. For the detailed accounts of its foundation which the literary sources provide are supplemented by a considerable number of archaeological reports which, however chaotic a general impression they may give, when taken together enable us to check the reports of the historians and geographers. In addition we have comparative material regarding the foundation of Baghdad collected and largely put in order by Le Strange.[3]

My aims have been two-fold. First, to throw some light on the topographical factors which influenced the rise and fall of Sāmarrā, and to contribute to discussion concerning the role of the *muhandisīn*, or engineers, in medieval Islam by showing the influence of topography upon their works. Secondly, to show that the building of Sāmarrā is not an isolated phenomenon, a new disease which the later 'Abbāsid Caliphs contracted and which led to their ruin, but is part of a development, which the Ummayads had expressed by building more or less isolated desert castles, of a concept of Islamic kingship where the glory of the ruler was manifested in the size and luxury of his works. A rather Aristotelian notion of *Megalopsuchia* or Magnificence, in fact. But whereas the personal magnificence of the Ummayads had developed in comparative privacy, the 'Abbāsids turned to the public life of the towns, from the development of which, however, they cut themselves off by their enormous extravagance. We see the beginnings of this in the palace which al-Manṣūr built for al-Mahdī in Baghdad where at least the gesture was made in the context of enormous social and economic development. But in Sāmarrā the building of palaces took the first place from the start and remained the first preoccupation of the Caliphate even after its return to Baghdad.

I should, of course, make it quite clear that in concentrating upon these aspects of the history of the 'Abbāsids I am not asserting that political and military considerations did not also play their part in their downfall. But even given a less disastrous political history, it does seem

---

[2] A considerable volume of material exists already collected conveniently in Tiesenhausen's *Sbornik Materialov Otnosyashchikhsya k Istorii Zolotoi Ordy* (Materials relating to the History of the Golden Horde): Arabic authors, St. Petersburg 1884; Persian authors, Moscow/Leningrad 1940.

[3] Le Strange, *Baghdad under the Abbasid Caliphate*, Oxford 1900 (*Baghdad*), which draws so largely upon al-Khaṭīb al-Baghdādī (cf. the review of Le Strange's book in *Journal of the Royal Asiatic Society*, 1901) that it may almost be regarded as an edition of the text with a topographical commentary. Compare also Salmon, *Introduction Topographique à 'Histoire de Baghdad*, Paris 1904.

that as far as the architectural history of the 'Abbāsids in Sāmarrā and later in Baghdad is concerned their building programmes would have come to a similarly sticky end.

The archaeological material, which is in a chaotic state, relies heavily on literary evidence, particularly on compilations of M. Streck (*Die alte Landschaft Babylonien,* Leiden 1901) and E. Reitermeyer (*Die Stadtgründungen der Araber im Islam,* Leipzig 1912) the usefulness of which is diminished by their authors' lack of acquaintance with the site and ignorance of E. Herzfeld's discoveries, and by a general inability to discriminate between different periods of building on the site of Sāmarrā (e.g. between the developments of al-Mu'taṣim and those of al-Mutawakkil). The site was excavated in two campaigns by Herzfeld, further work being prevented by the 1914–18 war and the British occupation of Mesopotamia. But although Herzfeld claimed to have enough material by 1914 for a complete publication of the site, the material was only partly published, the crucial volume on the buildings of Sāmarrā having just disappeared without trace. The result is that we only have preliminary reports to deal with for the most part, often highly speculative and invariably contradicting their predecessors in some respects. The task of reconciling the contradictions is frankly not worth the enormous labour involved, since in many cases only further excavation could show which of the opposing views is correct. But it means that the evidence can often only be used with the greatest of care. And the hardest blow is that the last of Herzfeld's volumes, the *Geschichte der Stadt Samarra* (Hamburg 1948, but delayed for nine years by the war, in which the blocks for the maps he had prepared were destroyed), which ought to have presented his maturest judgements, is a curious mixture of epigraphy, philology and prosopography, with only a little topography thrown in, often without references, and with a sufficient number of patent misattributions to make it impossible to rely upon his unchecked claims.

The reports I have consulted are as follows:

1. Herzfeld, *Samarra, Aufnahmen und Untersuchungen zur islamischen Archaeologie,* Berlin 1907 (*Aufnahmen*), which includes a map (Tafel 8) which attempts to reconstruct the town from the literary sources but which fails totally to correspond to the air photographs at the end of the *Geschichte.* It deals cursorily with a number of sites, including the Jawsaq and the Qaṣr al-'Ashīq, but very few of these early conclusions are substantiated in his later work.

2. Viollet: *Description du Palais d'al-Moutasim . . . à Samarra* etc. (*Description*) (Mémoires présentées par divers savants à l'Académie des

Inscriptions et Belles-Lettres: Vol. xii, part 2, Paris 1909; Vol. xii (*sic*) part 2, 1911), which contains a series of important plans of the Jawsaq (which he calls the Dar al-Khalif *sic*), the Qaṣr al-ʻAshīq and the Qubbat al-Ṣulaybiyya. The first article (Plates xi, xiii, xiv) gives a reconstruction of the Jawsaq, endowing it with a remarkable amphitheatre with a built-up entrance on one side, resembling the Madrid bull-ring. This entirely fanciful re-construction was unfortunately taken as the source for the model now in the Baghdad Museum (Seton Lloyd, *Iraq*, 1951).

3. Sarre and Herzfeld: *Archäologische Reise im Euphrat- und Tigrisgebiet*, Berlin 1911, Vol. i (*Reise*) is in many ways still the most useful, since it represents the maximum of surveying and recording of monuments with the minimum of interpretation. Particularly useful (pp. 53 ff.) for the canals of Sāmarrā and their construction.

4. Herzfeld: *Erster Vorläufiger Bericht über die Ausgrabungen von Samarra*, Berlin 1912 (*Bericht*), includes the evidence (decisive) for the identification of the Balkuwārā with good plans of this and the Qaṣr al-ʻAshīq, both of which were used by Creswell.

5. Herzfeld: " Mitteilungen über die Arbeiten der Zweiten Kampagne von Samarra ", *Der Islam*, v (1914), 196–204 (*Mitteilungen*) presenting the final draft of the plan of the Jawsaq (reproduced on a much larger scale by Creswell) and asserting that a plan of the whole town had been prepared. What happened to it? This seems to have marked the end of Herzfeld's excavating, since the 1914–18 war intervened and the finds were scattered as a result of the British occupation of Mesopotamia.

6. Iraq Government Department of Antiquities: *Excavations at Samarra 1936–1939*, Baghdad 1940: Vol. i, Architecture (*Excavations*) which in spite of dubious assertions, such as that the whole ruin-field belongs to a single clearly-defined period (p. 2), thereby neglecting the progression from al-Muʻtaṣim to al-Mutawakkil, is important for its report on a remarkable palace on the West bank at Ḥuwaysilāt.

The various volumes of the *Ausgrabungen von Samarra* are only of peripheral interest to us, though Vol. vi, mentioned above, Herzfeld's *Geschichte der Stadt Samarra*, Berlin 1948 (*Geschichte*), contains a set of air-photographs which, *faute de mieux*, form the basis for many of my conclusions regarding topography. The plates, often of landscapes, also give a good idea of the Tigris valley and the raised tablelands on either side of it which, particularly on the East side, were of importance for the development of the town of Sāmarrā.

7. Sousa: *The Irrigation System of Samarrah during the Abbasid Caliphate*, Baghdad 1948–9, 2 Vols. in Arabic (*Sousa*), is, particularly when it deals with irrigation problems, of great value. The maps are the

most detailed which exist, even though the precise identifications which he gives of streets or houses are often over-optimistic.

8. Creswell, *Early Muslim Architecture*, Vol. ii, Oxford 1950 (*EMA*), though dealing primarily with individual monuments is refreshingly clear, and the plans which he publishes present in the most accurate and convenient form the latest stages of our knowledge regarding the buildings. I am also much indebted to him for his comments and help.

II. THE CONSTITUTION OF THE SITE

A necessary preliminary to the examination of the problems concerned with the planning of Sāmarrā is to classify it: are we to compare it to the garrison towns of early Islam, the *amṣār* or the Khurāsānian *ribāṭ*-towns,[4] or is it more like the " pleasaunce "-towns of the Caliphate of Cordova such as Madīnat al-Zahrā'?[5] or would it be more correct to regard it as a diplomatic capital, comparable to the foundations of the Aghlabids in the neighbourhood of Qayrawān?[6] Again, is it convincing to regard it as *one* town? The site is thirty-five kilometres long and often more than five kilometres wide, and the air photographs show that there were considerable gaps in the built-up areas. One reading, not, I think, the correct one, of the literary sources would allow us to see Sāmarrā as a series of consecutively inhabited areas, starting in the South with al-Muʿtaṣim's Qādisiyya, going North to the Jawsaq, then across the Tigris to the West bank area populated by al-Wāthiq and finally going to al-Mutawakkil's palace in the extreme North of the area. This view is untenable since there is much evidence to show that expansion did not lead to depopulation of previously inhabited areas; however, it poses in topographical terms the same puzzle that we find in al-Mutawakkil's notorious assertion that in founding the Jaʿfariyya he had founded a town.[7]

---

[4] W. Barthold, *Istoria Kul'turnoi Zhizni Turkestana* (*Complete Works*, ii/1, Moscow 1963), pp. 200–5 lays down a general plan for Khurāsānian towns, which he describes as developing round the nucleus of the *ribāṭ*. This generalisation is refuted with copious examples by G. A. Pugachenkova, *Puti Razvitiya Arkhitektury Yuzhnogo Turkmenistana Pory Rabovladeniya i Feodalizma*, Moscow 1959, pp. 142–9.

[5] K. Brisch: " ' Madīnat az-Zahrā' in der modernen archäologischen Literatur Spaniens ", *Kunst des Orients*, iv (1963), 5–42.

[6] M. Solignac: " Recherches sur les Installations Hydrauliques de Kairouan et des Steppes Tunisiennes du VIIe au XIe siècle " in *Annales de l'Institut des Etudes Orientales de l'Université d'Alger*, 1952 and 1953 (*Recherches*).

[7] Al-Yaʿqūbī, *Kitāb al-Buldān*, translated as *Les Pays* by G. Wiet, Cairo 1937 (references to the de Goeje text always come first), p. 267/61.

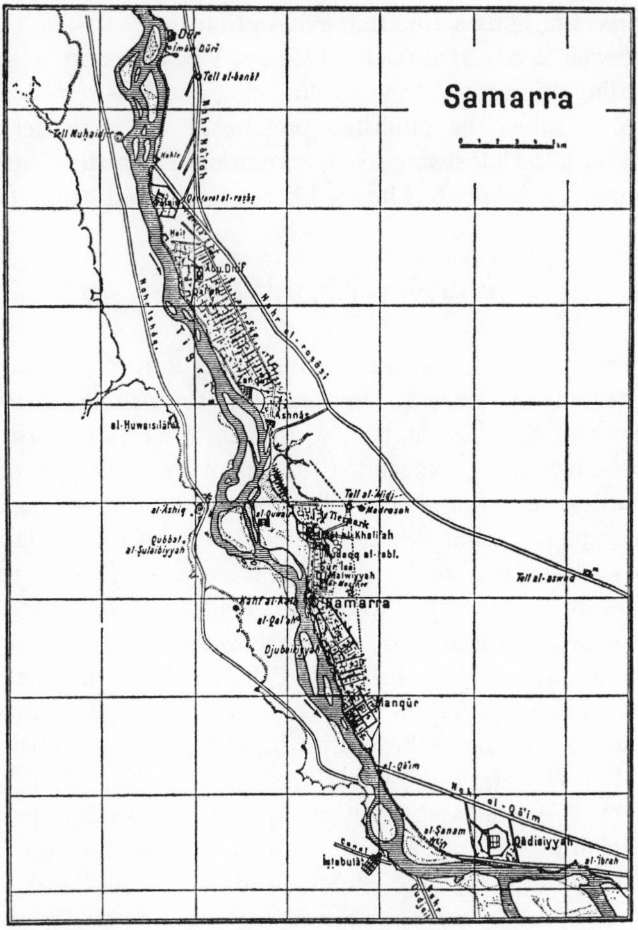

Map showing situation of Sāmarrā, Balkuwārā (Manqūr), Qādisiyya, Abū Dulaf., &c. (From Herzfeld *op. cit.*) Scale 1:100,000

Some of these suggested alternatives may be disposed of quite shortly. For example, the distance from Baghdad, the emphasis which all contemporary accounts place upon the importance of the port installations on the Tigris and the vastness of the street areas even round the Jawsaq and therefore, presumably, from the reign of al-Mu'taṣim alone, may all be regarded as decisive evidence against regarding Sāmarrā as a mere pleasaunce; and the fifty years' almost permanent residence of the Caliphate there serves to distinguish it from the " diplomatic " capitals of the Tunisian Aghlabids or, for example, the Ghaznawid palace of Lashkarī

Bazār near Bust.[8] Again, its sheer size, even if we except the constructions in the neighbourhood of the Ja'fariyya in the North, and the lack of any central walled area serve to distinguish it from the *ribāṭ* towns of Khurāsān with their *shahristāns*, the outgrowths, though perhaps not so invariably as Barthold imagined, of the early Arab invasions of Central Asia. And as far as the unity of the site is concerned, it is perhaps sufficient to point out that as the areas of habitation grew people tended to enlarge their estates, so that although we should naturally expect that the high officials of state would be forced to alter their residence to the vicinity of the ruler there was far from being anything like depopulation in the older areas.

There is a sense in which one could regard an Islamic capital as just that place where the ruler happened to be, as with the seasonal residence of the Aghlabids in various castles round Qayrawān, the population of which remained stable when the ruler left; though it would not be the usual sense we give to the word. But although the 'Abbāsids were away from Sāmarrā at various times, often for considerable periods, either engaged on campaigns or fleeing from their troops, it is interesting that except for the testimony that al-Wāthiq repaired the quarters of Baghdad which had been destroyed in a disastrous fire during his reign, we have no evidence that the Caliphs while at Sāmarrā considered any other city of equal importance.

The question of just what made Sāmarrā into the 'Abbāsid capital in the ninth century is, therefore, a complex one, which reflects a certain indecision on our part as to the modern usage of the word. Is, for example, a diplomatic capital like Canberra more *important* than other Australian cities, and if so in what sense? Or, if we are prepared to define " capital " as the centre of power represented by the concentration of Ministries and officials in any one area, how far does it have to move for us to say that a new capital has arisen? I do not think that there are any clear answers to these questions, and the fact that there are not should, as well as making us sympathetic to the difficulties of the medieval geographers in explaining how towns were, make us wary of taking all their classifications at their face value.

For example, a very widespread criterion in our sources for regarding a site as a city is the possession of a congregational mosque. However, Sāmarrā by A.D. 860 had two and tenth-century Baghdad three, so that one is inclined to agree with Le Strange when he points to the existence of many settled sites without a *minbar* and prefers to take the existence of a

---

[8] For 'Abbāsiyya and al-Qaṣr al-Qadīm see G. Marçais, *Manuel d'Art Musulman*, Paris, 1926, i, 40–4. For Bust see article by J. Sourdel-Thomine in *Encyclopaedia of Islam*, 2nd edition.

congregational mosque as a sign of the importance of a town, rather than as a necessary condition of there being a town at all.[9] Equally, the fact that we have mint cities shows more about the prestige, importance or independence of a ruler than about the place where coins are struck; and where, as very frequently happens, we find coins struck in different places at the same period, we can come to no conclusions at all as to which place must be regarded as the capital. In the case of Sāmarrā[10] coins were minted until 341 A.H., and although there are no gold *dīnārs* two years after the departure of al-Mu'tamid, we have a complete set of dirhams of the Caliphs (with the exception of the pretenders) from al-Mu'taṣim to al-Muttaqī, sometimes in several examples. This, while sufficient to attest the continuing importance of Sāmarrā, demonstrates also the lability of the criterion of mints for talking about a town as a capital.

In spite of our sources,[11] therefore, we may perhaps give the following description of Sāmarrā: first, although we know that there were monasteries on the site and some small villages before the coming of the 'Abbāsids, and although al-Ya'qūbi quotes Ja'far al-Khushshakī's story of a prophecy concerning the *re-building* of an ancient town,[12] the enormous population changes which al-Mu'taṣim brought about entitle us to regard Sāmarrā as an original foundation of the 'Abbāsids.[13] Secondly, we shall

[9] Le Strange, *Lands of the Eastern Caliphate* (*Lands*), Cambridge 1905, p. 35, note 2.

[10] G. C. Miles: " The Samarra Mint ", *Ars Orientalis*, 1954, pp. 187–91.

[11] Al-Manṣūr in his apostrophe of the site of Baghdad said that he would found four other towns and al-Ya'qūbī says that indeed he did (al-Ya'qūbī, p. 238/10): Malaṭya (the *Byzantine* city of Melitene), Maṣṣīṣa (the *Byzantine* city of Mopsuestia), al-Manṣūra in Sind, which is the archaic Hindu site of Brahminabad, and al-Rāfiqa which seems to have been laid out by al-Saffāḥ. This might give one a rather poor impression of al-Ya'qūbī's general reliability and perhaps he has indeed forgotten about the earlier existence of the towns. However, I think it would be more accurate to say that he made no distinction between comparatively minor re-building by a ruler, the addition of a considerable, though separable complex, on the lines of the Ja'fariyya, and beginning from scratch on a previously uninhabited site.

[12] Al-Ya'qūbī, p. 257/47.

[13] The fact of population change is perhaps the strongest criterion. Unlike Nīshāpūr where the Arabs seem to have inhabited the Sāsānian site until the ninth century (Wilkinson in *Bulletin of the Metropolitan Museum*, 1950, pp. 60–72) and merely to have moved then en masse to a new site (that is, the re-location of a town and not its re-foundation), we have the case of Tyana in Anatolia where under al-Ma'mūn not only were the walls rebuilt but a new population was imported. Or, to take a more recent example, Istanbul after the Turkish conquest (R. Mantran, *Istanbul dans la seconde moitié du XVIIe siècle*, Paris 1962): we find massive deportations of Byzantine Greeks and their replacement by Central Anatolian Turks or even Greeks from the Morea. This might perfectly well be regarded as the *creation* of a (Turkish) city, even though the amount of building or rebuilding during this early period remained small.

be prepared to think of the site as more or less inhabited *in toto* throughout the residence of the Caliphs but with a frequently changing centre of power represented by the Caliphal residence and the offices of his ministers.[14] This means that the Ja'fariyya was not a new foundation, since the population of the northern areas inhabited under al-Mutawakkil was no different from that of the old, the interesting feature of the move being that the inhabitants of Sāmarrā seemed not unwilling to move with him. We may compare the palace, therefore, with the suburb which the Mongol Vizier, Rashīd al-Dīn, added to Tabrīz at the end of the thirteenth century, the Rab'-i Rashīdī with its large-scale public works. Although, to judge from Herzfeld's air photographs, the Ja'fariyya is physically separate from the more southerly parts of Sāmarrā and although al-Mutawakkil spoke very grandly of what he had done, he was really no more than a ninth-century Rashīd al-Dīn, without even the latter's public-spiritedness.

These introductory remarks, brief and inadequate as they are, serve to underline one respect in which Sāmarrā is typical of Islamic towns founded in the early centuries of Islam, namely that it is quite different from a Hellenistic colony. Thus, although the names of towns tend to repeat themselves (for example, the Aghlabid sites of al-Ruṣāfa, al-Raqqāda and al-Khawarnaq, all of which are named after Mesopotamian or Iranian originals),[15] unlike the Hellenistic colonies where the newer cities which took the name of the parent also followed the parent plan, the Islamic sites frequently have nothing but names in common. In transmitting a plan the Hellenistic colonies also transmitted a type of social organization: but in Islam whether the site chosen became a desert castle, a fortress, a pleasaunce or a fully-fledged town seems to have been left to chance.

There will now follow a series of comparisons between Sāmarrā and other towns, designed to show that if indeed Sāmarrā can be seen as an act of folly on a vast scale, the various stages of its occupation are paralleled very closely in the development of Baghdad under al-Manṣūr and Hārūn al-Rashīd; and so far from being a ghastly lesson to the 'Abbāsids, the mania for building continued after the return of the Caliphate to Baghdad, though now as the last remaining occupation of the impotent rulers.

After an examination of the motives we can attribute to al-Manṣūr and al-Mu'taṣim for the foundation of their respective cities, which will

---

[14] The centre of power was re-inforced by the proximity of the Congregational Mosque, re-built by al-Mutawakkil in the vicinity of the Jawsaq before he conceived his project of a palace in the northern part of Sāmarrā, but supplanted by the Mosque of Abū Dulaf once the Ja'fariyya had been built. Cf. al-Ṭabarī, ed. de Goeje, iii, 1452.

[15] Marçais, *Manuel d'Art Musulman: L'Architecture* Paris 1926, i, 118–19.

suggest that Sāmarrā and Baghdad were different ways of coping with the same problems, I shall deal with the relationships between types of building in the two cities, which will lead to conclusions concerning the much-discussed role of the engineers or *muhandisīn* in medieval Islam. Finally I shall deal briefly with the topography of the site and its consequences for the planning, particularly with respect to the irrigation systems. This comparison can, of course, make no pretence of completeness, but perhaps it will at least enable us to refute the assertion, so commonly made, that the decline of Sāmarrā is in some peculiar way connected with the fact that it was created by royal fiat, rather than coming into being spontaneously.

III. MOTIVES FOR THE FOUNDING OF SĀMARRĀ

Although al-Ṭabarī[16] seems to be the only source for the view that both Baghdad and Sāmarrā were founded by the Caliphs from fear of their armies, there is considerable evidence in the plan of Baghdad as it has been described to us, as well as in the planning of Sāmarrā, that considerations of the ruler's personal safety were paramount.

Al-Manṣūr had found both Kūfa and Hāshimiyya uninhabitable because of rebellions or insurrections, and in the planning of the Round City of Baghdad we see a pronounced attempt to avoid trouble. The inner enceinte, in which stood al-Manṣūr's palace, the Bāb al-Dhahab, the Congregational Mosque and a number of government offices, an intermediate portion consisting of a ring of houses belonging to people whom al-Ya'qūbi actually says would be useful in an emergency, then the outer enceinte, the only communication between which and the Bāb al-Dhahab were four arterial roads,[17] gave a disposition which effectively divided the city into quarters, each one of which could be sealed off from the others by gates. In these circumstances, even if we do not take the legend seriously that al-Manṣūr was prompted to these measures by the warning of a Byzantine patrician that it was dangerous to have foreign, potentially treacherous, merchants so near to him, we can plausibly assume that he was aware of the dangers of civil or military disturbances in the comparatively narrow arterial streets,[18] since he cleared out the stalls from the arcaded arterial streets and filled them with his troops. And these

---

[16] Al-Ṭabarī, transld. Zotenberg, Paris 1867–1874, iv, 527.

[17] Le Strange, *Baghdad*, pp. 26–8; Creswell, *EMA*, ii, Figs. 2 (facing p. 8) and 3 (facing p. 12) gives a series of plans somewhat refining upon Herzfeld's reconstruction.

[18] Le Strange, *Baghdad*, p. 66.

measures can be seen as the reinforcement of his determination, initially expressed in his orders that soldiers from the various Arab tribes should be kept separately, that his city should be tranquil.

It is, of course, striking, given this evidence of al-Manṣūr's desire for security provided by the material arrangement of the Round City, that ten years or so after taking up residence in the Bāb al-Dhahab he should move to the Palace of Khuld outside the walls, the palace inside the walls remaining, apparently, as an official residence but certainly fallen into disrepair by A.D. 800. Perhaps the proximity of the new palace of Khuld to the river, with its control of the review ground and the pontoon bridge leading to East Baghdad, seemed adequate compensation: or the move may reflect al-Manṣūr's increasing confidence in the power of his troops to keep order.

However, it is clear that his successors realised that security had been sacrificed and attempted to remedy this in various ways. Hārūn al-Rashīd, for example, moved to Raqqa[19]—though the fact that our sources also admit that he left his wives, his children and his treasures behind in the palace of Khuld rather detracts from their claims that his motive also was fear of his army. Al-Ma'mūn[20] is said to have been able to live in Baghdad only by keeping his troops dispersed and by not allowing them into the city in too great numbers, but under al-Mu'taṣim even this became impossible. Because of the increasing military involvement of the 'Abbāsids the army grew, supplemented by enormous importations of Turkish *ghulāms*. Totally un-Arabised and non-Muslim to boot they must have seemed distressingly nomadic to the population of Baghdad, and although trained outside the city and, no doubt, carefully organized, we learn from all accounts that their presence was regarded as an intolerable affliction.

The subsequent history of the 'Abbāsids shows the extent of the Turks' power to cause their commanders anxiety. However, at the time of al-Mu'taṣim's removal from Baghdad in A.D. 836 it is perhaps more accurate to say that he lived in fear of a rising of exacerbated civilians rather than of a military rebellion. His first move, from Shammāsiyya, scarcely more than a northern suburb of Baghdad, may be explained, following the sources, by its proximity to the centre of Baghdad; but,

---

[19] Al-Fakhrī, transld. E. Amar, *Histoire des Dynasties Musulmanes*, Paris 1910, p. 402 (p. 319 of text). Al-Ṭabarī (Zotenberg) iv, p. 527, who supports this also says that before leaving for Raqqa Hārūn began to build on the site of al-Qāṭūl (see note 21), a tradition for which there is neither literary nor archaeological confirmation.

[20] Al-Ṭabarī, *ibid.*

supposing that Herzfeld's identification[21] of the octagonal walled area to the South of Sāmarrā and now called Qādisiyya be accepted, al-Mu'taṣim's second move to al-Qāṭūl, where a considerable amount of building was embarked upon before it was discovered that the ground was not suitable for canal-digging, can be taken as showing his determination to learn from his experiences in Baghdad and to build a walled city to keep himself safe from disturbance.

Supposing all this to be correct, when al-Mu'taṣim moved upstream from wherever al-Qāṭūl was, we have a similar reversal of policy to that which al-Manṣūr made when he moved to the palace of Khuld in Baghdad, an even more striking demonstration that he did not expect trouble from his troops. For his palace, the Jawsaq al-Khāqānī is unfortified, remains of buttresses reproduced on the plan in Creswell (*EMA*, Fig. 194 facing ii, 242)

[21] The evidence for the siting of " al-Qāṭūl " is not conclusive, particularly in view of the fact that it has not been shown that Herzfeld's conjecture (*Reise*, ii, 107) that the site was near the Qāṭūl Abu'l Jund, a canal which has been obliterated by changes in the bed of the Tigris, was unjustified. The only evidence we possess in the sources is (al-Ya'qūbī, p. 256/46) that it lay up the Tigris from Shammāsiyya and below Sāmarrā and that (Yāqūt, *Mu'jam*, iv, 922) glass was produced there. Nevertheless (*Sousa*: i, 261) Herzfeld was able to say in a letter dated 1947: " After having thought that the big octagon was the villa of Hārūn al-Rashīd (see note 19) on the Qāṭūl I later found out that this unfinished building belongs also (sic) to the abandoned foundation of al-Mu'taṣim ". This dogmatic conclusion would be interesting if Herzfeld had ever bothered to provide the evidence for it.

The octagonal walled area, the ruins of which appear on Herzfeld's air-photographs (*Geschichte*) and inside which there is scarcely anything visible except a ruined building in the centre and a few traces of canals which may or may not have been completed, corroborates the description (*Reise*, ii, 106–7) of the interior as showing " ganz schwache Resten " with habitation areas round the walls and a mound in the centre, two or three metres high. The walls are in the same style and are built of the same materials as those of Sāmarrā, and he judged from the exceptionally sparse sherd finds that the area had never been occupied for any considerable period. The general disposition he noted is, of course, very characteristic of the Round City.

More recent excavations in this area (Nājī al-Asīl, " La Ciudad de al-Mu'tasim en al-Qātūl " in *Al-Andalus*, 1947, pp. 349–57) have not, unfortunately, done more than Herzfeld was able to observe. Numbers of glass wasters were found, which fits Yāqūt's description, and the pottery fragments, still in remarkably small quantities, are much the same as those which have been found in Sāmarrā. However, since there is some doubt (E. Kühnel, " Die Abbasidischen Lüsterfayencen " in *Ars Islamica*, i (1934) 149–59; Lane, *Early Islamic Pottery*, London 1957, p. 11) that the pottery which is often called " Sāmarrā ware " was actually made there, the fragments need not show that habitation only started in the octagon during the later, " Sāmarrā " phase. The palace in the centre was also investigated, and it was discovered that the canal which surrounded it fed an ornamental lake on the far side of a large inner courtyard, a feature both of the Jawsaq and of the Qaṣr al-'Ashīq. So that if Qādisiyya was indeed " al-Qāṭūl " its plan had great influence.

being the standard device for strengthening a mud-brick or mud-cored outer wall and therefore not showing any defensive purpose; and indeed it must have been unfortifiable because of the vast area the complex covers and because its position, which commands a stretch of the higher ground overlooking the Tigris, merely leaves it as one palace among many and gives it no special strategic advantage.[22] Beside it, just to the North, is a vast series of barracks, which Herzfeld calculated could easily lodge three thousand men, even without an upper storey, clearly the residence of al-Muʿtaṣim's guards.

It is in these circumstances that I am inclined to view his very stringent regulations[23] regarding the conduct and disposition of his Turkish troops, which involved not only the isolation of the areas where they lived but also the regulation of their social and economic life, as being aimed at achieving what would otherwise have been done by fortification of his palace. The administrative ghetto in which they were placed was an alternative to the architectural stronghold which al-Manṣūr had planned for himself. And the most striking feature, perhaps connected also with the rigid division of the *sūqs* into trades which al-Yaʿqūbī remarks upon in both Sāmarrā and Baghdad, is the way in which civil and military were separated: we might even think that al-Muʿtaṣim saw himself as able to cope with either separately but feared the conjunction. By these speculations it is intended not so much to cast doubt on Professor Ayalon's contention (expressed during the colloquium) that the isolation of the Turks was motivated by al-Muʿtaṣim's desire to keep them unsullied by contact with the (inferior) local population, as to suggest that desire for security is the only factor which will properly explain the very detailed arrangements which al-Yaʿqūbī describes him as having made.

One may doubt whether, given the Turkish problem, any walled enceinte or any set of stringent regulations would have enabled the Caliphate to perpetuate itself. Al-Muʿtaṣim made the situation more difficult, however, by his policy of expansion on the West bank of the Tigris, with its tendency to substitute widely spaced palaces and estates[24] for the closely packed city round the Jawsaq, and which give neither the security of walls (those which appear on Herzfeld's air photographs, like those of the Jawsaq, have a delineatory function only) nor even that of the law and order of the East bank. And al-Yaʿqūbī, who is so explicit about

---

[22] One of the more striking features of the site is the long series of enclosures right at the edge of the bluff above the river, even in areas which are very densely populated further inland.

[23] Al-Yaʿqūbī, pp. 258–9/49–50

[24] id. p. 264/57.

al-Mu'taṣim's security regulations, says nothing about any issued by al-Mutawakkil or his successor, al-Muntaṣir, events which would have been much nearer to him in time:[25] so that it is fairly clear that al-Mutawakkil cannot have considered the effect of his move northwards to the Ja'fariyya upon the parts of the city which were previously inhabited. Indeed, the only concession to security that we find in the later history of Sāmarrā is the report that al-Mu'tamid moved over to the West bank to a site called the Qaṣr al-'Ashīq or the Qaṣr al-Ma'shūq[26] the only building in the whole of Sāmarrā which looks anything like a castle.

We thus have a very interesting pattern emerging, first of all in Baghdad and then in Sāmarrā: the ruler attempts to isolate and perhaps to defend himself from his civilian or military subjects and then, having done this, moves to an area which is neither isolated nor defended, taking refuge instead in some form of administrative measures. This system broke down increasingly as the 'Abbāsid Caliphs came and went, and the large number of mercenaries produced a situation, once al-Mu'taṣim's regulations had been relaxed, where no defensive measures on the part of the ruler were adequate. It is interesting, however, that the Caliphs did

---

[25] However, Al-Ya'qūbī's *Mushākalat al-Nās li-Zamānihim wa-mā yaghlibu 'alayhim fī kulli 'Aṣrīn*: translated by W. G. Millward, " The Adaptation of Men to their Time " in *Journal of the American Oriental Society*, 1964, pp. 329–44), a short treatise much more unfavourable to al-Mutawakkil than the *Kitāb al-Buldān*, says (p. 343) that he occasioned the building of " prisons and buildings with heavy doors " and that the population imitated him. It looks as though their imitations were prompted by desire for security.

[26] Although the de Goeje text of al-Ya'qūbī (pp. 264, 268) mentions the Qaṣr al-'Ashīq as being on the *east* bank I agree with Wiet (p. 56, footnote 6; p. 62, footnote 2) that this must be a lapsus on someone's part. For there would be no point in saying which bank unless al-Mu'tamid had crossed it, and the Jawsaq and the Ja'fariyya are both on the east bank. Al-Ya'qūbī (p. 264/56) also says that the *east* bank was abundantly watered and full of orchards, a flat contradiction of his remark on the previous page (p. 263/53–54) that water shortages there caused serious trouble and cf. the remark of al-Iṣṭakhrī (translated Mordtmann, *Das Buch der Länder von Schech Ebu Ishak el Farsi el Isztachri*, Hamburg 1845, p. 53) that apart from the Nahr al-Qāṭūl (that is, the Nahrawān) on the east bank of the Tigris all was a desert, the only waterworks being on the west bank.

The literary evidence, therefore, does not prevent us from identifying the Ma'shūq of al-Ya'qūbī with the Qaṣr al 'Ashīq. Herzfeld (*Reise*, ii, 82–3) had denied this, on the grounds that the de Goeje text must refer to some refurbishing of the Jawsaq, implausible even without the reading of Wiet which I have followed, since al-Ya'qūbī had actually referred to the Jawsaq only a few lines before (p. 268/62), and on the more convincing grounds that the building known as the Qaṣr al-'Ashīq showed signs of a restoration, which could hardly be compatible with its having been finished by at the earliest A.D. 878 and then deserted 10 years later when al-Mu'tamid went off to Baghdad. However, he later changed his mind (*Geschichte*, p. 129 and footnote) saying that further investigation had shown that it was much more difficult than had at first seemed the case to isolate two building periods.

not stop trying after their return to Baghdad, for a palace originally built by Ja'far the Barmecide in East Baghdad was turned into the Dār al-Khilāfa, two enormous complexes, the Tāj and the Firdaws, as well as many smaller buildings, being erected inside its confines.[27] Insofar, therefore, as the building of 'Abbāsid cities can be seen as concerned with responses to the constant problem of the ruler's personal safety, Sāmarrā is far from occupying a unique position. It represents one, though perhaps, as we shall see, the crucial, stage in the failure of the 'Abbāsids to come to (architectural) terms with their subjects.[28]

IV. FINANCIAL ASPECTS

It would be out of place to attempt to give a general account of the financial background to the building of 'Abbāsid cities, quite apart from the fact that it is difficult to make sense of al-Ya'qūbī's exaggerated

---

[27] Le Strange, *Baghdad*, pp. 243–63.

[28] One general motive which all the sources refer to and which therefore cannot be passed without comment is that of personal likes and dislikes on the part of a ruler; though widely as this motive has been attributed we should never, I think, be entitled to assume that a town was founded *merely* on the personal dislikes of a ruler. Thus, we know from al-Ya'qūbī (p. 238/10) that al-Manṣūr was believed to have congratulated his predecessors on not having discovered the site of Baghdad so that he should have the glory of developing it, and that al-Mu'taṣim (p. 264/46) conceived a distaste for Baghdad after his troops had so badly misbehaved themselves there, very comparable to the distaste for Paris after the miseries of the Fronde which led Louis XIV to move to Versailles. But although it is clear, as in Aghlabid and Fāṭimid Tunisia, for example, or under the Caliphate of Cordova, that the personal decision of a ruler may be sufficient to turn an isolated village or castle into a temporary capital, we are left in no doubt that the 'Abbāsids, in the case of both Baghdad and Sāmarrā, considered themselves to be founding something *permanent*.

Ineffective, however, as personal likes may be in causing a city to rise where none was before, we do know of two cases where the personal dislikes of a ruler were sufficient to cause the destruction of a centre of power—the Ja'fariyya, to which I have already alluded, when al-Mutawakkil's son and successor, al-Muntaṣir, ordered the inhabitants to raze the buildings, and, some years earlier, Tyana in Central Anatolia (now Kilisse Hisar, near Nighde). The city had been founded by al-Ma'mūn in the sense that it was rebuilt after its capture and a new population imported. But al-Mu'taṣim at the end of his Anatolian campaigns ordered the destruction of al-Ma'mūn's buildings and the dispersal of the population which he had brought together (al-Ṭabarī (de Goeje) iii, 1111–12, 1165; Yāqūt, *Mu'jam*, iii, 554). In addition al-Mu'taṣim ordered that any removable material (that is, all building materials, other than rubble or concrete, as well as any more valuable commodities) should be taken away—a command which is a striking precedent for the desertion of the Ja'fariyya.

figures.[29] But, extraordinary as the foundation of Sāmarrā may have been and colossal as the expenditure on it undoubtedly was, it could never have taken place but for the acquiescence of al-Mu'taṣim's subjects. Some account, therefore, is required of the sources of money required for building the various quarters, as well as a statement of the inducements to settle in the area which the population had received.

One feature is constant, the acquisition by the Caliphs of land for building, but this, although a financial operation to which the Caliphs paid scrupulous attention,[30] cannot have been, to judge from the prices quoted, more than a very minor cost.[31] It is in events after the land had been paid for that the interest lies and among these we can, I think, make a distinction—between the period from the foundation of Baghdad up to and including the foundation of Sāmarrā, and that covering the period of al-Mutawakkil and his successors. During the first period, which also covers the development of al-Ruṣāfa and the other quarters of East Baghdad, we are told of the wholesale distribution of concessions, first of all to the Caliph's family, friends and high officials, but eventually[32] to anyone who wanted land, the costs of building falling upon the concessionaire, particularly in the case of the commanders of the Turkish mercenaries at Sāmarrā who were made responsible for providing the public buildings of their quarters.[33] In the case of Baghdad at least, two cases cited by al-Ya'qūbī with respect to the development of al-Ruṣāfa under al-Mahdī[34] suggest that there may have been some reward for this: Faḍl b. Rabī' received land in the 'Askar al-Mahdī because he had turned the concession he had originally received in West Baghdad into markets and shops, and 'Abbās b. 'Abd al-Muṭṭalib because he had turned the concession which he had received from al-Manṣūr into orchards. (The first of these went on to build a hippodrome—*ḥalba*—on his new conces-

[29] For example, al-Ya'qūbī, p. 266/60, where we have the estimate of a million and a half dīnārs for the building of al-Mutawakkil's uncompleted canal. Al-Ṭabarī (de Goeje, iii, 1438) calculates that it only cost 200,000 dīnārs, while Yāqūt (*Mu'jam*, ii, 86) mentions a figure of only 10,000. For a more detailed evaluation of his expenditure see al-Juzūlī, *Maṭāli' al-Budūr fī Manāzil al-Surūr*, Cairo 1300 A.H., ii, 277–8.

[30] Al-Ya'qūbī, p. 258/48; al-Ṭabarī (de Goeje) iii, 1438, where it is pointed out that when the canal was being built up to the Ja'fariyya al-Mutawakkil bought up all the villages on the way and moved out all the inhabitants.

[31] Al-Ya'qūbī, *ibid.*

[32] Al-Ya'qūbī, p. 250/33.

[33] Al-Ya'qūbī, p. 258/48–9. It also appears (id., p. 264/57) that after land had been granted in the form of Caliphal concessions it could be sold. For when al-Mu'taṣim developed the west bank of Sāmarrā, such was the demand for land that a *jarīb* of land fetched a high price. It is, however, not clear who reaped the benefit of the rise in price.

[34] Al-Ya'qūbī, p. 252/37.

sion, an oddly public building for a private development.) Given, however, that al-Ya'qūbī is right to say that a system of inheritance grew up[35] and that the notables followed al-Mu'taṣim to Sāmarrā, it follows that a considerable proportion of them must have been absentee landlords in one or other place, a situation which must have been even more pronounced after the developments on the West bank by al-Mu'taṣim and al-Wāthiq. To some extent, also, there must have been a certain amount of Parkinsonian expansion to fill the space available, and indeed one advantage of Sāmarrā was said to be that construction on the grand scale was possible. However, neither this fact nor the interesting sequence of habitation of the Hārūnī palace[36] at Sāmarrā, originally built by al-Wāthiq, is sufficient to rule out the necessity of both pluralism and absenteeism among the notables.[37]

This first period is characterized by two interesting phenomena: a certain wariness on the part of the Caliphs of spending too much money, but an equal readiness on the part of the notables to squander large sums. Al-Manṣūr, who was apparently notorious for his meanness, was prepared to abandon the demolition of the Sāsānian palace of Ctesiphon, which he had intended to provide building materials for his palace of Khuld, when it became too expensive, in spite of the fact that it was made clear to him that by admitting defeat in the face of the Sāsānians he would inevitably

---

[35] Al-Ya'qūbī, p. 250/33, 254/43.

[36] When Afshīn moved nearer to the Hārūnī palace on al-Wāthiq's accession (al-Ya'qūbī, p. 264/58) Waṣīf moved into Afshīn's palace; as for the Hārūnī it became under al-Mutawakkil (p. 261/53) the residence of Yaḥyā b. Aktham, who was chief *qāḍī*.

[37] A cursory survey of al-Ya'qūbī and al-Ṭabarī has revealed the curious fact that very few families are mentioned by either as having property in both Sāmarrā and Baghdad. We should not of course expect many of the *same* names to recur, both because of the difference in generations and because so many of the names mentioned in connexion with Sāmarrā are of Turks. But when al-Ya'qūbī (p. 254/42) mentions the change and decay among the proprietors of Baghdad, it cannot have been total by any means. And in fact we have two examples of what must have been a very general phenomenon: (al-Ya'qūbī, p. 249/33, 260/52) Isḥāq b. Ibrāhīm had concessions at both Sāmarrā and Baghdad and even abandoned some of his lands under al-Mutawakkil in order to build near the mouth of a canal, afterwards called the Isḥāqī; and (id., p. 253/39, 260/52) Mu'ādh b. Muslim al-Rāzī in Baghdad who was the grandfather of Isḥāq b. Yaḥyā b. Mu'ādh in Sāmarrā. That there cannot have been a limitless crowd of landowners is also suggested by al-Ṭabarī (de Goeje, iii, 1452), who says that when al-Mutawakkil held the Ramaḍān prayers in the Ja'fariyya no-one prayed in Sāmarrā (that is, when prayers were held in the Mosque of Abū Dulaf there was no-one who remained behind in the quarter of al-Ḥayr to pray in the Great Mosque which al-Mutawakkil had built there). The paucity of references to plurality of landholdings, therefore, does not mean that we must admit that it was rare.

lose face.[38] Although al-Mahdī was so generous with his distribution of land in al-Ruṣāfa he issued a sumptuary edict forbidding spacious buildings.[39] And al-Mu'taṣim who, al-Ṭabarī says[40] refused to send money to re-dig the canal at Shāsh (the modern Tashkent), although he accepted its inhabitants as his subjects, clearly was on the mean side even in his distribution of land at Sāmarrā, since in the quarter of al-Ḥayr the walls had to be demolished on more than one occasion to ease the pressure on housing.

In contrast to this meanness or economy we have the readiness of the notables to spend money on building, first of all at al-Qāṭūl, which was then abandoned for Sāmarrā proper, and again in Sāmarrā towards the end of al-Mu'taṣim's reign. For when al-Wāthiq succeeded[41] it was only his building of the Hārūniyya which gave the local landowners the urge to restore their houses, since up to this time they had only regarded Sāmarrā as an encampment, building on a colossal scale even though they imagined that their buildings could only be occupied temporarily. It is, of course, this readiness to spend without regard to considerations of permanence which in the second period infected so disastrously al-Mutawakkil and his successors.

One qualification is needed, namely that with the exception of special luxuries like imported cedar and teak, carved stucco,[42] fresco painting, glass mosaic and marble panelling,[43] building costs must have been kept down very much and speed of construction enormously increased by the fact that the principal building material was unbaked brick. When after the assassination of al-Mutawakkil[44] al-Muntaṣir gave the order to demolish the Ja'fariyya and to transport the materials back to the centre of Sāmarrā this can only have applied to the baked brick facings and arches of doors or windows, for it would have been neither necessary nor possible

---

[38] Le Strange, *Baghdad*, pp. 38–9.

[39] Al-Ya'qūbī, p. 251/36.

[40] Al-Ṭabarī (de Goeje: iii, 1326) who also says (ibid.) that al-Mu'taṣim, being chiefly interested in military expenditure, did not like decoration on his buildings. This assertion is hardly borne out by the considerable finds of lavish decoration, both in carved stucco and marble, which were made at the Jawsaq.

[41] Al-Ya'qūbī, p. 265/58.

[42] Herzfeld (*Bericht*, pp. 14–15) points out that the moulded style of stucco decoration, the *Schrägschnitt* style (Creswell's *Style C*, *EMA*, ii, 283), which is capable of being indefinitely reproduced, is considerably more economical of labour than the elaborately *carved* stucco friezes.

[43] Al-Ya'qūbī (p. 258/39) speaks of al-Mu'taṣim's importation of marble workers and of his orders for marble from Lattakya, which were substantiated by the discovery in the Jawsaq (*EMA*, ii, 237) of considerable fragments of a marble frieze.

[44] Al-Ya'qūbī, p. 267/62.

to remove everything. The stucco must have been left in place (a conclusion borne out by the lavish finds in the area of the Ja'fariyya), only marble allowing of safe removal. In fact Herzfeld remarks[45] on the minute quantities of baked brick found in the ruins in this area, so that it looks as though al-Muntaṣir's orders were carried out with some efficiency. In view of the building materials used, therefore, the massive migrations and depopulations need not have been quite so spectacularly prodigal as the accounts we obtain from the sources might suggest; but even given this extenuation, the nonchalant attitude which the notables showed in leaving their dwellings and settling elsewhere is very remarkable.

The second period, covering the activities of al-Mutawakkil and his successors, where the vast building programme of the Ja'fariyya is followed, after the return of the Caliphate to Baghdad, by that equally vast complex, the Dār al-Khilāfa, would seem to be characterized by the fact that the principal sources of expenditure on building are now Caliphal rather than private. One hesitates to say that they represent *public* expenditure, since apart from the Great Mosque of al-Mutawakkil in the quarter of Ḥayr, that of Abū Dulaf which he built to the South of the Ja'fariyya and that which was added to the Dār al-Khilāfa in the tenth century in Baghdad, which in any case do not represent expenditure *the first aim of which* is public benefit, the Caliphs merely built bigger and better palaces with their appurtenances—game reserves (in al-Musharrahāt to the South of the Balkuwārā, as well as in the Dār al-Khilāfa in Baghdad), elaborate ornamental arrangements of landscaped ponds, race-tracks and grand-stands.[46] They all have in common one feature—their conspicuousness, their attempt to manifest the power of the ruler in works of architecture rather than in the economic prosperity of the city and its inhabitants. Al-Manṣūr in his eulogy of the site of Baghdad showed himself aware of the need to re-create the glories of the Sāsānian Empire but at the same time was fully alive to the importance of trade. But in the later 'Abbāsids the desire to emulate, and excel, the past has become paramount, and this

[45] Herzfeld, *Reise*, ii, 65–9.

[46] The Tall al-'Alīq/al-'Alīj at Sāmarrā is not, as we might think, the remains of a pre-Islamic settlement, but the work of al-Mutawakkil who (Herzfeld, *Geschichte*, p. 131; Qazwīnī, *Nuzhat al-Qulūb*, transl. Le Strange, p. 42) commanded earth to be brought together and a pavilion built on top from which he could watch his horses. It is paralleled by the Qubbat al-Ḥimār (Le Strange, *Baghdad*, p. 254), part of the Tāj palace in the Dār al-Khilāfa at Baghdad, built as a belvedere, even though its helical form with an exterior ramp suggests a comparison with the Malwiyya, the helical minaret of al-Mutawakkil's Great Mosque.

is a fundamental change of attitude which in other spheres soon visited the Caliphate with its effects.

V. THE PART PLAYED BY THE "ENGINEERS" (*muhandisīn*)

That there is considerable difficulty in determining the exact function of the people called *muhandisīn* in medieval Islam is well known;[47] so that it is particularly difficult to decide just how far their role in the foundation of Islamic cities was decisive, or whether they merely existed to carry out the planning and construction of some of the main buildings of the city, the ruler's palace, for example, or the Congregational Mosque, once other, non-architectural, considerations had determined where the city was to be. For one thing, all our sources lay enormous stress on the astrological factors, and even where there is no astrology precisely involved, omens and portents still occupy an excessively important part of the accounts we possess. This is the case over a very wide range, from the account of the foundation of Fusṭāṭ by 'Amr, with the omen of the dove in the tent, and the hunting scene which al-Ya'qūbī retails from Ibn Khushshakī,[48] in which the appearance of an owl apparently had a crucial importance in the siting of Sāmarrā, to the astrological considerations which governed the Fāṭimid attack on Egypt and possibly also the foundation of Cairo. Just how far is all the astrology *a posteriori*, reflecting the leanings of our sources and therefore discountable? or does it genuinely reflect the overwhelming importance of superstition, as opposed to an eye for land and the economic or strategic importance of a site? Although, perhaps, no general answer can ever be given to these questions, we can nevertheless begin to provide an answer for the special case of Sāmarrā.

For example, the eulogy of the site of Baghdad which al-Ya'qūbī[49] puts into the mouth of al-Manṣūr shows itself to be conscious of pre-Islamic tradition and suggests at least partly the desire to recreate its glories, and moreover is largely in terms of the future economic prosperity of the place, mentioning nothing at all about astrology. This is in marked contrast to his account of the choice of Sāmarrā as a building site.[50] But the difference, so far as the *muhandisīn* are concerned, is only apparent, since in each case they were called in only after it had been decided that the city should be in

[47] O. Grabar, review of L. A. Mayer's *Islamic Architects and their Works* (Geneva 1956, pp. 18–29) in *Ars Orientalis*, 1959, pp. 220–4.

[48] Al-Ya'qūbī, p. 257/47. [49] Al-Ya'qūbī, p. 237/10. [50] Al-Ya'qūbī, p. 257/48.

some particular place; so that in Sāmarrā they seem to have been told to make the best of the site,[51] since it was only after the East bank had been developed that al-Mu'taṣim turned to the much more fertile West bank. And although in the case of the Ja'fariyya it is not clear whether al-Mutawakkil's astrologers or his *muhandisīn* had the determining voice, the subsequent history of the canal there (see note 29), which was still unfinished when the site was abandoned, shows either that the role of the engineers was secondary or else that they were incompetent surveyors. If we also bear in mind the experience of al-Mu'taṣim with " al-Qāṭūl " (see note 21) before it was discovered that the site was unsuitable, it would follow that the role of the *muhandis* was executive only, to carry out what the Caliph or the astrologer wanted and, in some cases at least, to make the best of a bad job.

The whole process, of course, must have been far less a matter of chance than might appear from what has been said. For the countryside of Mesopotamia, largely desert and irrigated by ancient canals from the Tigris or the Euphrates, cannot have offered much of a choice of sites for building at any period. It requires no specially trained eye to see that the water supply in one area is good, and it may well be, for example, that although the East bank of Sāmarrā was in fact developed first it was chosen by al-Mu'taṣim because of the potentialities of the West bank; more obviously, Baghdad with its many canals, some of which connected with the Euphrates and which, like the Karkhāyā, were navigable along their whole length, was pre-eminently suitable as a centre of communications.

However, the behaviour of al-Mu'taṣim and al-Mutawakkil, who forged ahead without considering whether the sites they had chosen were suitable or not, is far from exceptional in Islam. Qayrawān, for example, seems to have been established, for strategic reasons, during the second Arab raid on Ifrīqiya in A.D. 654 on a site which shows no remains of Roman waterworks and where the Islamic waterworks date at the earliest from the reign of the Caliph Hishām. The first fifty years of its history show continuous migrations to sites very much in the vicinity,[52] none of which shows much sign of waterworks either, and it seems most plausible to suppose that this semi-nomadism was in fact a series of attempts to find suitable alternatives for inadequately provided sites.

It would involve too much of a digression to deal in any detail with the systems of canals in Baghdad and Sāmarrā. What seems, however, to be true of each is that the 'Abbāsids were better at utilizing previously

---

[51] Ibid.

[52] M. Solignac, *Recherches*, 1952, pp. 16–22.

existent systems of canals than at digging or planning their own.[53] Impressive as the waterways of Baghdad were, with even a piped water supply inside[54] the Round City of al-Manṣūr, they are fundamentally an adaptation of the great Sāsānian canals, excellent in their way but presupposing something to begin with. The same situation seems[55] to have applied in Sāmarrā where the Nahrawān (also, confusingly, called the Nahr al-Raṣāṣī and the Qāṭūl al-Kisrāwī) on the East bank and the Nahr 'Īsā on the West bank are Sāsānian, as is the triple canal which Ibn Serapion describes as branching off somewhere below the octagon of Qadisiyya but no longer extant. However, not only were there fewer canals in Sāmarrā dating from the pre-Islamic period, they were also much less exploited than those of Baghdad: it is clear from Herzfeld's air-photographs that nothing like the Baghdad network was ever in existence and that, in addition, *qanāt* systems were inadequately exploited. The conclusive proof of this is a remark by al-Iṣṭakhrī, who[56] says that the only flowing water on the East bank is the Nahrawān, all around being desert and trees, houses and waterworks all being on the opposite bank, a description which if exaggerated is certainly significant.

Herzfeld remarks[57] that the water supply of modern Sāmarrā is now taken from the Tigris and that there are no springs at all on the East bank, so that the system of water carriers which al-Ya'qūbī describes[58] must, even at its most efficient, have led to extraordinary inconveniences. The houses in the concession from al-Ḥayr northwards, for example, seem to have been up to 2,500 metres[59] from a source of running water, and the large

---

[53] Al-Ya'qūbī, 266/59; Le Strange, *Baghdad*, passim; Herzfeld, *Geschichte*, pp. 66 ff.; *Reise*, ii, 55 ff.; Ibn Serapion, *Description of Mesopotamia and Baghdad*, ed. and transl. Le Strange in *Journal of the Royal Asiatic Society*, 1895, pp. 1–76, 255–315; *Sousa* passim. In spite of Cahen's justified point (" Le service de l'irrigation en Iraq au début du Xie siècle ": *Bulletin d'Etudes Orientales*, xiii (1949–1951), 117–43) that considerable work is still needed to ascertain just how much of the irrigation systems of Mesopotamia are pre-Islamic, the sherd finds of Sāsānian earthenware in the vicinity of both the Nahrawān and the Nahr 'Īsā at Sāmarrā, and which justify us in ascribing them to pre-Islamic workmanship, enable us to advance tentatively the suggestion that where, as on the East bank, there were few canals, no considerable exploitation in Islamic times occurred.

[54] Al-Ṭabarī (Zotenberg), iii, 322–4.

[55] Herzfeld, *Samarra*, pp. 3, 51, 75, 84 says that the part of the Nahrawān (*alias* Qāṭūl al-Kisrāwī) to the North of the Mosque of Abū Dulaf is the unfinished work of al-Mutawakkil. However, no junction is visible in his later air-photographs, nor do the ruins of the bridge, the Qanṭarat al-Raṣāṣī, in the vicinity of the Ja'fariyya bear him out. At best it would seem that there was some widening of the canal, around the time the Ja'fariyya was being built, near the intake, that is just below the village of Dūr 'Arabāyā.

[56] Op. cit. (see note 26).

[57] Herzfeld, *Samarra*, pp. 1–2.

[58] Al-Ya'qūbī, p. 263/56.

[59] Herzfeld, *Geschichte*, Air Photograph 3.

houses on the banks of the Tigris anything up to 1,500 metres from the river, since, in order to avoid the danger of flooding, they were built on rising ground. Even the waterworks inside the Jawsaq and the Ja'fariyya, to judge from the very sparse remains of canals visible, seem to have been more for ornament than for use, the elaborate *pièces d'eau* which Viollet[60] observed representing the least economic use possible of a scanty water supply.

The water difficulty was aggravated by a surprising lack of bridges. In contrast to the numerous bridges of Baghdad we have only a handful for Sāmarrā, almost all across the Nahrawān canal, with a few associated with the triple canal to the South of Sāmarrā, though since there are very few remains of habitation areas or irrigation systems to the East of these canals the bridges might be thought rather a luxury. And archaeological investigation has done little to add to the contemporary accounts of Ibn Serapion.

Again, in contrast to the three pontoon bridges which linked East and West Baghdad there was only one linking the two banks of Sāmarrā, a link which, in view of the water difficulties and the large areas of habitation on the East side, with a consequent lack of cultivation, was even more necessary than in Baghdad.[61]

It seems, therefore, that we are faced with a situation where there was " water, water everywhere, and not a drop to drink ".[62]

---

[60] Viollet, *Description*, 1911, p. 12.

[61] G. L. Bell, *Amurath to Amurath*, London, 1911, p. 237: 'I rode to . . . al-'Ashīq and was rewarded for my trouble by finding indubitable traces of a masonry bridge in the low ground almost opposite a curious building called the Ṣlebiyeh (Herzfeld's Qubbat al-Ṣulaibiyya). My attention was called to this by seeing men dig out the brick piers and arches for building material. The peasants told me that when the river is low piers can be seen in the bed of the stream and that the bridge went in the direction of the Beit al-Khalīfeh (Herzfeld's Jawsaq). I give this information for what it is worth." She goes on, nevertheless, to suggest that the central portion may have been a pontoon, an arrangement corresponding with a bridge at Mosul which certainly existed in her lifetime. And although Herzfeld (*Samarra*, pp. 1–2) says that the current of the Tigris allows of a pontoon bridge in only one place, namely more or less where the modern pontoon bridge at Sāmarrā is located, it does not follow that the same was true of the currents in the 'Abbāsid period. Gertrude Bell's suggestion is certainly therefore worth considering.

[62] More recent excavations (*Excavations*) have demonstrated this point in an amusing way. They covered a series of about twenty-one houses on the West bank of the Tigris, all with rich stucco decoration. However, unlike the houses on the East bank, the walls bearing the stucco were all coated with bitumen and had nails to hold the stucco in position. This double precaution suggests very strongly that the houses suffered from damp, a very clear demonstration that the *muhandisīn* had no say in what would be the best situation, their status here having apparently dropped to that of interior decorators.

This combination of difficult communications and defective water supply, each factor aggravating the other, produces a persuasive reason, apart from the motive of personal dislike which al-Ya'qūbī implies,[63] for the desertion of the Ja'fariyya after al-Mutawakkil's death. And it illustrates once again the secondary role which the *muhandisīn* played in the planning of Sāmarrā. The site was chosen and building ordered before it could be determined whether it was suitable or not; and given the situation at Sāmarrā, where previous habitation had not produced a state of affairs congenial to further settlement, the *muhandisīn* showed themselves unable to persuade the Caliphs to be less extravagant or, alternatively, to produce a solution of the water problem which progressed beyond the Sāsānian irrigation systems. Their function, therefore, must have been executive rather than architectonic: they existed to realize the orders of others, and this they attempted to do, without being able to say whether the task with which they were faced was reasonable or not. For had they had the choice it is scarcely conceivable that they could have wished to develop the East bank of Sāmarrā.[64]

VI. ARCHITECTURAL CONSIDERATIONS—STREETS

Interesting as it would certainly be to trace connexions between Sāmarrā, Baghdad and other incompletely surveyed 'Abbāsid cities like Raqqa and Heracleia, we are faced with a crucial blank in the literary sources which makes even tentative reconstruction of their plans impossible. Nor can we even compare the defensive arrangements since there is no suggestion that Sāmarrā, even initially, was intended as a garrison town. The only areas in which comparison is possible are the street-systems, for which the air-photographs in Herzfeld's *Geschichte* are even adequate, and the various types of palace architecture, which the extant plans, few as they are, provide us with material for at least tentative judgements. My general thesis is the same as before, however: namely, that despite the enormous differences between the cities Sāmarrā was the

---

[63] Al-Ya'qūbī, p. 267/61.

[64] Herzfeld (*Bericht* p. 27 and plan on Pl. IX) when discussing the three-aisled pavilion on the Tigris side of the Qaṣr al-'Ashīq remarks that it gives a wonderful view of the East bank and then goes on to cite the views from the Jawsaq, the Mosque of al-Mutawakkil, the Balkuwārā, and the Qubbat al-Ṣulaybiyya (most probably a tomb!) as evidence for the feeling for terrain of the Samarra *muhandisīn*, quoting also (al-Ya'qūbī, p. 258/48) al-Mu'taṣim's command to them to choose the *most suitable* sites. But Herzfeld's evidence makes them more like a collection of aesthetes than professional engineers or surveyors.

extension, indeed the exaggeration, of tendencies which had manifested themselves in Baghdad under al-Manṣūr and in Raqqa under Hārūn al-Rashīd, and that after the return of the Caliphate to Baghdad the exaggeration became even more marked, with magnificence now as the only aim of any new construction.

Whereas with Baghdad we have the evidence of literary sources that the city was planned, in the case of Raqqa and Sāmarrā we have only the evidence of the map, in the latter case a long street, the Shāri' al-A'ẓam, from which a series of side streets, all more or less parallel, goes off. This is sufficient to be regarded as planning if we bear in mind that Fusṭāṭ as excavated by Gabriel and Bahgat[65] is in fact typical of medieval Islamic cities in having no two streets parallel and scarcely ten yards without a bend. We have already remarked that the striking differences in water communications in Sāmarrā and Baghdad is due not to intent but to the nature of the soil and to the absence of Sāsānian canals in the former place, but that we can assume that on the West bank of Sāmarrā, where the canals were exploited, the irrigators imported by al-Mu'taṣim took Baghdad or Baṣra as their model.[66] The question arises, therefore, whether we can trace any connexion between the land communications in the two towns.

The Round City of Baghdad where the streets of the four quarters seem actually to have been concentric[67] is clearly excluded, since the walled area of Qādisiyya shows no signs of any streets at all. And the really striking feature of Sāmarrā, the Shāri' al-A'ẓam, which reached a length of 11 km. (3 *farsakhs*) measured by the map[68] and which in at least some sections reached an astonishing width,[69] so that it was more like an indefinitely extended *maydān* or square than an avenue, again appears to be a feature without precedent.

Both literary and archaeological sources, however, provide some evidence. Al-Ya'qūbī, for example, in his account of Baghdad thinks it worth while to point out that in al-Ruṣāfa[70] there was a straight street (*ṭarīq mustaqīm*) in which the Great Mosque and the palace of al-Mahdī

[65] A Bahgat and A Gabriel, *Fouilles d'al-Fusṭāṭ*, Cairo 1921, general map of the excavations, Fig. 3, facing p. 31. This conclusion is now admirably supplemented by Scanlon's controlled excavation, preliminary reports of which can be found in the *Journal of the American Research Center in Egypt*, 1966, 1967.

[66] Al-Ya'qūbī, p. 264/57.

[67] Al-Ya'qūbī, p. 241/17.

[68] Herzfeld, *Geschichte*, air-photographs. It is pertinent to remark that a day's journey on a caravan route was generally fixed (Qazwīnī, *The Geographical Part of the Nuzhat al-Qulūb . . .*, transl. Le Strange, London 1919, pp. 161–79) at five *farsakhs*.

[69] Al-Ya'qūbī, p. 266/60: 200 ells or 98 metres.

[70] Al-Ya'qūbī, p. 253/40.

were situated. And clearly such a street must have been remarkable in a site where there can have been few influences from Hellenistic or Roman town-planning. Secondly, in describing the area between the Syrian gate and the quarter of Ḥarb[71] he mentions that it was traversed by a great avenue crossed by many streets, a description which must apply to its width rather than its length, for the distance was not great. Archaeological evidence, however, presents striking precursors, for example in Egypt where the oases of Khārga and Dākhla cover an enormous area, though perhaps it would be more proper to regard each of these as a collection of separate villages, some of which are contiguous, but which even in antiquity must have regarded themselves as separate units.

But in Khurāsān we have an even more surprising series of analogues. From at least the seventh century onwards villages, and later towns, present a remarkably constant form,[72] the centre of the town being a canal (compare al-Mutawakkil's projected re-digging of the canal up to the Ja'fariyya, one channel to go along each side of the main avenue),[73] which could stretch for as much as six kilometres, with the houses arranged on either side of it, the villages lands behind them and the *dihqān*'s castle somewhere off the axis. It has been calculated[74] that by the tenth century there were as many as six thousand villages of this type in Khurāsān, and where, as in the more considerable towns of Sinj and Yaz Tepe in the Merv area,[75] this plan persisted, we find towns of inconsiderable width but up to two farsakhs in length. The general resemblance to Sāmarrā, therefore, is very striking.

However, tempting as it is to postulate a connexion between the two, it must be remarked that the differences are more significant. First, so far from forming the centre of Sāmarrā, the Nahrawān and the Nahr 'Īsā seem to have acted as the boundaries North and South of the inhabited areas on each bank, and the first mention of a central canal comes with al-Mutawakkil. Yet even in this case, where the plan was at least partially realized, the air-photographs show[76] that there were very considerable gaps in the built-up areas. Not only, therefore, can we not understand

---

[71] Al-Ya'qūbī, p. 248/30.

[72] Pugachenkova, *Puti Razvitiya Arkhitektury* . . . , pp. 144 ff., 194 ff.

[73] Sarre and Herzfeld, *Reise*, ii, 67. Its beds still exist on either side of the upper section of the Shāri' al-A'ẓam, above the Mosque of Abū Dulaf.

[74] Pugachenkova, p. 144. [75] Pugachenkova, p. 194.

[76] Herzfeld, *Geschichte*, photographs 1–3, which show an empty gap of three kilometres to the South of the Ja'fariyya between it and the Mosque of Abū Dulaf, and again to the South of the Turkish concessions at Karkh, as far as the region of the Tall al-'Alīq, of five kilometres.

al-Ya'qūbī literally[77] when he says that the whole seven farsakhs or thirty-five kilometres of Sāmarrā was built-up continuously (any more than we can believe his assertion that the Tigris was inhabited continuously from Baghdad up to Sāmarrā); we also have to deal with a site which, if never more than one town essentially, was far from being the planned unity of these Khurāsānian towns. Al-Mutawakkil's canal, moreover, must be seen not as the artery of the new site, as the Khurāsānian canals seem to have been, but as a grandiose project of little utility designed, like his other buildings, to add lustre to his name.

Why then was Sāmarrā so long? It is clear from the discussion of water communications above that to have the city on both banks of the Tigris and to neglect the possibilities of the Nahrawān and the Nahr 'Īsā was almost the worst of all possible solutions. However, given that the choice was fixed on the East bank we can see why the city tended to extend and its streets to widen. For as time went on the elaborate political segregation of the non-Arab populations needed reinforcement by geographical segregation, the ruler, as in the case of al-Mutawakkil, being connected with the apparently more stable central trading areas by the lengthened Shāri' al-A'ẓam. But, obviously, the longer the main street the more difficult to reach areas of disturbance.[78] The only solution can have been to widen the street, though it is arguable that by the time the Ja'fariyya had been built, the distance from the quarters of al-Ḥayr and al-Karkh was so great that merely to widen the street can hardly have made any difference. And indeed, as we have seen above, the extension had the fatal result of maximizing the water losses, already serious because of the absence of anything corresponding to the sophisticated Khurāsānian *qanāt* systems, by percolation and evaporation.[79]

The principle feature of the habitation of Sāmarrā, therefore, is a naturally deficient site aggravated by extensive rather than intensive settlement, a feature of the expansion of Baghdad to al-Ruṣāfa under

---

[77] Al-Ya'qūbī, p. 267/60.

[78] Herzfeld (*Geschichte*) quotes the *Kitāb al-Aghānī* (xx, 42) to the effect that during heavy rainstorms none of the Sāmarrā streets was passable and life came to an absolute standstill.

[79] Herzfeld, *Geschichte*, air-photographs 1–5. Also compare *Sousa* (i, Map 8, facing p. 248) which shows a double line of *qanāts* passing more or less East–West through the Northern sector of the octagon of Qādisiyya, where the canal which enters the NW wall intersects them, so that they must be pre-Islamic. And although it is so far impossible to distinguish clearly between Sāsānian and post-Sāsānian work in 'Irāq, it can be remarked that there is nothing in *Sousa* to show that any *qanāt* systems were incorporated into 'Abbāsid buildings as part of the waterworks.

al-Mahdī but in Sāmarrā carried by al-Mutawakkil to absurd lengths. The intensively settled area round about al-Karkh which al-Mu'taṣim laid aside for his followers and their troops on his first arrival and which al-Ya'qūbī designates as the real centre of Sāmarrā,[80] roughly circular as it was, seems to have represented the optimum size and shape for the town, and this, after the desertion of the Ja'fariyya and the removal of the Caliphate to Baghdad, is very much what it had returned to by the time of al-Iṣṭakhrī's visit and, indeed, retains very much until recent times.

The pattern of settlement in Baghdad and Sāmarrā takes an interesting form, therefore: (*a*) first stages of magnificence in Baghdad under al-Manṣūr and al-Mahdī; (*b*) feelings of freedom at the spaciousness of Sāmarrā, which lead to the developments of al-Mu'taṣim and al-Wāthiq on the West bank; (*c*) prodigality of al-Mutawakkil at the cost of all economy and convenience; (*d*) disaster, followed by immediate contraction but (*e*) return to Baghdad and even greater architectural excesses. However, the gross expansion of Sāmarrā could not be repeated, for the good reason that by the time al-Mu'tamid returned to Baghdad the city must have been so built up that the only kind of display possible was in individual buildings, a display which, needless to say, the late Caliphs indulged to a degree even more extreme than Mutawakkil himself.

VII. BUILDINGS

In this final section I wish to make a few, very incomplete, observations about the relations between *types* of buildings in Baghdad and Sāmarrā. With the proviso that the site of Sāmarrā encouraged the 'Abbāsids to spread themselves, I think we have already produced some evidence to show that Sāmarrā is the development of a phenomenon already present in Baghdad under al-Manṣūr, namely of the town as the glorious garment of the ruler, and this evidence can be supplemented by considerations of the architecture of the two cities.

It should be emphasized that the discussion does not pretend to provide a history of architectural developments during the 'Abbāsid period, the use, for example, of the triple-arched facade as decoration for the courtyards of Ummayad and 'Abbāsid palaces, since this is to tread ground already well mapped out by Creswell.[81] But as an alternative to this we can trace the development of various types of building in association,

[80] Al-Ya'qūbī, p. 259/51.

[81] Creswell *EMA*, ii, chapters on Mshatta, Ukhayḍir and Sāmarrā.

of palaces and open squares, for example, of kiosks and game reserves and of gateways like the Bāb al-'Āmma at the entrance to the Jawsaq which are also loggias and which occupied an important place in court ceremonial. It is these associations of buildings, which, for better or for worse, we might describe as " public architecture ", which constitute almost the only evidence, apart from the lay out of the streets of Sāmarrā, that there was such a thing as town-planning in medieval 'Irāq. Even were there space for an extended treatment, however, there would, unfortunately not be sufficient material for the kind of comparison which would be more illuminating. For whereas the archaeological material at Sāmarrā is certainly as rich as the literary sources, Baghdad, thanks to the disturbances of the Buwayhids and the destruction of the Mongols, provides no topographical evidence whatsoever. But despite this essential incompleteness of the comparative material, the comparison is a necessary start to the study of Islamic town-planning.

1. Palaces

Neither al-Ya'qūbī nor the Khaṭīb are at all informative about the *interior* disposition of the 'Abbāsid palaces of Baghdad.[82] But it is interesting that al-Manṣūr's palace of Khuld, to which he moved from the centre of the Round City, repeats its general scheme, overlooking a large square, in this case the Review Ground outside the Khurāsān Gate, with the office of the Shurṭa or Chief of Police overlooking it and the western end of the pontoon bridge[83] leading from it. And with the palace in al-Ruṣāfa we know[84] that in this case also the Great Maydān was nearby. In Sāmarrā the Jawsaq was on the Stone Square[85] (Taş Meydanı is still a common Anatolian name for the main square of a town or a village); the Mosques of Abū Dulaf and al-Mutawakkil both show traces of a widening of the street at the approaches to them and the same is true of the Ja'fariyya itself.[86] That the phenomenon does not recur in Baghdad in the Dār al-Khilāfa must, I think, be put down to lack of space only, for the adjunction of important public buildings and a large open space seems to be very much an 'Abbāsid feature. The palace of Ibn Ṭūlūn, for example,

[82] G. Makdisi in two articles on the topography of eleventh-century Baghdad (*Arabica*, vi, 1951, pp. 178–97, 281–309) provides valuable information on this subject which is, he emphasizes, not to be read back into the earlier history of the town because of the enormous changes which took place under the Buwayhids. He remarks (p. 301) that the building of the enclosure walls under al-Mustaẓhir in 408 A.H. had nothing to do with the Dār al-Khilāfa, as Le Strange had suggested.

[83] Le Strange, *Baghdad*, p. 106.

[84] Le Strange, *Baghdad*, p. 189.

[85] Herzfeld, *Geschichte*, p. 132.

[86] Herzfeld, *Geschichte*, air photographs 1, 2 and 3.

built at the foot of what is now the citadel of Cairo in his city of al-Qaṭā'i', was actually called al-Maydān, and presents a striking contrast with the parts of Fusṭāṭ to the south of it but probably contemporary where we see signs of squares only in slight widenings at street junctions. The square was the sort of grandiose conception which one had to be more than a mere noble to achieve.

Whereas the early palaces of Baghdad seem to have been basically unitary buildings, Sāmarrā initiates a trend which continues in Baghdad under the later 'Abbāsids—of building various separate entities within the same enclosing wall. This is suggested by a list which Herzfeld ascribes to Yāqūt[87] of palaces attributed to al-Mutawakkil where, if we leave aside questions concerning the general accuracy of the costing, only four of the palaces that he gives are confirmed by al-Ya'qūbī.[88] The reason for the considerable discrepancy in the two lists is not, I think, invention or omission on the part of either author (though, obviously, this cannot be excluded) so much as unclarity as to what " a palace " actually was—a comparable difficulty to the problems of understanding the word " city " with respect to early Islamic foundations which we discussed at the beginning of this paper. Al-Ṭabarī, for example,[89] says that al-Mutawakkil built a palace in the Ja'fariyya called al-Lu'lu'a, which Herzfeld construes as a vast building on the scale of the isolated mansions to the south of Sāmarrā identified as al-Iṣṭablāt and al-Musharrahāt. However, nothing in the air photographs of the Ja'fariyya supports this view, and if we are not to suppose that al-Ṭabarī is tiresomely re-naming a site already familiar to us it seems most reasonable to take al-Lu'lu'a as a kiosk or even just a courtyard. And, of course, in the case of the Ja'fariyya itself[90] it seems to do least violence to the archaeological data to interpret al-Mutawakkil's assertion that he had founded a new town as potential rather than actual, so that, on this view, he had built a large palace, inside an enclosure but to which almost unlimited additions could be made. But still, to become a town instead of this isolated palace-complex it needed time, which was denied to it by the early assassination of al-Mutawakkil.

The history of the Hārūnī palace in Baghdad demonstrates even more clearly the difficulty of distinguishing between a complex of palaces and

---

[87] *Yāqūts Geographisches Wörterbuch*, ed. Wüstenfeld, iii, 17.

[88] Al-Ya'qūbī, *History*, ed. Houtsma, Leiden 1883, ii, 600. The four palaces are al-'Arūs (the Bridegroom), al-Gharīb (the Solitary), al-Shibdāz (a proper name?) and al-Burj.

[89] Al-Ṭabarī (de Goeje), iii, 1348.

[90] Qazwīnī, *Nuzhat al-Qulūb*, transl. Le Strange, p. 49, actually says that al-Mutawakkil built a magnificent palace at Sāmarrā, the Ja'fariyya, using the word *kushk*—a late source but one which at least reflects the current traditions.

several separate ones. Built by Ja'far the Barmecide, who prudently handed it over to Hārūn al-Rashīd, it was then presented to Hārūn's son, al-Ma'mūn, who proceeded to construct a *maydān* there[91] and founded within the palace enceinte a quarter where his attendants and followers built houses for themselves. But although al-Mu'taṣim resided there for a short time in 833 A.D. the site was not fully exploited until the return of the Caliphate from Sāmarrā, when the single enclosure[92] is described as being more than a square mile in area and, although still called the Hārūniyya, housed the palaces of al-Firdaws and al-Tāj as well as the Qaṣr al-Thurayya, the famous house of the Pleiades. The Tāj, built out over the Tigris on a series of arches made of brick from Ctesiphon, even dwarfed the follies of al-Mutawakkil in its decoration and appurtenances.[93] And under the Buwayhids the whole enclosure, now dignified with the empty title of Dār al-Khilāfa, became the tomb of the 'Abbāsid Caliphate, where each ruler whiled away the impotence of his days by building splendid and useless kiosks within it.

The difficulty is, of course, far from being restricted to Baghdad and Sāmarrā. Marçais, for example, remarks on the problems of disentangling accounts of the Fāṭīmid city of Ṣabra-Manṣūriyya and of deciding just how many palaces it contained,[94] and in Fusṭāṭ Bahgat and Gabriel were frequently forced to use sewer systems as a means of dividing up the complexes of buildings they excavated, finding no ready criterion in the series of courtyards which they had brought to light, a difficulty great enough on the domestic scale but considerably magnified when we come to palaces. And, of course, this style of construction, with its groups of houses or of courtyards all within a private enclosure, goes very much against the social developments of town life.

2. Ceremonial gateways[95]

The gateways of, for example, al-Manṣūr's Round City[96] and even the elaborate entrances of palaces like the 'Abbāsid Ukhayḍir are distinguished

---

[91] Le Strange, *Baghdad*, p. 244. [92] Le Strange, *Baghdad*, p. 263.

[93] Le Strange, *Baghdad*, pp. 253–62.

[94] Marçais, *Manuel d'Art Musulman*, Paris, 1926, i, 118–19.

[95] O. Grabar: " Baghdad, al-Mushatta and Wāṣit " in *The World of Islam, Studies in Honour of Philip K. Hitti*, ed. Kritzeck and Bayly Winder, London 1959, pp. 99–108. This provides some account of the *adventus* under the early Caliphs and states that the gate complex at Ukhayḍir, for example, " corresponded to a gate ceremonial, for which, to my knowledge, no real evidence exists in Ummayad times, but which becomes more and more emphasized under the 'Abbāsids . . .".

[96] Al-Ya'qūbī, pp. 239–40/14.

chiefly by their defensive intention (in particular, no-one was allowed to ride through the gates of the Round City). In contrast to this type, which we shall not expect to exist in Sāmarrā, because of the absence of city walls, we find a peculiar type of porch or loggia developing in which the Caliphs would hold audience, as for example with the Bāb al-'Āmma which formed the entrance to the Jawsaq.

It is known that on the great arch of Ctesiphon in front of the *īwān* there was a crown,[97] and Grabar has conjectured that as a general rule the Sāsānian kings held their audiences at the entrance to the *iwans* of their palaces rather than in the domed halls behind them.[98] However although we must obviously take these antique examples into account, since the 'Abbāsids were obsessed by the glory of the Sāsānian empire, we have also a record of a very interesting gate in Baghdad, the Bāb al-Ṭāq, which was situated at the eastern end of the principal pontoon bridge and which seems to have been originally part of a palace built for the daughter of al-Manṣūr.[99] In the days of Hārūn al-Rashīd it was often used as a meeting place, poets coming there to recite before him, so that it actually became known as the Majlis al-Shu'arā', and it is tempting to suppose that this was the immediate origin of the Bāb al-'Āmma in Sāmarrā which with its triple portico occupied the whole of the entrance to the Jawsaq, and where the Caliphs sat in audience twice a week.[100] On the other hand, the triple entrance of the Ja'fariyya seems merely to have been an imposing facade without either ceremonial or defensive purpose. In Baghdad the Dār al-Khilāfa also possessed a Bāb al-'Āmma, the entrance to the palace both for visitors and for the private canal which furnished the grounds with water but obviously also of importance since it was provided with iron gates said to have been taken from Amorium by al-Mu'taṣim after his victory there, as a result of which it was called by some the Bāb 'Ammūriya.[101] There is, however, no evidence that it was used like its namesake in Sāmarrā for Caliphal audiences, and, indeed, it is probable that the Baghdad Bāb al-'Āmma, like the gate of the Ja'fariyya, as well as

---

[97] A. Christensen, *L'Iran sous les Sassanides*, Copenhagen 1944, p. 397.

[98] Grabar, op. cit., p. 103, footnote.

[99] Le Strange, *Baghdad*, p. 218.

[100] Al-Ya'qūbī, p. 261/63.

[101] Le Strange, *Baghdad*, p. 275; *al-Fakhrī*, ed. Ahlwardt, p. 275; see Creswell, *Muslim Architecture of Egypt* (Oxford 1952), i, 32, for the strangely peripatetic history of these doors. It should be noted that Ibn Shiḥna (*Al-Durr al-Muntakhab fī Ta'rīkh Mamlakat Ḥalab*, Beirut 1909, p. 39) says that al-Mu'taṣim brought the gates back to Sāmarrā. The procedure had precedents: for example, the gate of Zandaward was brought to Wāṣit and then transferred to Baghdad (Creswell, *EMA*, ii, 14; al-Ṭabarī (Zotenberg), iii, 321).

the raised pavilion at the entrance to the Qaṣr al-ʻAshīq and the courtyard and garden facades of the[102] Balkuwārā, all of which were triple-arched, approximated more to the general pattern of entrances to ʻAbbāsid palaces in not having more than a decorative function. Once again, therefore, we have a case of magnificence without content.

3. Hippodromes and Game reserves[103]

According to al-Masʻūdī Hārūn al-Rashīd was the first ruler to play polo in Baghdad: after the extermination of the Barmecides al-Ma'mūn built a *maydān* for polo within the grounds of the Hārūnī palace and also constructed a game reserve (*ḥayr*) there which by the twelfth century in the time of Ibn Jubayr had been separated from the complex by a wall. Al-Yaʻqubī's testimony that a concession in al-Ruṣāfa at the time that al-Mahdī was building his palace there was turned into a hippodrome (*ḥalba*)[104] is then paralleled by his account of Waṣīf and his companions in Sāmarrā[105] who on receiving land from al-Muʻtaṣim proceeded to build a large enclosure called al-Ḥayr where, beyond a wall in the midst of a spacious plain, there was a circular enclosure containing all kinds of animals. Al-Yaʻqūbī does not actually state who these animals belonged to, though it would be strange to suppose that Waṣīf built only the outer wall of the area. But each of these cases represents rather an odd development of a grant of land by a private individual: for the area they occupied and the nature of their purpose demand necessarily a large audience or many participants.[106]

The other hippodromes and game reserves are Caliphal without a doubt. The palace of Musharrahāt, which is ascribed to al-Muʻtaṣim and identified by Herzfeld[107] on the strength of its surrounding walls with an isolated palace to the south of Sāmarrā and on the opposite bank of the Nahr al-Qā'im to the octagon of Qādisiyya, certainly had a game preserve and even a tower, the Burj al-Qāʻim, ascribed to al-Mutawakkil by Yāqūt and surviving as a ruin, probably originally of ziggurat shape.[108] But much more impressive is the complex associated with the Jawsaq—an

---

[102] Herzfeld, *Bericht*, p. 38 for Balkuwārā; p. 26 for Qaṣr al-ʻAshīq.

[103] The evidence for interpreting *Ḥayr* as " game preserve " (cf. Creswell, *EMA*, i: chapters on Qaṣr al-Ḥayr al-Gharbī and Qaṣr al-Ḥayr al-Sharqī) is not complete, and unfortunately for our investigation, uses the evidence of al-Yaʻqūbī with respect to the quarter of Ḥayr in Sāmarrā very largely. However, Bar Hebraeus (transl. E. A. Wallis Budge, *Chronography*, Oxford 1932, i, 118) in describing Hārūn al-Rashīd's removal to Callynicus (i.e. Raqqa) in 780 A.D., says that he planted many *paradeiseis* there.

[104] Al-Yaʻqūbī, p. 252/37. [105] Al-Yaʻqūbī, p. 258/50. [106] Al-Yaʻqūbī, p. 263/55.

[107] Herzfeld, *Geschichte*, p. 73. [108] Herzfeld, *Geschichte*, p. 131; Yāqūt, iv, 22.

almost bottle-shaped race-track, the neck lying on the axis of the palace, and a quatrefoil to the South of this without an entrance, divided inside by a sort of cross-shaped *spina*, so that it contains four circular compartments with a corridor running round the outside.[109] To use the term *spina*, of course, begs the question of whether it was really a peculiar shaped racecourse (Herzfeld's " *kleeblattformige Rennbahn* "). But the fact that it has no entrance and that al-Mutawakkil's pavilion, the Tall al-ʿAlīq (see below) is much better adapted to overlook the unambiguous race-track on the axis of the Jawsaq, this being the only vantage point, makes the hypothesis that it was another race-track very dubious. Although it is about a kilometre north of the quarter identified by Herzfeld with al-Yaʿqūbī's al-Ḥayr its position, which lies off the axis of any building, and its general form suggest that in fact it is the Ḥayr which al-Yaʿqūbī described.[110]

These sports grounds seem to have sufficed, once built, for in the later history of Sāmarrā and again in Baghdad it is rather vantage-points and belvederes which are described for us. As well as the Burj al-Qā'im mentioned above al-Mutawakkil made an enormous mound, the Tall al-ʿAlīq, with a nine-roomed kiosk on top from which he could watch his horses.[111] And even the helical minarets of the Great Mosque and of the Mosque of

---

[109] Herzfeld, *Geschichte*, air-photographs 3 and 4. The east side of the Jawsaq with its vast rectangular enclosure and a number of transverse walls behind it has been identified (Herzfeld, *Mitteilungen*, pp. 196–204; Viollet, *Description*, pp. 695–8) with the palace polo ground, the bottle-shaped race-course to the East of this being something entirely different. Herzfeld's plan (*EMA*, ii, 242) also shows a square building between this " polo ground " and the race-course, still on the axis of the Jawsaq, which he identifies (Creswell, ibid.) with the grandstand. However, these identifications must remain debatable because of the difficulty of reconstructing the elevations of the buildings of Sāmarrā. At most therefore we can regard the fact that the building is on the axis of the palace as significant.

The fact that al-Mutawakkil had to build the Tall al-ʿAlīj as a grandstand is itself a pointer to the absence in the Jawsaq of any point from which an adequate view of the bottle-shaped race-course could be had. So that although Herzfeld's square building within the Jawsaq looks like a pavilion in plan, it may well have been nothing of the sort.

[110] Al-Yaʿqūbī, 263/55. On air-photograph 4 (*Geschichte*) (cf. *ibid.* Pl. 23b, Pl. 24) one can see clearly a wall which forms the easterly limit of building on the east bank of the Tigris and which curves round, parallel to the wall of the clover-leaf, about five hundred metres from it. The careful husbanding of space round the clover-leaf at the expense of the building area suggests that it may even be the rebuilt wall which al-Yaʿqūbī states (261/53) to have been demolished several times for lack of building space.

[111] Qazwīnī, *Nuzha* . . . , p. 42. He later (*ibid.*, p. 48) calls the hill Tall al-Makhālī (Nose-Bag hill), but since he shows his unreliability in ascribing al-Mutawakkil's Great Mosque to al-Muʿtaṣim the name is perhaps not to be taken too seriously. G. L. Bell (*Amurath to Amurath*, pp. 242–3) mentions that the tell was surrounded by a moat.

Abū Dulaf, although not primarily secular monuments, can be included in this category, for the archaism of their form is sufficient to characterize them as the products of a controlling imagination. And of these the Qubbat al-Ḥimār,[112] with a semicircular plan and an exterior spiral staircase which was the prospect-tower of the Tāj palace in the Dār al-Khilāfa at Baghdad, was clearly a reminiscience.

The incompleteness of this account of the features of Baghdad and Sāmarrā which might properly be considered as town-planning is not wholly to be ascribed to the destructive effects of time, nor to the silence of contemporaries, nor to the deplorable failure of Herzfeld to complete the publication of his reports. For, even if we had the opportunity to consult more material than actually survives, a complete picture of Sāmarrā would have been strikingly different from either a Hellenistic or a Roman community on the one hand or a later medieval Islamic city on the other.

Pauty[113] has suggested that what was lacking was the appearance of a merchant class, but Sāmarrā was clearly not underdeveloped from the point of view of trade. Al-Ya'qūbī's accounts[114] of the volume of trade which passed through Sāmarrā are completely confirmed even in the comparatively restricted realm of porcelain by the rich finds of Chinese wares published by Sarre,[115] and although subsequent changes in the course of the Tigris and the disastrous opening of the Diyālā canal in A.D. 938[116] have altogether succeeded in obliterating traces of the port installations, there is no need to assume that contemporary accounts are

---

[112] Le Strange, *Baghdad*, p. 254.

[113] E. Pauty: " Villes Spontanées et Villes Créées en Islam ": in *Annales de l'Institut d'Etudes Orientales*, ix, 52–75.

[114] Al-Ya'qūbī, p. 263/55–6.

[115] Sarre (*Die Keramik von Samarra*, vol. ii of the *Ausgrabungen*, pp. 54–5) states that the greater part of the porcelain sherds came from the Jawsaq and very few from private houses, all these Far Eastern wares being imported. (It is worth while to remark that the Sāmarrā finds still constitute one of the most important sources for the study of T'ang pottery.) Later (*ibid.*, pp. 67, 101) he suggests rather wildly that some imitations of T'ang porcelains and earthenwares are so good that he cannot dismiss the possibility that Chinese workers were actually employed. But, of course, expertise with porcelain guarantees nothing when it comes to other materials and may even be a gross handicap. However, whether or not this was actually the case, the possibility itself points to a flourishing trade situation.

[116] The attempt to increase the flow of water in the Diyālā canal (cf. Yāqūt, iv, 849) in fact destroyed the whole irrigation system and Canard (" Baghdad au IVe siècle ": *Arabica*, ix, 1962, pp. 267–87) suggests that a great deal of the depopulation of the east bank of the Tigris can be traced to this event.

grossly in error when they compare them with Baghdad. But what was lacking was social cohesion. The ordinances of al-Mu'taṣim had to a considerable extent isolated the non-Islamic elements of the population, and whatever view we take of their numbers it is clear that they represented a substantial proportion of the total inhabitants. But apart from these ghetto areas, which at least were intended to be socially self-sufficient, what we have is merely a series of large enclosed palaces, Caliphal or otherwise, each with its community of soldiers and retainers and related to the inhabitants of the other palaces only by geographical proximity (and when we consider the length of Sāmarrā even this relationship can hardly be maintained).

The grandiose projects of the Caliphs which concentrated, as accounts of their finances show, upon the exterior manifestations of prosperity, had very little to do with the city as such. Public as the ceremonial architecture of the palaces and their sports grounds may seem, therefore, it had hardly more than private significance. The totally isolated desert castles of the Ummayads persisted in Sāmarrā in a way of life: the population of Sāmarrā existed for al-Mu'taṣim and Mutawakkil as filling material for the new areas they built, as books are bought by some people to furnish rooms with rather than to read. So that the architecture of magnificence initiated by al-Manṣūr in Baghdad, developed in Sāmarrā and then returned to Baghdad, isolated rather than uniting and thus went against the development of the *town* viewed as a community. And in the case of Sāmarrā the desire for display aggravated the lack of social cohesion since the impossibly defective communications, the terrible water supply and the great demands made upon it in the name of magnificence, the ethnic difficulties and the instability of the Caliphs' position all stemmed from it. It was the chief cause of the spectacular collapse of the site, as much the cause as the effect of the return of the Caliphate to Baghdad, a collapse which but for the adventitious importance which the site later acquired as a centre of Shī'ite pilgrimage would have been total.

In this paper I have tried to produce evidence for regarding the Sāmarrā adventure not as an isolated episode in the history of the 'Abbāsids but as the development of a theory of kingship already existing at the time of the foundation of Baghdad and applied there also under the later 'Abbāsids—namely, of the town as the living sign of the glory of the ruler. But if the similarity between Sāmarrā and Baghdad is more striking than the differences, why did Baghdad survive? The real answer would seem to lie in the period of Seljuk domination when the essentially centrifugal effect of the vast isolated complexes, of which the tenth-century Dār al-Khilāfa constitutes the latest important example, was counteracted by the rise of public institutions like the *madrasa*, unifying where the palaces complexes, each self-sufficient, divided. And it is indeed this type of institution which Sāmarrā above all lacked; without it the apparently unconquerable combination of Caliphal patronage, trade and the lure of space and property produced a town which faded almost as quickly as it grew.[117] It is interesting to speculate what would have happened had it been, for example, Malik Shāh and not al-Mu'taṣim who had decided to found a city on the Tigris above Baghdad—and perhaps all the more interesting when we remember that of all conquerors the Seljuks were the least ready to found towns.

---

[117] Even the magnificence has not always impressed commentators: e.g. J. Sourdel-Thomine (*Arabica*, ix, 1962, p. 453) who remarks on the " caractère à la fois grandiose et sommaire " of the monuments of Sāmarrā. It is true that one's general impression, like that of the Hadrianic villa at Tivoli, is more of extent and variety than of originality or taste. However one building, apart from the two helical minarets still standing, unfortunately only very summarily published (*Excavations*, Part I), is worthy of remark on the west bank of the Tigris and perhaps to be identified with the Qaṣr al-Jiṣṣ which Ibn Serapion reports as lying on the Isḥāqī canal. It consists of a square with cylindrical towers at each corner and twenty-four free-standing buttresses [*sic*] on each side. " The buttresses stand 80 cm. from the wall, to which their heads were probably connected by some system of vaulting." Supposing these to be some sort of flying buttress we have here a remarkable innovation, since they ante-date the earliest examples generally recognized (those of the Masjid-i Jāmi' in Isfahan, which are fourteenth century) by almost five hundred years.

DAMAS À LA LUMIÈRE DES THÉORIES DE JEAN SAUVAGET

Par

Nikita Elisséeff

I

Le propos de l'exposé qui va suivre est d'analyser les théories de Jean Sauvaget sur le développement de la ville de Damas et d'examiner dans quelle mesure ses conclusions sont encore valables aujourd'hui.

Lorsque Jean Sauvaget publiait en 1934 dans la *Revue des Etudes Islamiques*[1] son " Esquisse d'une histoire de la ville de Damas " il précisait qu'il faisait paraître ce texte sans aucune référence et sans discussion des faits nouveaux, annonçant pour plus tard des études plus approfondies; c'est ainsi que paru en 1949 dans *Syria* sa restitution du plan antique de Damas.[2] Une mort prématurée empêcha malheureusement Jean Sauvaget de parfaire son œuvre.

II

Pourquoi Jean Sauvaget a-t-il considéré Damas comme le type des villes syriennes? Ce choix se justifie, pour lui, par les faits suivants:

(1) les villes de la côte sont des ports de mer à caractère particulier, elles ont été saccagées, leur évolution n'apparait pas clairement.

(2) Nous manquons de sources anciennes pour retracer l'histoire des villes de l'intérieur.

(3) " Des trois grandes villes sur lesquelles les renseignements abondent: Jérusalem, Alep, Damas, la première est à écarter en raison de sa fonction de sanctuaire longtemps occupé par les Francs. Entre Alep et Damas, c'est Damas qui doit être choisie car elle n'a jamais cessé depuis la conquête musulmane d'être la capitale de la Syrie."[3]

Le dessein de Jean Sauvaget était d'étudier la croissance de la ville de

---

[1] *REI*, Cahier iv, 422–80.

[2] *Syria*, xxvi (1949), 314–58.

[3] Jean Sauvaget, " Esquisse " . . . , *REI*, 1934, 423–4.

Damas et de montrer ses transformations au cours des temps. Nous allons aujourd'hui rappeler brièvement les théories de notre regretté maître en matière d'histoire urbaine, puis, en suivant son plan général, nous évoquerons les problèmes essentiels qu'il a abordés pour son étude et signalerons quelques points qu'il n'a pas eu le temps de préciser dans l'étude de Damas que Jacques Berque considère comme le prototype de la métropole orientale musulmane.

L'histoire ne se déroule pas dans l'abstrait, aimait à rappeler Sauvaget, c'est pourquoi historiens et archéologues doivent s'épauler. On ne peut écrire l'histoire uniquement avec les textes, certes ceux-ci sont explicites mais trop souvent sujets à caution, il convient donc de procéder à une confrontation incessante des témoignages littéraires avec les vestiges de la culture matérielle. Ressources trop délaissées, les documents archéologiques ont servi de cadre et de support à la vie sociale, pour connaître et comprendre les hommes c'est donc la documentation archéologique qu'il convient d'interroger à cause de son caractère irrécusable mais il faut prendre garde de ne pas se laisser aller à la solliciter. Les documents archéologiques sont muets mais authentiques aussi " on demandera aux textes l'enrichissement et l'explication des faits que la seule consultation du monument ne nous aura pas permis d'établir ". " C'est Jean Sauvaget qui a su déceler par des études minutieuses les vestiges des villes créées par les Séleucides et à qui revient le mérite d'avoir précisé ainsi un chapitre de l'histoire de l'urbanisme complètement obscur avant lui " note Roland Martin.[4]

Les vestiges architecturaux sont parfois des données de faible importance, il convient alors pour l'histoire urbaine de s'appuyer sur les indices topographiques qui permettent de retrouver l'ordonnance primitive du plan dans un réseau de rues altéré par les modifications apportées au cours des siècles. C'est en partant de la topographie actuelle de la ville de Damas que Sauvaget restitue le tracé antique, vérifiant ainsi la loi de la persistance du plan. Il faut établir d'abord un tracé théorique et y inscrire ensuite les vestiges dont on dispose, à notre avis toute conclusion devra être contrôlée sur le terrain car, trop souvent, les plans urbains ne signalent pas les courbes de niveau ou bien notent des vestiges ou des inscriptions qui peuvent n'être plus à leur place d'origine. Jean Sauvaget précise le cadre de la ville et souligne son évolution en s'appuyant sur des données classiques comme la loi de la permanence topique du sanctuaire, le phénomène de la persistance des habitudes commerciales et l'interdépendance des édifices publics. Après avoir restitué le plan antique, il prête

[4] Roland Martin, *L'Urbanisme dans la Grèce antique*, 163.

attention au développement des éléments caractéristiques de la cité musulmane, étudie les édifices et leur relation avec la vie urbaine et leur influence réciproque.

Sauvaget a mis l'accent sur le développement des éléments caractéristiques de la cité musulmane, ces éléments sont pour l'aspect religieux de la ville: la Grande Mosquée Omeyyade, les mosquées, les *ḥammām*-s, qui en sont les annexes, les *madāris*, les *khānaqāh*-s, pour l'aspect administratif: la citadelle (*qal'a*), le palais de Justice (*dār al-'Adl*), le *dār al-Sa'āda*, siège du pouvoir civil à partir du XIIIe siècle, enfin pour l'aspect économique, les centres spécialisés comme les souks, les *qaysāriyya*-s et les *funduq*-s. L'étude d'une ville comme Damas permet, ainsi que le notait Sauvaget, de voir et de comparer à l'intérieur d'un seul et même cadre les effets qu'ont produits sur le même sol des mouvements historiques qui s'y sont succédés. Nous rappelerons très schématiquement l'histoire de cette ville au destin exceptionnel; rares sont, en effet, les cités qui ont pu garder durant plusieurs millénaires une place remarquable dans l'histoire du monde.[5]

III

Damas est une cité très particulière avec une histoire multimillénaire.

Déjà en 1750 avant notre ère elle joue un rôle important en bordure du désert, elle est alors la capitale du pays d'Aram. Pendant une durée ininterrompue de neuf siècles Damas fut régie par des civilisations étrangères au pays et au monde sémitique. De 333 avant notre ère, après l'occupation de la ville par Parménion, à 64 avant notre ère ce fut le règne des descendants d'Alexandre, puis après que Pompée ait réduit la Syrie, l'autorité de la " Paix romaine " s'étendit sur Damas, c'est alors que les Nabatéens, appelés pour maintenir l'ordre, vinrent occuper Damas à deux reprises et y bâtirent un quartier. Enfin à partir de la mort de Théodose (395) ce fut l'emprise byzantine jusqu'à l'arrivée des troupes musulmanes en 635. Dès lors Damas reprendra sa place dans le monde sémitique et devient une grande cité musulmane.

Pendant près de cent cinquante ans Damas sera la capitale rayonnante de l'Empire omeyyade, mais après l'avènement des Abbassides commence pour elle une sombre période de troubles qui durera trois siècles pendant lesquels, devenue métropole provinciale, elle dépendra, suivant les fluctuations politiques, tantôt de Bagdad, tantôt du Caire. L'installation à

[5] Pour l'histoire de Damas nous renvoyons à Jean Sauvaget, " Esquisse ", et à notre article " Dimashḳ " dans *Encyclopaedia of Islam*, 2nd ed., ii, 286–99.

Damas d'*atabegs* aux ordres des Seldjouqides place la ville sous la domination des Turcs. Avec le règne de Nūr al-Dīn, Damas redevient, au milieu du XIIe siècle, la capitale d'un état indépendant. Si, à l'avènement

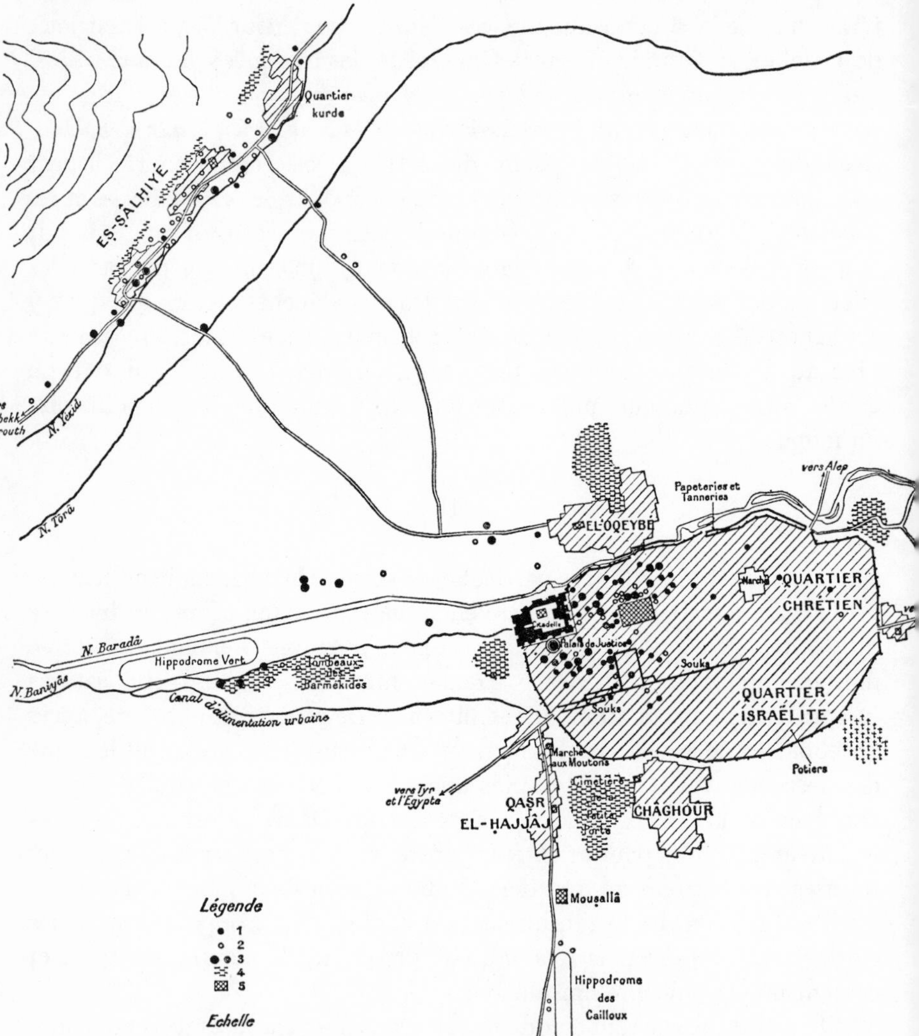

Damas au milieu du XIIIe siècle
1. Couvent 2. Mausolée 3. Médrésé 4. Cimetière musulman
5. Grande-mosquée
(*d'après Sauvaget, Revue des Etudes Islamiques 1934*)

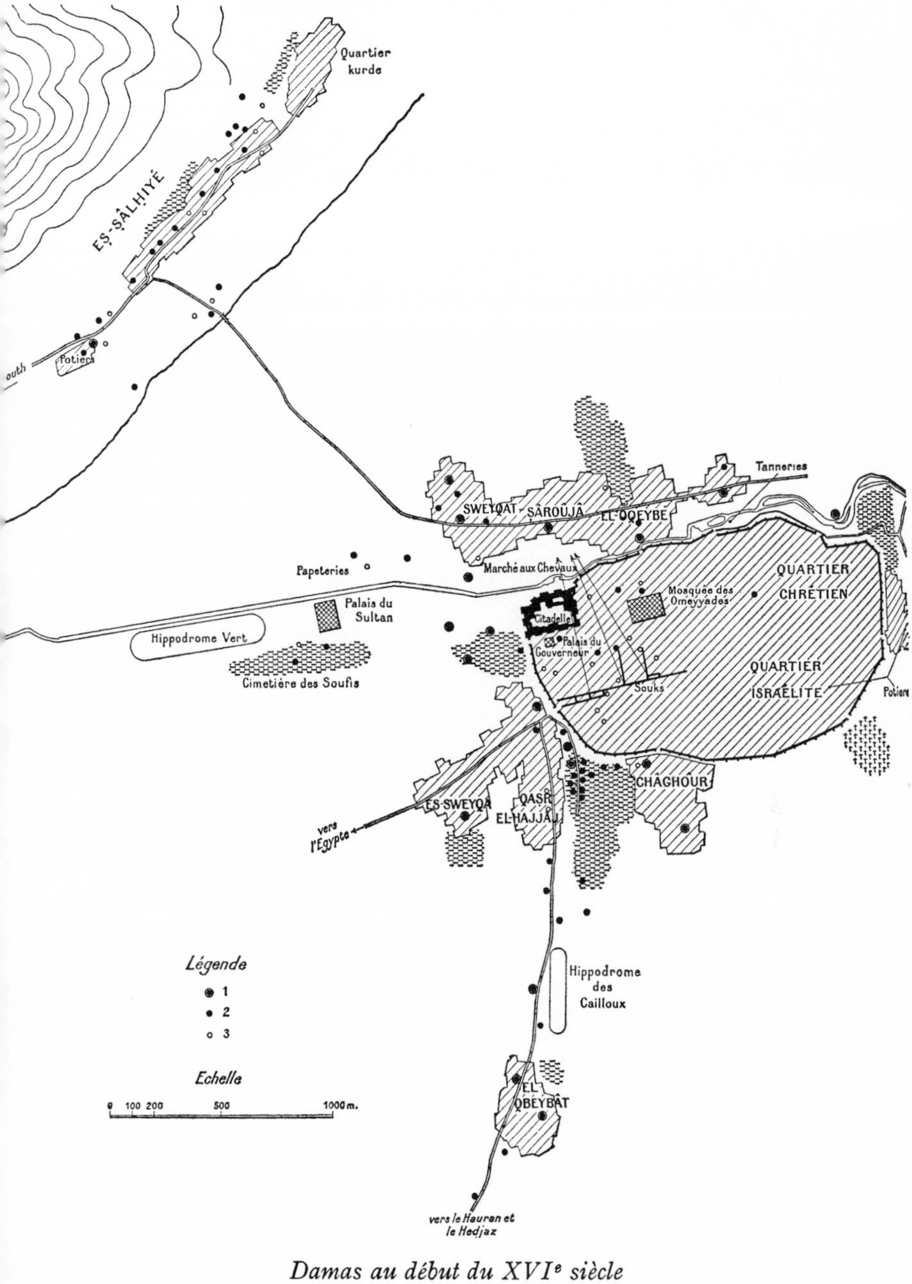

Damas au début du XVIe siècle
1. Grande-mosquée 2. Mausolée 3. Médrésé
(d'après Sauvaget, ibid.)

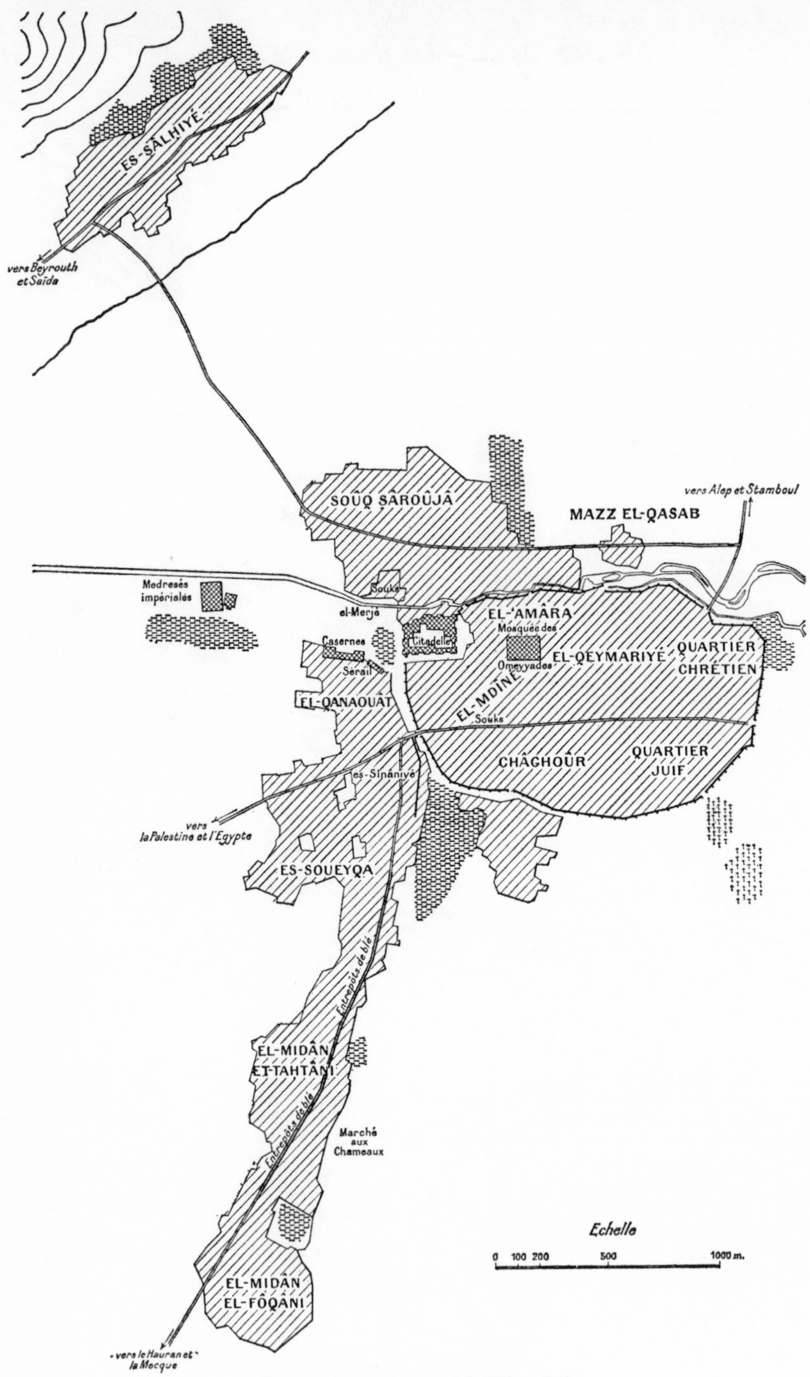

Damas au milieu du XIXe siècle
(d'après Sauvaget, ibid.)

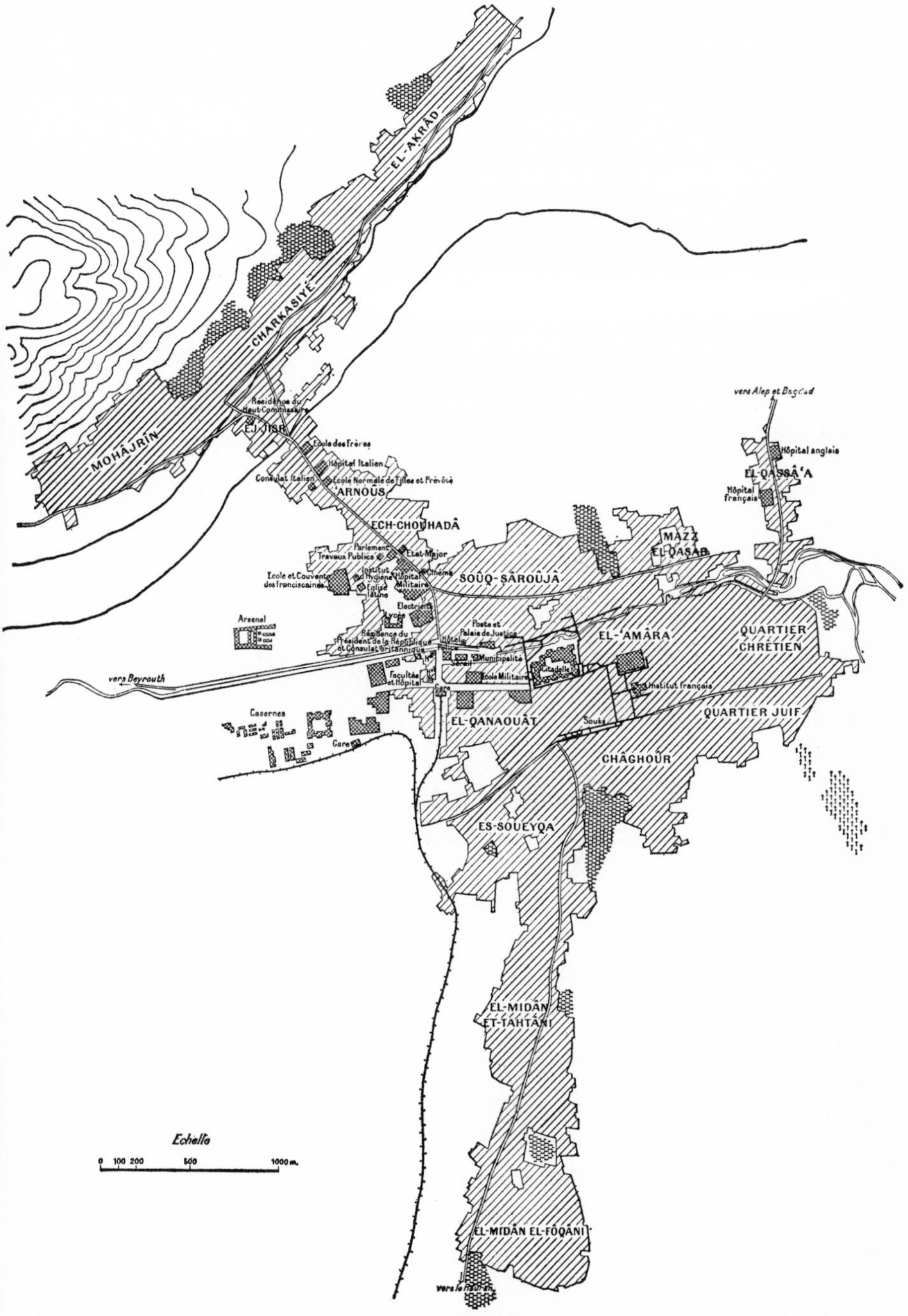

Damas contemporaire
(d'après Sauvaget, ibid.)

des princes kurdes ayyoubides, l'indépendance n'est plus qu'un mythe car le chef de la famille réside au Caire, elle n'en reste pas moins le siège d'une cour princière vivante. Sous les Mamelouks, mis à part les années de quasi indépendance que lui vaut le règne de Tengiz, au début du XIVe siècle, Damas reste vassale du Caire. L'arrivée des Ottomans en 1516 n'apparaît tout d'abord que comme une substitution de maîtres, les janissaires succédent aux mamelouks, mais rapidement Damas perd de son éclat et n'est plus, pendant quatre siècles, que le centre d'une province de l'Empire ottoman. En 1920 elle devient la capitale d'un pays sous mandat, qui est confié à la France, un quart de siècle plus tard elle est la capitale de la Syrie indépendante.

IV

Lorsque l'on étudie les problèmes de l'urbanisme des villes musulmanes il faut, d'après Mez,[6] distinguer quatre types très différents:

(*a*) les villes du monde méditerranéen héllénistique,
(*b*) les villes de type sud-arabique comme Ṣan'ā' et La Mecque,
(*c*) les villes mésopotamiennes,
(*d*) les villes orientales.

L'empire romain et l'empire byzantin étaient comme la Perse et la Transoxiane hautement civilisés et urbanisés, aussi les problèmes sont-ils très différents en Afrique du Nord pour laquelle il faudrait ajouter un cinquième type de villes plus particulièrement étudiées par Georges et William Marçais. Il ne nous est pas possible de retenir pour Damas l'axiome de William Marçais[7] que " dans l'Islam médiéval tout avènement de dynastie se traduit par un développement de la vie urbaine notamment par l'édification d'une cité ", non plus que la formule " à situation nouvelle il faut un cadre nouveau ". Ces principes, qui pourraient être valables pour les Abbassides en Iraq, ne sauraient convenir en Syrie ni pour les Omeyyades, ni pour les Seldjouqides, ni pour les Zenguides, ni pour les Ayyoubides, ni pour les Mamelouks, ni pour les Ottomans.

En Syrie, les Arabes n'ont pas fondé de villes nouvelles, ils se sont établis dans des villes antiques demeurées intactes avec leurs monuments et leurs institutions, les grandes villes se maintinrent et de là proviennent les caractères saillants de l'urbanisme syrien et la continuité qui se

---

[6] A. Mez, *Die Renaissance des Islams*, Heidelberg 1922, chap. xxii.

[7] " L'Islamisme et la vie urbaine ", *Comptes-rendus de l'Académie des Inscriptions et Belles-lettres*, 1928, 94.

manifeste dans le développement des cadres urbains pendant plusieurs générations. Il convient de rappeler avec Claude Cahen[8] que la ville dont hérite l'Islam n'est plus la cité antique. En effet on peut noter à Damas trois faits d'urbanisme: à l'époque héllénistique création " a fundamentis " d'une ville neuve à l'est de la vieille cité araméenne, aux alentours de notre ère, fondation de nouveaux quartiers nabatéens à l'est de la ville séleucide, enfin, à l'époque impériale, remaniement profond avec reconstruction du temple, construction de l'enceinte, aménagement de la Grand' Rue transversale est-ouest et embellissement de la rue à l'est du Temple ainsi que la réfection du système d'adduction d'eau.

L'ordonnance antique subit encore, entre l'époque impériale et le conquête arabe, à l'époque byzantine, d'importantes modifications sur lesquelles nous reviendrons dans une étude prochaine. A la conquête musulmane Damas, comme Jérusalem, a un long passé. Le développement urbain ininterrompu, et d'une remarquable intensité depuis l'Antiquité, communique aux agglomérations musulmanes de Syrie un caractère particulier; en effet, notait Ashtor-Strauss[9] il diffère sur plusieurs points de celui de la vie urbaine dans les pays musulmans voisins quoique les institutions aient été les mêmes. Le facies musulman des villes syriennes, remarque Sauvaget, n'est que le produit d'une évolution multiséculaire dont il importe de connaître le détail pour en comprendre les caractéristiques.

V

Un des principaux problèmes de l'histoire de Damas est le passage de la ville hellénistique à la cité musulmane.

Robert Brunschvig posait, en 1947, la question de savoir " comment sur le même site la ville antique romaine d'allure ouverte, régulière et bien dessinée a-t-elle pu se transformer en une ville musulmane aux voies tortueuses et compliquées à allure parfois de labyrinthes aux demeures claquemurées, qui se complait aux culs de sac, aux replis d'ombre, aux coins secrets."[10] L'auteur expliquait cette métamorphose par des causes juridiques tandis que Sauvaget l'explique par des données archéologiques. Nous donnerons plus loin notre opinion personnelle.

---

[8] Cl. Cahen, " Mouvements populaires et autonomisme urbain dans l'Asie musulmane au Moyen Age ", *Arabica*, 1958, 226.

[9] Ashtor-Strauss, " L'Administration urbaine en Syrie médiévale ", *Rivista degli Studi Orientali*, xxxi, 74.

[10] " Urbanisme médiéval et droit musulman ", *Revue des Etudes Islamiques*, 1947, 155.

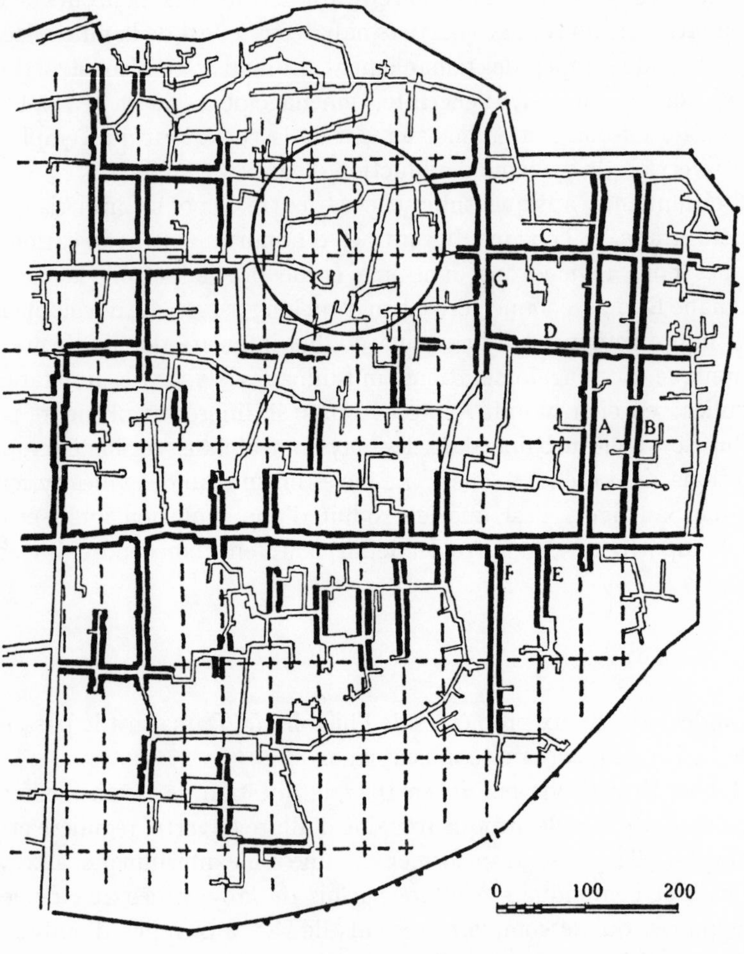

Damas antique, partie orientale
(d'après Sauvaget, Syria, 1949)

Petit à petit d'hellénistique, Damas va devenir islamique et dans un cadre antique va se former une civilisation musulmane. Tout au long de cette métamorphose il reste des éléments permanents: le sanctuaire autour duquel s'articule toute l'évolution de la ville depuis ses origines: au Temple de Jupiter a succédé l'Eglise de Saint-Jean qu'a remplacée à son tour la Grande Mosquée Omeyyade, le mur d'enceinte d'époque romaine qui ne subit que peu de changements, et les centres d'activité artisanale et commerciale. Le plan réticulé commence à se dégrader à partir de l'époque byzantine et peut-être avant, l'ordonnance géométrique se disloque alors, remarque Gustav von Grunebaum,[11] et sous la domination musulmane c'est un fait accompli. La clarté architecturale du plan a disparu mais ce n'est pas l'Islam qui est à l'origine de la dégradation de l'urbanisme de Damas. Nous allons voir les différents problèmes abordés par Jean Sauvaget dans ses études sur Damas, comme l'évolution du plan réticulé, le cloisonnement de la ville en quartiers, la transformation de la Grand' Rue antique en souk, le problème de l'eau.

Grâce au terrain pratiquement plat sur lequel elle est bâtie Damas, par son plan, est très proche de l'image de la cité théorique. Bien que tous les vestiges conservés, remarque Roland Martin, datent de l'époque romaine Jean Sauvaget attribue aux occupants hellénistiques le réseau des rues. Que celui-ci soit d'époque hellénistique il n'y a pas de doute; Damas ne présente-t-elle pas, rappelle Martin, les caractéristiques des villes séleucides: simplicité, régularité géométrique, préoccupation pratique plus qu'esthétique, c'est une ville de lotissement plus qu'une ville à structure monumentale. Toutefois bien des traits attestent des remaniements datant de l'époque romaine, en particulier l'ensemble Temple de Jupiter—avenue à colonnades—Grande Place est composé selon des règles de symétrie d'axialité contraire à l'esprit hellénistique mais conforme à l'esthétique romaine.

Nous signalerons pour notre part qu'il a existé des villes à plan en damier chez les Assyriens qui se différenciaient des cités à plan concentrique d'origine hittite. Il n'est pas impossible que les Araméens, venus de l'est, aient apporté à Damas ce genre de plan qui répondait à un but pratique: permettre un système équitable de répartition des terres, le plan en damier facilite beaucoup les opérations de lotissement. En effet entre le tell (*Bāris*), où l'on situe la première résidence royale, et le Temple, les deux pôles de l'agglomération primitive, on pourrait peut-être déceler un quadrillage remontant à l'époque araméenne. A l'époque hellénistique on s'est contenté d'ajouter à l'est de la ville de nouvelles " insulae " sans

---

[11] G. von Grunebaum, " The structure of the Muslim Town ", *Islam*, 1955, 141–58.

appliquer un plan général d'urbanisme. Les Séleucides furent fidèles au tracé en damier si pratique et si simple à réaliser, ce tracé, que nous retrouvons dans leurs fondations comme Laodicée, Alep ou Doura Europos, offrait à chacun son lot et son domaine dans un réseau de rues orthogonales. Dans l'évolution d'une ville bâtie sur un plan en damier " les étapes successives ne se laissent pas discerner ", remarque Sauvaget,[12] " si l'on a pris soin, lors de chaque nouvel agrandissement, de prolonger exactement le quadrillage et de se régler sur le même gabarit que dans l'agglomération primitive, car alors les nouvelles " insulae " ne se différencient pas des anciennes, du moins pas par leur plan: de là une homogénéité fallacieuse qui peut induire en erreur quant à la date de construction des nouveaux quartiers." Il a fallu attendre l'occupation romaine pour voir Damas vraiment transformée. Certes les Romains ont du adapter leurs procédés d'urbanisme à la ville qu'ils trouvaient. Sans rompre avec la régularité du plan hellénistique, ils ont agrandi le cadre créant alors un urbanisme hellénistico-romain dont l'époque byzantine n'oubliera pas les traits. Ne bâtissant pas une ville nouvelle, ils n'ont tracé ni *cardo* ni *decumanus* ce qui amena l'absence d'un *forum* au centre de la ville. En construisant une enceinte rectangulaire les Romains ont tracé une voie large de plus de vingt cinq mètres joignant la Porte Orientale (Bāb Sharqī) à la porte dite Bāb al-Jābiya à l'ouest. En ce qui concerne la restitution du plan primitif de Damas par Sauvaget l'emplacement du tell primitif, l'actuel tell Samaka en bordure de cette voie, ne soulève pas de problèmes, ses dimensions, sa hauteur, son site laissent à penser que nous avions jadis sur cette croupe le palais araméen, le nom de *Bāris* le confirme. En revanche l'emplacement proposé pour le théâtre antique appelle quelques remarques; Jean Sauvaget suivait, faute de mieux, l'hypothèse des deux savants allemends Wulzinger et Watzinger[13] mais sur le terrain, en dehors d'une rue au tracé curviligne, et qui suit d'ailleurs le cours du nahr Qulayt, il n'y a aucune trace ni des gradins ni de la scène ni du mur de fond. Peut-être l'édifice servit-il de carrière? L'appellation de *ṭāḥūn al-sijn* donnée à un moulin construit sur le nahr, et remontant au moins au VIe/XIIe siècle, peut laisser supposer que le théâtre a été, à une certaine époque, transformé en prison; ce fait n'aurait rien d'étonnant, en effet le théâtre romain de Boṣrā ne fut-il pas aménagé en citadelle? De nos jours, l'emplacement supposé est occupé par un admirable palais du XVIIIe siècle en relativement bon état de conservation mais occupé par divers ateliers d'artisans.

---

[12] Jean Sauvaget, " Le plan de Laodicée sur Mer ", *Bulletin d'Etudes Orientales*, iv (1934), 111–12.

[13] *Damaskus*, i, *Die Antike Stadt*, Leipzig 1921.

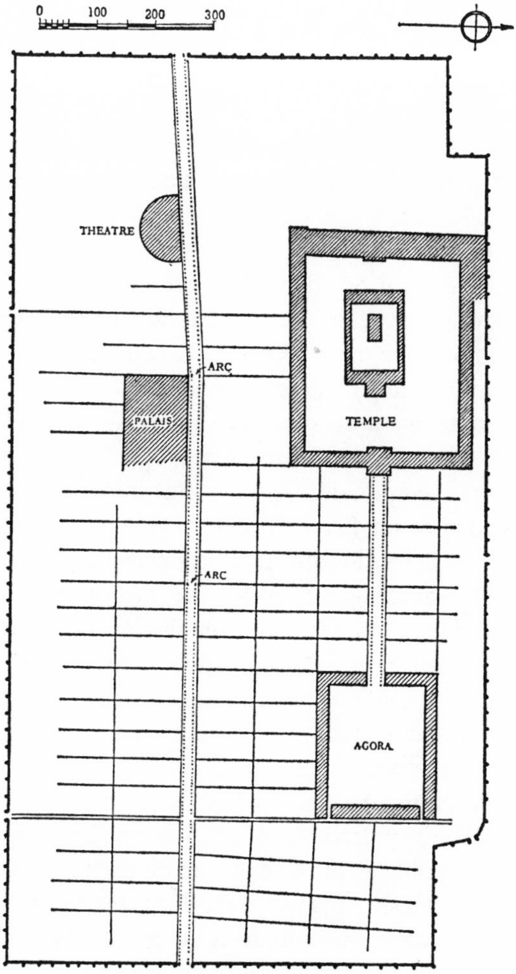

Damas antique: plan restitué
(d'après Sauvaget, ibid.)

Nous n'avons donc jusqu'à présent aucun indice certain pour localiser le théâtre de Damas.

Le problème le plus important nous semble celui de la localisation de l'*agora* par Jean Sauvaget. Dans le quadrillage restitué par Wulzinger et Watzinger ainsi que par Sauvaget l'emplacement de l'*agora* est satisfaisant à première vue mais lorsque l'on examine ce même quadrillage sur un plan portant des courbes de niveaux et que l'on se rend sur le terrain on constate l'existence d'un tell de deux cents mètres avec une plateforme de cent mètres au milieu du côté méridional de l'*agora*. Certes au nord, une rue oblique, le Darb al-Raḥba, longeant le pied du tell rappelle l'existence déjà ancienne d'une place oblongue ou carrée qui se nommait au Moyen Age: Raḥbat al-Khālid et dont le souvenir se perpétue dans l'actuelle place al-Diwāna, bordée de maisons dont les cours sont à trois ou quatre mètres au dessous du niveau actuel et dont les bassins seraient donc au niveau de l'époque romaine puisque nous savons qu'à Damas le sol s'est exhaussé de quatre mètres environ depuis l'ère impériale. On ne pourrait, dit Roland Martin, citer aucune *agora* hellénistique placée comme celle que Sauvaget restitue à Damas axée sur une Grand' Rue en parfaite correspondance avec la façade du grand temple alors que de multiples compositions romaines viendraient témoigner en faveur d'une datation de leur époque. Pour Martin il y a de sérieux doutes sur l'origine grecque de ce dispositif et, d'après lui, seul le quadrillage des rues parait remonter à la fondation de la ville par les Séleucides. A l'époque romaine se situe une grande œuvre d'urbanisme répondant à une politique de prestige et correspondant à des conditions économiques favorables. Les Romains reçoivent l'héritage grec mais adoptent des techniques nouvelles et font preuve d'un goût réel du décor et d'un sens profond du grandiose. L'ensemble Temple—avenue—place a été entièrement remanié à l'époque romaine dans la seconde moitié du IIIe siècle de notre ère. C'est alors que le Temple de Jupiter est rebâti de fond en comble en grand appareil de pierre, du propylée oriental, dont une partie subsiste, partait vers l'est une large voie bordée de colonnades, au bout de la rue, comme à Corinthe, une *agora* qui, ainsi que nous venons de le voir n'avait rien de classique, fermait la perspective.

VI

Un autre problème important est la transformation de la Grand' Rue antique au souk médiéval.

C'est au cours des deux premiers siècles de notre ère que la rue se transforme, elle n'est plus bordée de murs nus alignés, on introduit une

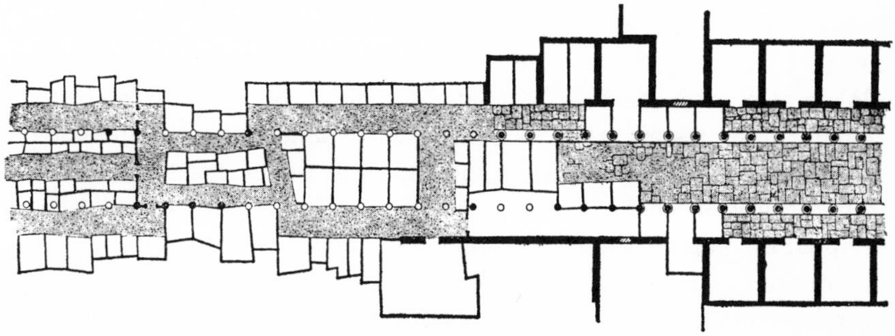

Schéma montrant le mode de transformation en souk d'une avenue antique à colonnades
(*d'après Sauvaget, Bulletin d'Etudes Orientales, 1934*)

parure architecturale, les rues sont bordées de portiques et de somptueuses colonnades, il y a aussi des effets de perspective avec des portes monumentales, des arcs et des tétrapyles.[14] Nous retrouvons des voies de ce genre à Jerash, à Palmyre et à Damas.

Pour Jean Sauvaget il y a une loi générale d'évolution des villes syriennes suivant laquelle les souks se développent au Moyen Orient sur le site d'une grande avenue à colonnades et à portiques latéraux. Petit à petit les boutiques s'installent sous les portiques, puis des échoppes se fixent entre les colonnes et finissent même par mordre sur la chaussée; le meilleur exemple de cet envahissement est l'extremité occidentale de la Rue Droite à Damas, nous y voyons en effet trois souks paralléles qui ont envahi non seulement les portiques mais la chaussée centrale.

Dès l'époque romaine la Grand' Rue à colonnades joue à Damas le rôle de principale artère commerciale, à l'époque byzantine cette voie aura les mêmes fonctions que le *mésé* où était groupée, dans les grandes villes, la majeure partie de la vie économique, les divers corps de métiers y étaient alignés les uns après les autres. Les ateliers et quelques activités artisanales étaient installés sur des emplacements réservés. Seule l'alimentation courante était dispersée dans la ville. L'envahissement de la voie antique par les boutiques, souligne Robert Brunschvig, est dû à la force des intérêts privés qui ont joué pendant des siècles contre l'ordonnance antique. La dégradation a commencé avant l'Islam mais elle semble s'être particulièrement accélérée au Moyen Age ce qui a amené Ashtor-Strauss à dire que " si le *muḥtasib* avait fait son devoir de veiller à ce que les bâtiments n'envahissent pas la voie publique, les villes musulmanes auraient gardé le plan que leur avaient donné les Romains et les Byzantins au lieu de

[14] R. Martin, *op. cit.*, 176–99.

changer les rues alignées et larges en ruelles tortueuses étroites et encombrées. L'école chaféite, qui, était la plus répandue en Syrie, était très indulgente sur ce chapitre, les hanafites admettaient l'empiétement si personne ne protestait, seuls les hanbalites demandaient la permission des autorités ".[15] La carence des pouvoirs est certes responsable de la prolifération des échoppes empiétant sur la voie publique mais l'égoisme et l'appât du gain ne furent pas étrangers à cette transformation. A notre avis, ne sont étrangers à la transformation de la voie antique en souk ni l'accroissement de la population urbaine ni les périodes de calme et de paix qui au cours de l'histoire permettent un regain de prospérité d'où découle un essor de l'activité urbaine. Ainsi le commerce international influence-t-il la structure socio-économique de la cité, ces changements sont en relation avec les évolutions du volume, de la direction et de la nature du commerce méditerranéen, en énonçant cela Jean Sauvaget songeait principalement à Alep, il me semble que les fluctuations du trafic méditerranéen sont moins sensibles à Damas placée sur l'axe Euphrate—Nil.

L'élément fondamental et permanent pour l'installation des quartiers commerciaux est l'habitude: on regroupe le commerce pour permettre de faire les achats les plus divers au même endroit, de génération en génération on se rend au même marché pour son ravitaillement, le déplacement d'un centre commercial est chose rare car on heurterait des habitudes ancestrales, aussi les souks de Damas n'ont-ils fait que reprendre la tradition antique. Les souks en pays d'Islam ont partout la même structure générale: un même produit groupe les mêmes artisans et chaque commerce a sa rue, il y a aussi des centres spécialisés comme la *qaysāriyya*, héritière de la *basiliké* byzantine. Dés 1920, Louis Massignon notait la fixité de la répartition topographique, suivant une règle constante les bazars forment un bloc compact autour de la mosquée principale, ils constituent ainsi une véritable " cité marchande ". Damas présente un cas particulier, en effet, les souks n'y connaissent pas de localisation rigoureuse, ils forment des chapelets et ne se marquent pas sur la carte par une tâche mais par deux axes principaux ayant une série de ramifications. Au début du XIIIe siècle, l'afflux de population qu'avait attiré à Damas la cour princière ayyoubide amène un bouleversement de la vie économique: de nouveaux souks s'installent " sous la Citadelle " après le remaniement de celle-ci, le *dār al-biṭṭīkh* est transféré extra-muros au nord de la ville. C'est en vertu du phénomène de la persistance des habitudes commerciales que ce marché aux primeurs, fruits et légumes, fonctionne encore de nos jours et que les

[15] "L'administration urbaine . . .", *RSO*, xxxi, 81–2.

souks situés au cœur de la ville poursuivent leur existence sur l'emplacement qu'ils occupent depuis l'époque romaine.[16]

Lorsque Jean Sauvaget parle de la dislocation de la ville en quartiers il entend ce terme dans le sens particulier d'un secteur restreint et non pas celui d'une région de la ville. Il existait, en effet, depuis longtemps à Damas un quartier officiel administratif qui groupait les organes du gouvernement, au début au sud de la Grande Mosquée puis, au Moyen Age, au sud de la Citadelle, un quartier universitaire proche de la Grande Mosquée, où dominaient les *madrasa*-s, un quartier commerçant le long de la Grand' Rue axiale, enfin des quartiers d'habitation où les gens se trouvaient groupés tantôt par ethnies: par exemple nabatéens, kurdes ou turcomans, tantôt par religion: musulmans, chrétiens ou juifs. A ces divisions s'ajoute un fractionnement en micro-quartiers juxtaposés, compartiments étanches, véritables cités en miniature. Chacun de ces micro-quartiers groupe toutes les classes sociales, il jouit de l'autonomie économique et religieuse; il a sa mosquée, qui deviendra plus tard dans certains cas une Grande Mosquée (*jāmi'*), son bain public (*ḥammām*), son partiteur d'eau (*ṭāli'*), son four (*furn*) et son petit marché (*suwayqa*). Il a aussi un chef (*ra'īs*) et son contingent de milice (*aḥdāth*).

Du point de vue topographique, le quartier se distingue de l'insula gréco-romaine: dans la ville antique, la circulation et les accès aux maisons se font par les mêmes rues, dans la ville musulmane, au Moyen Age, seulement un certain nombre d'artères à circulation sont libres, sur ces artères s'amorcent des ruelles: *darb*, *ḥāra*, dont une porte aux lourds vantaux interdit l'accès, ces ruelles se ramifient en impasses: *zuqāq*, *dahla*, que ferment des portes dans lesquelles est généralement aménagé un portillon, ainsi, avant de pénétrer dans une demeure, on franchit la porte du quartier, celle de l'impasse et finalement celle de la maison.

Pour Jean Sauvaget, le facteur d'évolution urbaine de Damas est l'insécurité chronique. Le fractionnement par quartiers, dû aux trois siècles de troubles qui ont précédé l'arrivée des Zenguides, supprima la vie urbaine, la notion de ville disparut en tant que collectivité humaine, une et solidaire, la ville n'eut plus d'unité morale et devint un agrégat de quartiers. Pour Jacques Weulersse aussi " la hantise du massacre est une des causes déterminantes de la morphologie urbaine en Orient, chaque communauté se retracte dans son quartier clos comme un animal en sa carapace." Enfin pour Ashtor-Strauss, c'est l'insécurité et l'instabilité qui poussèrent les bourgeois à se grouper à Damas.[17] Pour nous, l'insécurité

---

[16] Elisséeff, " Corporations de Damas sous Nūr al-Dīn ", *Arabica*, iii (1956), 61–79.

[17] " L'administration urbaine . . .", *RSO*, xxxi, 85.

n'est pas la seule explication du fractionnement en quartiers. Il conviendrait d'étudier la tendance générale au fractionnement urbain, examiner le développement du quartier, suivre son évolution avec ses activités économiques. En fait, dans quelle mesure ce phénomène est-il spécifiquement islamique? N'existait-il pas déjà dans les cités hellénistiques? Sauvaget ne tend-il pas à déformer l'image en donnant trop d'importance au centre urbain planifié et symétrique, ignorant le conglomérat indigène qui pouvait exister autour. A notre avis, une des causes de la dislocation de la ville en quartiers pourrait être d'origine religieuse. En effet, les Romains avaient un grand temple de Jupiter, centre de leur vie religieuse officielle, et des autels de dieux lares à domicile, chez les Byzantins, si l'icône avec sa lampe à huile avait pris la place de l'autel domestique, on vit apparaître à côté de l'Eglise-cathédrale des églises de paroisse, celles-ci ne furent-elles pas à l'origine du cloisonnement? Les limites de la paroisse ne correspondraient-elles pas avec celles du quartier? Les mosquées de quartier, plus tard, permirent aussi aux gens de ne pas sortir de leur petit univers pour s'acquitter de leurs devoirs religieux. On vécut groupé autour du lieu de prière en commun.

Sauvaget n'a évoqué l'habitat damascain que de façon fort vague lorsqu'il a rappelé que la maison servait de module à l'insula gréco-romaine. Certes les logis se pressent denses le long des ruelles étroites, articulées sur des rues plus larges donnant accès aux portes de la ville. La maison urbaine n'a pas de cave, elle est tournée vers l'intérieur et ordonnée autour d'une cour centrale généralement dotée d'un bassin. Sur cette cour, rectangulaire ou carrée, s'ouvrent les portes des chambres, sur la face sud une large baie donne accès à une vaste pièce, l'*īwān*, dont il faut rechercher l'origine dans l'empire sassanide. Les matériaux de construction sont surtout le peuplier et la brique d'argile, mais, pour les édifices importants et pour les riches demeures on faisait venir de la pierre calcaire et du basalte du Hauran. La maison damascaine, qui n'a pas encore fait l'objet d'une étude systématique, est couverte en terrasse sur laquelle au long des soirées et des nuits de la belle saison, lorsque le vent ne souffle pas trop fort, on rêve, on mange et on dort même.

Sans y consacrer d'étude particulière, Jean Sauvaget s'est intéressé à l'un des principaux problèmes de l'urbanisme, celui de l'adduction d'eau. Pourvoir les citadins en eau pure a été de tout temps une préoccupation importante pour Damas. Si les premiers canaux semblent bien être l'œuvre des Araméens, l'essentiel du réseau hydraulique extra et intramuros est l'héritage des Romains. A l'époque musulmane l'adduction d'eau relève du domaine de la bienfaisance comme l'attestent de nombreuses traditions (*ḥadīth*); il ne faut pas oublier que l'eau, dans l'Islam, est associée au culte pour les ablutions ce qui donne au bain public (*ḥammām*) le caractère d'annexe de la mosquée. L'intérêt de Sauvaget pour le problème de l'eau et pour le plan des canalisations nous en trouvons le témoignage dans les encouragements et les conseils qu'il prodigua à Michel Ecochard lorsque ce dernier rédigea en 1940 son ouvrage sur les bains de Damas. En soulignant l'intérêt d'une étude sur les partiteurs d'eau (*ṭāli'*) de Damas il n'a pas été étranger aux travaux de Richard Thoumin et de René Tresse sur la répartition de l'eau à Damas, mais il reste encore à préciser les localisations, les débits et les dénominations des partiteurs (*ṭāli'*) et des fontaines publiques (*sabīl*) en confrontant les monuments et les textes comme celui d'Ibn 'Asākir. Nous ne connaissons d'étude ni sur l'évacuation des eaux usées ni sur les latrines publiques de Damas.

L'analyse architecturale de la ville ne permettant de donner que peu de précisions sur les habitants d'une cité, les indications sur la société urbaine font défaut dans les travaux de Sauvaget. Le manque de documents antérieurs au XVIe siècle sur la structure sociale de la population damascaine l'a empêché de confronter textes et monuments pour faire une étude sociologique. Nous ne possédons pour Damas de renseignements précis sur la population, les quartiers, les maisons et les boutiques qu'à partir de la période ottomane grâce aux registres fiscaux conservés aux archives d'Istanbul et étudiés par Bernard Lewis, mais Sauvaget n'eut pas le loisir d'aborder cette période car ses travaux s'arrêtent à la fin de la période ayyoubide (milieu du XIIIe siècle).

On connait bien peu de chose de la structure de la vie municipale de Damas dans l'Antiquité et au Moyen Age. Pour cette ville, qui fut le centre d'une vie matérielle florissante et d'une activité spirituelle rayonnante et dont une partie de la population—militaires, fonctionnaires, agents du fisc—y réside tandis que l'autre—artisans, marchands, bourgeois—y habite, on a souvent évoqué l'absence d'une organisation municipale. Sauvaget ne voit plus dans la ville à partir du Moyen Age qu'une réunion d'individus aux intérêts contradictoires, pourtant les travaux d'édilité n'ont jamais cessé—on dalle les souks sous le régne de Nūr al-Dīn par exemple—les impôts immobiliers ont toujours été collectés. Certes il n'y a aucune unité morale comparable à celle des cités médiévales européennes, aucune personnalité juridique ou municipale, mais peut-être est-ce le manque de documents qui fait dire qu'il n'y a pas de " ville ". Les fonctions de *ra'īs*, de *shiḥna* et de *muḥtasib*, qui impliquent des responsabilités administratives, des institutions comme la *shurṭa*, les *aḥdāth* et le *bayt al-māl* s'inscrivent en fait dans une organisation municipale sur laquelle les renseignements nous font défaut. Le citadin musulman a bien conscience d'appartenir à une ville bien que le concept de ville, tel que nous l'entendons, lui manque, en effet n'a-t-il pas dans la suite de ses noms un ou plusieurs adjectifs toponymiques qui indiquent son lieu d'origine, la ville où il vit ou bien celle où il exerce son métier?

VII

Il faut essayer de voir dans les vestiges archéologiques le reflet de la politique. L'évolution des structures politiques est transcrite dans l'architecture de Damas, c'est en tant que témoins irréfutables de la vie que les monuments, tous les monuments, prennent un sens, telle est la leçon de Jean Sauvaget. La définition courante des villes du monde musulman est précisée par les aspects communs suivants: elles sont " closes par des remparts, environnées de sanctuaires et d'immenses cimetières; elles se composent de quartiers distincts par leurs fonctions et leur population. Toutes les villes importantes ont une citadelle . . . souvent juchée sur des buttes, collines résiduelles ou tells comme à Alep, Hama et Hims. . . . Au centre de la ville ancienne se dressent les monuments religieux les plus vénérables au voisinnage des souks, du moins des souks les plus anciens. . . . Partout pénombre, fourmillement humain, bruit, odeurs, poussière." En nous reportant à cette définition d'un manuel de géographie[18] nous pouvons conclure que Damas répond bien aux normes classiques d'une ville musulmane. Damas constitue un ensemble historique, archéologique et architectural unique, un mélange de documents relatifs à de nombreux siècles. Damas est une ville musulmane sévère, fermée et traditionnaliste, elle a pour symbole la Grande Mosquée Omeyyade avec ses trois minarets dominant une mer de maisons uniformes de hauteur et de couleur, avec des toits en terrasse au milieu desquels surgissent les coupoles des madrasas, des mausolées, des *ḥammām*-s et des *khān*-s. Deci delà se dressent des minarets carrés d'où est lancé, à heures régulières, l'appel à la prière qui couvre avec peine les bruits tintamaresques et les cris des marchands dont résonnent les souks. Par son genre de vie et par ses monuments Damas est bien, comme Sauvaget l'a justement senti, corps et âme, une cité islamique.

Pour voir l'originalité des villes musulmanes il faudrait, dit Claude Cahen[19] comparer celles-ci avec les villes qui à la même époque représentent, hors du domaine de l'Islam, d'autres branches de l'héritage antique, c'est à dire les villes byzantines et italiennes antérieures aux grandes évolutions

---

[18] Birot et Dresch, *La Méditerranée et le Moyen-Orient*, ii, 328.

[19] *Arabica*, v (1958), 226–7.

du milieu du Moyen Age. Les recherches sur la parenté entre les villes hellénistiques et les villes islamiques de Syrie pourraient amener des recherches homologues entre les cités sassanides et les cités islamiques d'Iran.

VIII

En revoyant les travaux de Jean Sauvaget, nous constatons que ses idées sur l'évolution de la ville de Damas, sur les rapports entre les monuments et la politique sont toujours valables. Laissant à ses successeurs le rôle d'historien de la société, Jean Sauvaget s'est attaché à l'étude de l'évolution du cadre urbain, à celle de la géographie et de la topographie historiques de Damas, et son grand mérite aura été de montrer une voie très féconde de recherches en confrontant constamment les textes historiques et les vestiges archéologiques.

HOUSING AND SANITATION:

Some aspects of Medieval Islamic Public Service[1]

by

George T. Scanlon

I

Limited to considerations of religion and administration, a study of the cities within the Muslim world does present an appertainable aspect of unity, to such a degree that one may speak of *the* Islamic City.[2] It is true that the Islamic city lacked internally evolved municipal institutions, on the one hand, and any fructifying sense of citizenship, on the other; but the appointment from on high of the *qāḍī* and the *muḥtasib* and the identity of the scope of their work and powers throughout *dār al-Islām* does yield a " patina " of administrative similarity.

Too often our sense of the medieval Islamic city springs from a re-creation of its civic life from texts and memoirs, and we thus pass over significant differences in physical character and in the differing solutions to problems raised by such characteristics. These differences are within an overall unity, but they are important, for each city had, as it were, its own heat, odour, cries, tumult and motion through which it gained its distinction.

We must attend distinctions in character which grow out of historical placement. The Islamic city perhaps evolved from an older city captured or ceded in war, alive and growing after occupation by Muslim forces. Such

---

[1] For the research and composition of this paper, the author was supported by a grant from the Center of Middle Eastern Studies of Harvard University, which is not responsible for the opinions stated herein.

[2] For the older view, *cf.* George Marçais, " L'Urbanisme Musulman ", *Mélanges d'Histoire et d'Archaeologie de l'Occident Musulman,* Alger 1957, i, 219–31. A far more synoptic view can be secured from Louis Gardet, *La Cité Musulman* (Paris 1954), particularly on the theological basis for urban social and political expression; and on the problems of antecedents and organization, Gustave von Grunebaum's essay, " The Structure of the Muslim Town ", is the most mettlesome and satisfying statement of the classical case (in *Islam,* Essays in the Nature and Growth of a Cultural Tradition, London 1955, pp. 141–58).

a city then had one of three fates in store: a renewal and extension of the conquered model, splendidly exemplified by Damascus; an adaptation of the earlier model to accommodate peculiar Islamic demands, most particularly the erection of Friday mosques and central government buildings, which ensued in the major cities of Transoxiana; or the bridging for purposes of better government of two formerly disparate but not distant civic entities, as an example of which I would suggest the merging of Jayy and Yahūdiyya to form pre-Buwayhid Isfahan.

Or if the city be an entirely new entity, it may evolve spontaneously, without recourse to plan or model, except for the advantageous positioning of the Friday mosque and the *dār al-imāra*. The best models here are the pure Arab Islamic camp-capitals of Baṣra, Kūfa, Fusṭāṭ and Ifrīqiya.[3] Or the new city can be built along the lines of a preconceived model, best exemplified by the ʻAbbāsid capital, the round-city of Baghdad. The various capitals in Fāṭimid Sicily and Tunisia and in Ummayad Spain could be put in the same category, though I hazard the guess that they were all really Royal Quarters, each a *dār al-salṭana* perhaps, or somewhat less ambitious Sāmarrās, since all were built at some distance from a powerful urban centre. Such cities are almost entirely within the purview of the archaeologist, who in the case of Sāmarrā, has led the historian to exaggerate its ephemeral history when compared with the great and long-lived Islamic city (like Baghdad) whose bustling continum has made archaeology impossible.

Three sub-categories should be noted:

(*a*) a thoroughly planned addition to an evolved older city, whereby the mint-new entity combines characteristics of most of the types noted above. Such was the " Versailles " which the Ṣafavids hinged to Saljūq Isfahan, and the walled quarter of al-Qāhira, which the Fāṭimids set a bit apart from the sprawl of Fusṭāṭ and Ibn Ṭūlūn's al-Qaṭā'iʻ, but connected to both by roads running from the Bāb al-Zuwayla to the Mosque of ʻAmr and to roads leading to the mosque of Ibn Ṭūlūn.[4] The older sections in

---

[3] These two large categories of conquered and created cities are well surveyed by Edmond Pauty, " Villes spontanées et villes créées en Islam ", *Annales de l'Institut d'Études Orientales*, Université d'Alger, ix (1951), 52–7. The former would be considered by Pauty and von Grunebaum as " spontaneous " additions to extant, evolving cities. But a change does take place which I consider other than " spontaneous ". Thus I choose the terms *renewal, adaptation, jointure* to make specific the purely Islamic transition.

[4] For a discussion of such connections see Paul Casanova, *Essai de Reconstitution Topographique de la Ville d'Al Fousṭāṭ ou Miṣr* (Memoires de l'Institut Francais d'Archeologie Orientale, xxv), i Cairo 1919), pp. 51–63, and especially Plan I, showing a

both instances are examples of chance-planning, or what I choose to call " town-happening ", eventually superseded in administrative and religious importance by the better planned addition. (It is well to recall that unless the older section was destroyed or abandoned, it continued to maintain a commercial parity.)

(*b*) subsequent renewal within the planned addition and/or removal of parts of a city based on an earlier model. The Mamlūks took advantage of earthquakes to re-design a good deal of al-Qāhira. Further, they added new wide arteries, such as the Sūq al-Silāḥ to connect the Rumayla plain fronting the Citadel and the Bāb al-Zuwayla, and, in the 14th century, a great highway connecting the Citadel with their new Nile port of Būlāq.

(*c*) the establishment of new residential quarters in the geographical lacunae within the defined capital; and of *faubourgs* immediately adjacent to the walls or within sight of the city along predetermined thoroughfares. Thus, in Cairo, there was the " filling-in " process between al-Qaṭā'i' and the southern wall of al-Qāhira and between both of these and the Citadel. The route to Būlāq dictated a line of development in the 14th century and in the 13th there is the establishment of a quarter around Babybars' mosque in Daher (al-Ẓāhir) from whence he would have to ride less than a kilometre to be in sight of the NW bastion of al-Qāhira. Finally in the 15th century there is the Mamlūk creation of Ezbekiyah (Azbakiyya) Gardens, a " development " around a gimmick—an artificial lake.

Such a working typology of the great Islamic cities points to inherent differences: modes of building and services were inherited or adapted from the large conquered centres; others construed or evolved from purely Islamic experience and ethos, novel physical conditions, emergent temperament and taste. From a variety of such factors we should construct the physical profile of most cities, a profile which when complete should give the essential difference of each city. (The social profile should enhance but not contradict the purely physical one, for the social norms can more easily be imposed from above, but the physical truths of a city stem from the reverse.) Climate dictates much, the mode of laying streets for instance: stamped earth in Iraq and Persia, tamped earth and crushed stone in layers in Egypt and Syria, stone slabs and cobbles in northern Syria and throughout Anatolia, etc. It shapes the form of the congregational mosque; in some places it points to large, cavernous warehouses and *khāns* while elsewhere it allows goods to lie in the open.

---

road running north from the *mashhad* of Sayyida Nafīsa, with another running into it from the vicinity of the mosque of Ibn Ṭūlūn: it is this road which runs to the southern wall of al-Qāhira.

No less important is terrain: Fusṭāṭ was built on an undulant shelf of *gabal*, it had to store water from a river somewhat distant and in places in which dirt and rubbish could not be dumped; hence the need for civic rubbish-heaps and for the direction of possible expansion, for the river was too wide at flooding to consider anything but temporary pontoon-type bridges. Isfahan and Damascus were green-belt cities whose obedient rivers could keep the water flowing (and hopefully clean) along the main routes of the city, and the supply gardens were almost immediate to its gates. Ethnic and religious considerations prompted certain arrangements within one city which were quite different in another; economic feasibility and civic health were concomitant considerations placing industry and crafts within or without the city boundaries; finally, mores gave reasons for domestic arrangements, such that housing was always oriented away from the streets, doors seldom faced one another, for the citizen sought to maintain his privacy and achieve " as complete a withdrawal from the public as possible ".[5]

Factors such as these worked for the ultimate disposition of the physical elements of the city, and consequently of the scope and disposition of the public services required to keep the Islamic metropolis alive and in motion. The prime needs were housing and water, connected with the former was sanitation, and with the latter, storage. Sanitation required a system of intelligently spread and scrupulously maintained generous supplies of water to keep the city clean and some system of canalization or collection to remove wastes. Each city evolved its own systems, and the individual Muslim gave much thought and time to the need for personal cleanliness and the best mode to achieve it for his family. To the degree that he was willing to co-operate and achieve it for his fellow craftsmen and/or guild-members, or for his " quarter " we can see this Muslim inhabitant tending towards our concept of " citizen ".[6]

---

[5] Von Grunebaum, *op. cit.*, p. 148.

[6] " Classical antiquity could not separate civilization from city life ", von Grunebaum, *op. cit.*, p. 143. Quite obviously the Muslim urbanite who sought from the corporate entity the right to and maintenance of the skeleton necessities of living, such as water and sanitation, but who demanded and secured instant privacy from the city once his daily work was accomplished was most definitely making such a separation. Charity was dispensed through religious channels and for religious reasons. If it were not for the possibly mixed-motived generosity of the ruling groups and the inherited sense of the need for community on the part of the religious leaders, it is highly doubtful if any Islamic city would have any great open areas, or piazzas or gardens, beautifully conceived *maydāns* and truly spacious buildings. There would be beauty and magnificence within private domestic complexes; but it was a rare Muslim bourgeois who would make a comparable non-religious contribution to the civic or aesthetic well-being of his city.

That the authorities would provide him with the water was a *donnée* of medieval life; that he built his house and his place of business in relation to that supply was a foregone conclusion. He, in turn, was subject to almost daily inspection should he be remiss in any matter contingent on water or sanitation.[7] The *muḥtasib*'s role as supervisor and regulator of streets, his unheralded but direct relation to Public Services, becomes more important. It is from the street that the water is supplied, the cess-pools (if there be any) cleaned and the general health of the city maintained. He saw that the streets were watered daily, that drinking water be available in those purlieux of the city lacking any public fountain (*sabīl*), and that all fountains be working and the water therein potable.[8] Merchants could be fined for not keeping the streets fronting their shops well-watered and free of dust, or could be held responsible for repairing and heightening the streets when ordered to do so.

When considered simply as arteries of traffic, streets presented problems which could not be solved in any uniform manner throughout the medieval Islamic world. How wide should they be? Who should use them? and when? and how? Though the rules varied, newer cities and those undergoing reconstruction generally opted for at least two wide cross streets, between 15 and 30 feet wide. Such highways were related to arrangements of city walls, to Friday mosques, to military needs, or as moves towards sounder administrative organization, particularly in capital cities. Otherwise the beast of burden or ridden animal was the gauge of width. In Fusṭāṭ, each street had to afford the passage of at least two horsemen abreast, while the great N–S street in al-Qāhira, called Bayn al-Qaṣrayn, varied slightly in width, affording the passage of between seven and ten mounted men. Jawhar insisted that the ramparts of

---

[7] Here the role of the *muḥtasib* was decisive and invariable. For the best picture of his role as overseer of the economic and social life of the city see Ibn al-Ukhuwwa, *Ma'ālim al-Qurbā fī Aḥkām al-Ḥisba*, ed. R. Levy, London 1938. Unlike the *qāḍī* he could investigate without written complaints (p. 5), though he could not enter private homes to investigate a suspected offence (p. 13). Indeed, on the whole, one sees his role as purely external, related to the actions and misdemeanours of the inhabitant in his *public* role (p. 88); reserving all other aspects of personal life to the courts of the *qāḍī* and of the civil ruler. It is interesting to note that he can make decisions about *'urf* (p. 5), and one may even think of him as the decision-maker about "common usage" (p. 33). Though it is easier to see him as the censor of public morals, it is more than relevant here to see him as the supervisor of Public Services, a role with great possibilities for quiet innovation. Ibn al-Ukhuwwa died in 1329 (729 A.H.), so it remains for future research to assess just how much the *ḥisba* had changed from the earliest period of Islamic domination.

[8] *Ibid.*, p. 96 f. for the regulation of water-carriers and water-sellers.

al-Qāhira's original walls be thick enough for two horsemen to ride abreast.[9]

When animals enter the picture their regulation becomes another of the *muḥtasib*'s " public services ". What types should be permitted into the recesses of the city, and how many at a time? Grave problems of congestion abided; and the *muḥtasib* and his men were forever inveighing against and fining the uncaring merchant or tycoon who tied up traffic for hours with his string of camels plunging amid the donkeys and pedestrians. Since the streets were intimately related to caravanserais and warehouses, it became a problem of whether to allow the animals in with the merchandise and the drovers, or to insist that they be kept outside the gates or " parked " in the open squares. The solutions differed: in Mamlūk Cairo there was the *wakāla*, which, while for human habitation exclusively, was never far from the city gate or entrance-way beyond which were the pack-animals and merchandise, or that part of it which they did not carry into the hostelry. The Saljūq *khāns* of Anatolia were another matter, for the animals could be stabled either below the sleeping galleries or around the forecourt, a practice and mode of architecture continued by the Ottomans. The personnel of such establishments were under the surveillance of the *muḥtasib* and to him they reported disease, heresy, and economic malpractices; likewise were they responsible to him as to the owners for the safety of any goods left in their care.

The location and width of streets counted for much in the placing of shops, markets and factories. Access was all, though custom dictated the position of the craft markets and ateliers throughout the city.[10] Where factories were concerned some relations had to be maintained between them, the place of purchase of raw materials, and the sale of finished goods. As much as possible the roads had to be kept free of inhibiting traffic, and, though the street system seems tortuous to a later observer, an amazing degree of ingress and egress during working hours was maintained. The police were especially vigilant about getting the daily supplies of food to the markets and to effect the return of the peasant and his cart to the countryside by sundown on market days. It was in the market and factory life of the city that the full force of the *muḥtasib*'s authority was felt: he scrutinized all weights and measures and maintained an incessant inspection of raw materials and products, foodstuffs and services.

Finally the personnel attached to the *muḥtasib* provided two other

---

[9] K. A. C. Cresswell, *The Muslim Architecture of Egypt*, i (London 1952), p. 21.

[10] Von Grunebaum, *op. cit.*, p. 146 f., especially the role and position of the covered *sūq* or *qaisāriyya*, which from the evidence available did not seem to exist in Fusṭāṭ.

services for the populace. They inspected all baths, tested water and drainage, and kept close watch on the activities of the bath-keepers. Lastly there was the execution of the ordinance of burial within twenty-four hours of death. The death was reported and registered by the police, who generally checked with the *qāḍī* of the quarter in which the deceased lived. The police official escorted the bier to the city walls and set down rules for public display of grief. Yet it is odd that this official had no jurisdiction in the cemetery itself, if it lay outside the city precincts, and it is this lack of civic surveillance of the cemeteries of Cairo, in particular, which contributed to their evolution into the abode of the criminal fugitive from the urban community.

II

On the two questions of housing and sanitation, the recent excavations at Fusṭāṭ can be most illuminating, for they exhibit a completely individual approach, one dictated by the physiogonomy of the setting. It was a camp-capital, originally a " tent-city " erected to effect the investment of the Byzantine fortress of Babylon in 640 (19–20 A.H.). As far as archaeology has surmised to date, it was founded upon unoccupied fields and out-croppings slightly to the north of the fortress, around which lay a town which contained a series of important Coptic religious buildings. Heliopolis (the ancient city of On) lay to the northeast, and the remains of famous temple-sites were not far distant. Though Fusṭāṭ eventually absorbed the population of this town, it can be considered a " created " entity within our typology.[11]

[11] For the fullest discussion of the early settlements and their evolved congealing, see Casanova, *op. cit.* Cf. A. R. Guest, " The Foundations of Fustat ", *JRAS*, 1907, pp. 80 ff.; Gaston Wiet, *Cairo: City of Art and Commerce* (Centers of Civilization Series), Norman 1964); and the two articles in the Encyclopedia of Islam: by Becker on " Cairo " in the 1st edition, and by Jomier on " al-Fusṭāṭ " in the 2nd edition.

A synopsis of Aly Baghat's excavations until 1920 will be found in Aly Bahgat and Albert Gabriel, *Les Fouilles d'al Foustat*, Paris 1921 (hereinafter referred to as *Bahgat*), and for the subsequent years in *Comptes Rendus des Exercises* of the Comité de Conservation, published by the Egyptian *Service des Antiquités*, in the volume 1920–24, pp. 159–64. A discussion of the houses excavated by Bahgat will be found in K. A. C. Cresswell, *Muslim Architecture of Egypt*, i (Oxford 1952), pp. 116–30. The results of a shorter season of work will be found in Ḥassan al-Ḥawāry, " Une maison de l'epoque toulounide ", *Bulletin de l'Institut Égyptien*, xv, 79–87.

Three seasons of excavation have been conducted at Fusṭāṭ under the auspices of the American Research Center in Egypt, and directed by the author of this article. The results are to be published in the Journal of the Center (*JARCE*) and they form the basis of the

When Alexandria was captured in 641–2 (20–21 A.H.), the army returned to Fusṭāṭ on the orders of the Caliph 'Umar and it became the capital of the newest Islamic province. Tents had been set up under tribal banners; these were now replaced by buildings of brick, but along streets which had represented divisions among the tribes. These divisions were just sufficient for the passage of two horsemen abreast, and this width seldom exceeded two metres: a distinction which already places Fusṭāṭ in contrast to such established centres as Jerusalem and Damascus.

Two other factors made for distinction: first, the city was built on an undulant shelf of sandstone, loping out of the Muqaṭṭam hills (to the east) towards the Nile. This meant that one built on bed-rock, and one built in terms of it, i.e., one never levelled *it*, one built on it, laying foundations and floors up to an even level.[12] In a later day one could simply build on these foundations entirely new upper structures[13] or different levels of flooring.[14] Or rarely, one would tear down to bed-rock and start rebuilding from there. One may quarrel with the lack of wisdom in such a method, but once accepted, the Fusṭāṭ mason showed rare ingenuity in manipulating this *gabal* shelf.

This ingenuity was again demonstrable in the heights he could reach when bed-rock was involved. The 1965 season revealed that the earliest settlers in Fusṭāṭ used mud mortar, which could never have allowed more than one-storey buildings. Though the evidence is not yet conclusive, one may hazard that this situation obtained up to the advent of Ibn Ṭūlūn.[15] With the introduction of lime mortar, strengthening could be achieved by

---

remarks made in this section of the article. The report of the 1964 season has already appeared: " Preliminary Report: Excavations at Fustat: 1964 ", *JARCE*, iv (1965), 7–30 with 15 plates (hereinafter referred to as *Fustat:* '64). Part I of the Preliminary Report for 1965 is in *JARCE*, v (1966), 83–112 and Pls. XXIX–XXXVII (hereinafter referred to as *Fustat: '65*); Part II will appear in 1968, and the report of the 1966 season in the 1969 issue. A fourth and final season is contemplated for the autumn of 1968.

For an interesting eye-witness account of Fusṭāṭ at its medieval apogee, though his statistics must be taken with a grain of salt, see Nassiri Khosrau, *Sefer Nameh*: Relation du Voyage, ed. and tr. Charles Schefer, Paris 1881, pp. 145–56.

[12] Cf. *Fustat: '64*, Pl. VI, fig. 13 where the *gabal* shelf is clear beneath the paving, and Pl. VII, fig. 15 where one sees the uneven foundation walls up to the string courses. Also *Fustat: '65 I*, Pl. XXXVI, fig. 18, for laying such foundations with kiln-wasters.

[13] *Fustat: '64*, sections on p. 14 and Pl. XIII, figs. 33 and 35, and *Fustat: '65 I*, p. 90.

[14] *Fustat: '64*, Pl. III, figs. 6, 7 and 8.

[15] *Fustat: '65 I*, *passim* and Pl. XXXIV, figs 16 and 17. Traces of mud-mortar construction were found throughout the major area excavated in 1965, and the objects found associated with such construction were all definitely eighth century, *op. cit.*, Figs 3–d, 6–b and c, 7–b, and 13–a and b.

inserting sand-stone columns or pillars within the walls at strategic points. (See Plate I–a and *Bahgat*, pl. VII–2, IX, XV–2 and XVI.) Heights of five and six storeys became the norm until the city was destroyed or abandoned in 1168 (564 A.H.).[16]

The second factor was water and its corollary, sanitation. At the time of the conquest, the Nile was under very little control. The island of Rawḍa protected Babylon from the full force of the annual flood, which spread unimpeded on the western banks, leaving at subsidence islands tillable for ten months of the year, as it does to this day. It is true that the army of ʿAmr came from the east, but it was this possible control of the river from the eastern bank which made settlement there rather than on the opposite shore feasible.[17] Further, with the protection of the island, this section of the eastern bank could be, and was, the river-port for the Islamic capital of Egypt, a position it maintained in parity with al-Maqs, built farther to the north by Saladin, even after the destruction of the southern section of Fusṭāṭ in 1168, and from which it was not totally ousted until the Mamlūks built Būlāq in the early 14th century.[18] It was this protected port facility which kept Fusṭāṭ the entrepôt of Egypt, in which one could purchase the wares of al-Andalus and of China, and from whence went the merchants of Egypt to sell her wheat and flax, textiles, glass and ceramics, even after Ibn Ṭūlūn had removed the administrative heart to al-Qaṭā'iʿ and the Fāṭimids even farther north to al-Qāhira. Thus Fusṭāṭ must be considered a port-city, one with a necessarily international flavour, and one which made additional calls on her appointed officials for surveillance and service.[19]

However, it was sanitation which brought out the genius in the Fusṭāṭ architect. Without a constant supply of running water, the simple one-storey family complex was impossible to realize; and, in the early period,

---

[16] *Fustat: '64*, Pl. II, fig. 4. In Pl. XXXI, fig. 9 (*Fustat: '65 I*), the walls of *līwān*-A sheathe sand-stone pillars as do all the walls of the rooms to the west of the courtyard containing the basin system.

[17] Cf. Bahgat, pp. 17 f. and fig. 2.

[18] Cf. Casanova, pp. 72–112 for the organization of life along the river-front. It must be recalled that a good deal of Casanova's re-rendering comes from Ibn Duqmāq who was writing at the close of the fourteenth century, when traces of this life were still in evidence.

[19] Goitein recounts how the economically distressed synagogue of the Palestinians in Old Cairo (Fusṭāṭ) attempted to secure the patronage of the rich Maghribi Jewish merchants who had always used the synagogue of the ʿIrāqis there. (*Studies in Islamic History and Institutions*, Leiden 1966, pp. 312 f.) More than anyone heretofore, Prof. Goitein evokes this international flavour, speaking from documents relating to Jewish merchants and communities. The archaeologist does little but substantiate the breadth of the perspective he presents.

when these were the mode, simple cess-pools cleaned from within the complex sufficed. The moment higher building became possible (and they were a godsend in such a congested commercial and industrial entrepôt which had never thought to forego its inherited street planning) other solutions were incumbent. First the houses were planned as complexes, four to five storeys high, built around courtyards which generally contained a basin-system. More than one family lodged within, and ownership was divided, yielding, in a non-pejorative sense, a medieval " tenement ". In certain instances, more than a hundred persons lived within a complex, and privies had to be available on each floor, which in turn meant that flues had to be constructed within the walls. Such flues can be found throughout the extant structures uncovered in Fusṭāṭ.[20]

All of these flues gave on to deeply cut canals in the *gabal*, which ran beneath walls, floors, and courtyards; all covered, at times vaulted, running individually or *en système* to cess-pools which were cleaned from without the complex. These canals were constantly watered from within, and the cess-pools covered daily with sand.[21]

With a bed-rock foundation and a river barely under control, the early settlers eschewed any canalizing from the Nile. Rather they used the *gabal* shelf and pack animals to solve their problems. At strategic points along the edges of the sprawling city, huge, roughly hewn pits were dug out of the bed-rock, the rock so secured being planed into shafts for building purposes or ground down to make street and flooring *dakka* (see below). Pack animals with skins of water would keep these reservoirs filled, moving day and night from the Nile to the pits.[22] From thence

[20] Cf. Bahgat, Pl. XIX–1; *Fustat: '64*, Pls. VI–16, VII–17, VIII–18; *Fustat: '65 I*, Pl. XXXIII, fig. 14, where there is a flue to the left of the hole in the impasse.

[21] Cf. Bahgat, Pl. XVIII–3 and 4; *Fustat: '64*, Pls. VIII–19 and IX–21; *Fustat: '65 I*, Pl. XXXII, fig. 13 and XXXIII, fig. 14, where beneath the entire impasse there runs a canal, whose total length is over forty metres (see Plan II of this article where this immense system can be seen commencing in the centre of the plan.)

[22] *Fustat: '65 I*, Pl. I–a; at the edge of the excavation two huge openings in the *gabal* will be noted. (In the same source on Plan II, these are " C " in IX–25 and " M " in XII–21.) Spot excavations to the east of this particular area proved there was no habitation, but a number of such pits. Thus for this particular area of Fusṭāṭ, we reached an eastern boundary. (This can be seen in Pl. II of this article: above centre and running up to the right-hand corner we encountered this edge. Trenching in the 1966 season to the north of the upper right-hand corner pointed to a continuation of the *edge* of the inhabited area. And slightly to the NE of this upper right-hand corner, the Department of Antiquities excavated an enormous storage pit, more than five metres in diameter at its lip. Though it is not a storage pit, but rather a cistern, Pl. V–a (*Fustat: '65 I*) gives a fair idea of the contours of such hewing.)

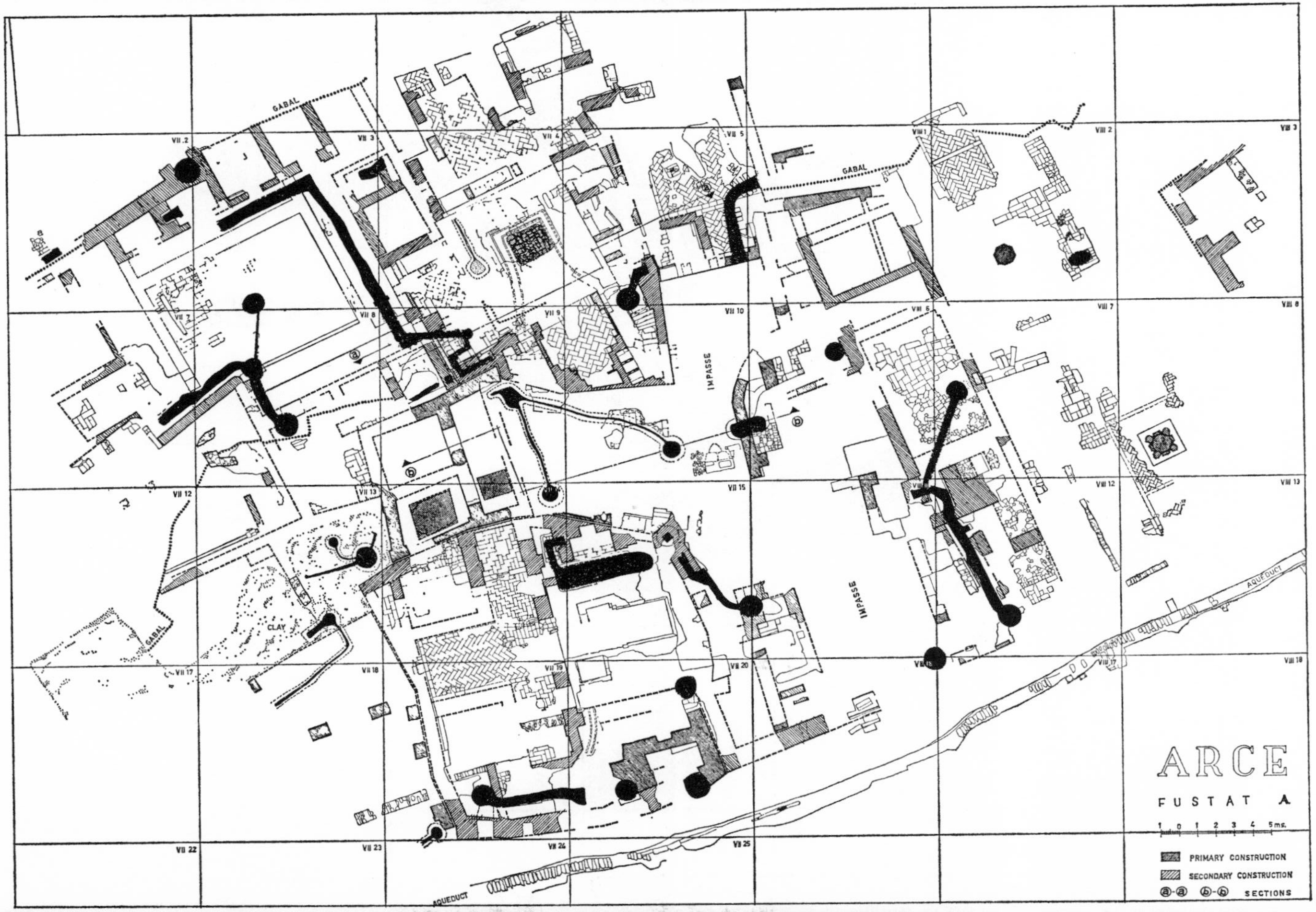
ARCE
FUSTAT A
1 0 1 2 3 4 5 ms.
PRIMARY CONSTRUCTION
SECONDARY CONSTRUCTION
ⓐ-ⓐ ⓑ-ⓑ SECTIONS
GABAL
IMPASSE
IMPASSE
CLAY
AQUEDUCT
AQUEDUCT
VII 2
VII 3
VII 4
VII 5
VIII 1
VIII 2
VIII 3
VII 7
VII 8
VII 9
VII 10
VIII 6
VIII 7
VIII 8
VII 12
VII 13
VII 15
VIII 12
VIII 13
VII 17
VII 18
VII 19
VII 20
VIII 17
VIII 18
VII 22
VII 23
VII 24
VII 25

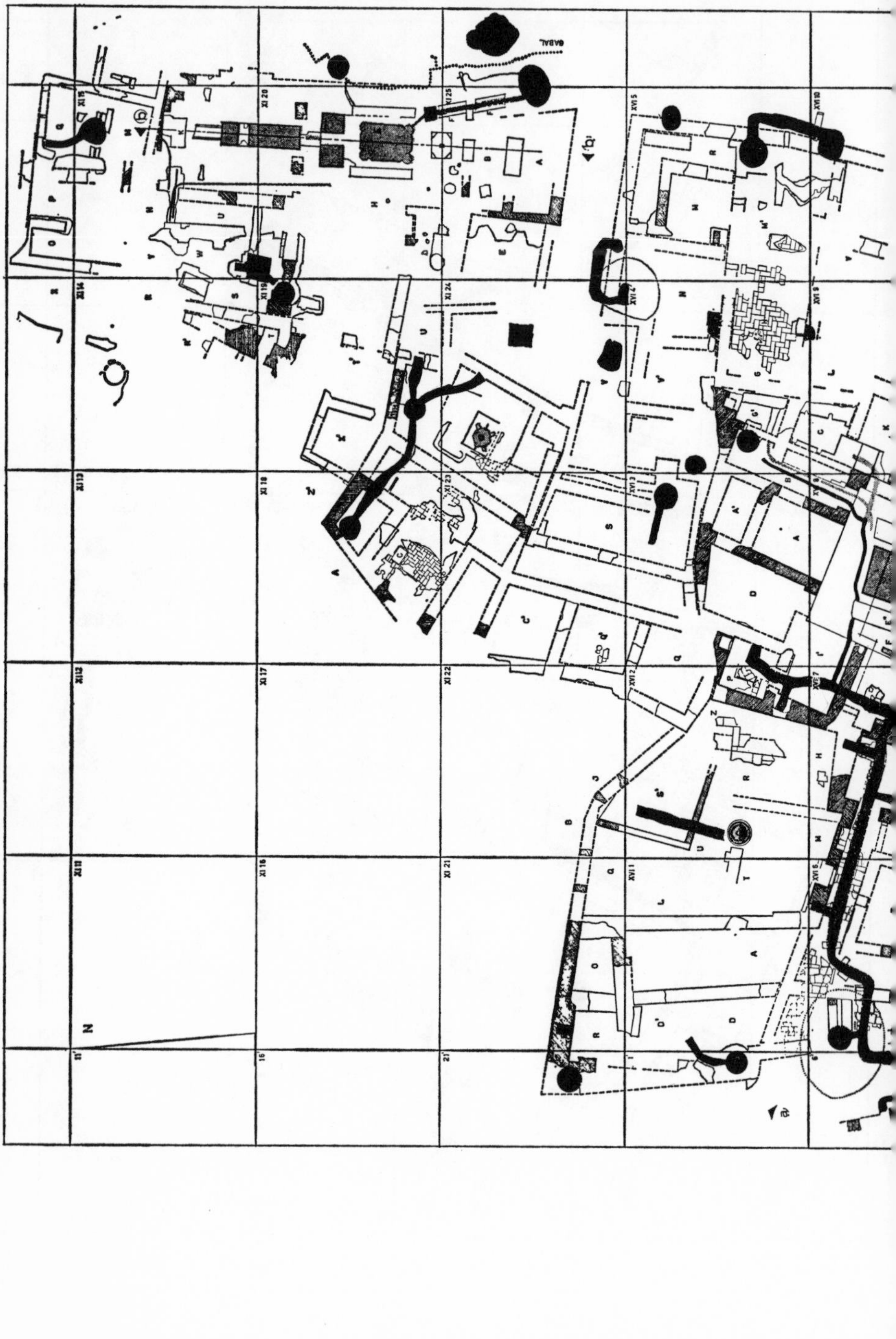
GABAL
N

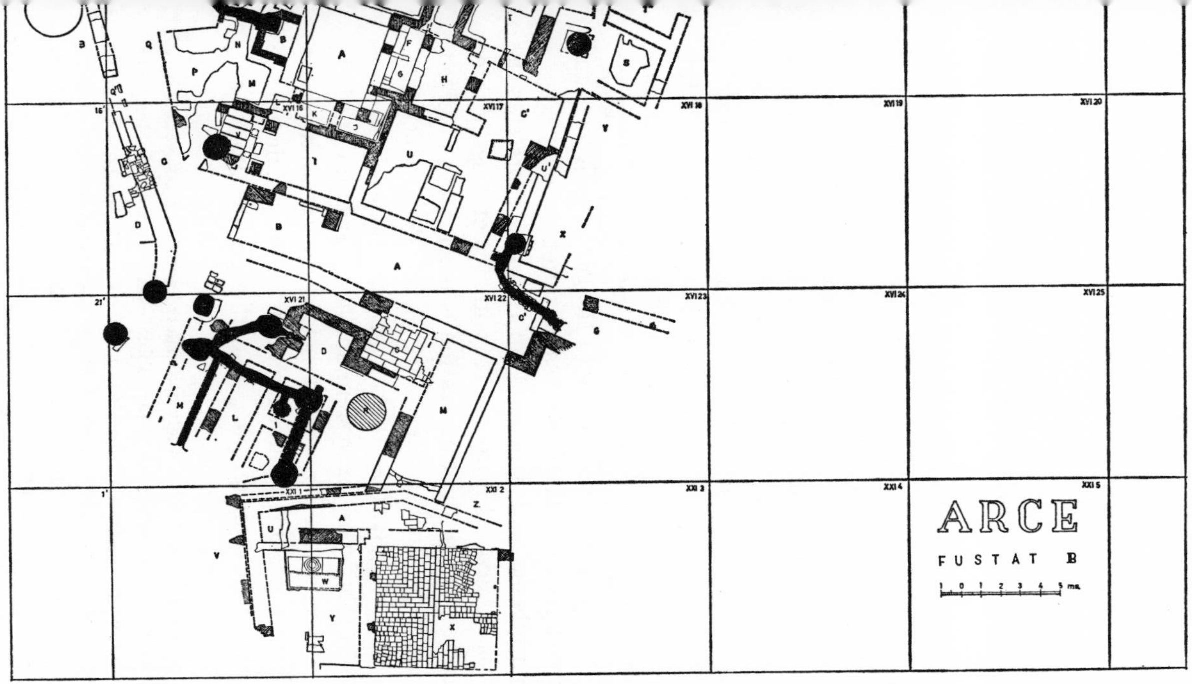

Plan II

water-carriers using donkeys or their own backs would move to and fro fulfilling the needs of houses, shops, ateliers, baths, mosques and public fountains. In time the internal hydraulic system became quite ingenious, and the water would be pumped by simple pressure to flow down into fountains and basins in court-yards. Within the domestic complex, distinction would be made between water for cleaning and cooking and that for drinking. The former would simply be put into a straight hewing into the *gabal*, bricked round and brought up to floor level; the latter into holds meticulously cut into the rock, smoothed, plastered and in some cases covered by vaulting (see Plate I–b).

Plan I represents the area excavated at Fusṭāṭ in 1964, one measuring roughly 70 × 50 metres. The solid black areas indicate the sanitation system, and those pits without attendant canalization which were adjacent to the street or easily accessible from the mews; pits in which the carriers poured the water which was to be used for all purposes within the housing complex and/or atelier. The holds for drinking water mentioned above and the courtyard basin systems are marked in dark grey.[23] The area contains twenty-seven pits hewn into the *gabal*, with flues and effluxes directly connected with the covered canalization.

The same colour scheme holds true for Plan II, which represents the larger of the two areas excavated in 1965. It is an area of roughly three thousand square metres. Here the canalization is much more involved, most particularly the long canal in the centre of the Plan, which runs beneath a paved mews serving (as does the canalization) no less than three domestic complexes.[24] This complex system, including two intermediate sumps, had to be conceived and executed before the erection of the complexes could commence. It no doubt required the heightening of the street to cover its path to the drainage pit. An earlier pit was cleaned out,

---

[23] The long line at the base of Plan I is a crudely constructed aqueduct, not yet entirely excavated, but traces of which can be seen through the rubble leading back to the Mosque of 'Amr. For a discussion of the aqueduct see *Fustat: '64*, pp. 16–17 and Pl. V–12 and VI–14.

It is my belief that this aqueduct, crude and jerry-built, represents the eastern extremity of the rebuilt area of Fusṭāṭ, work undertaken by Shīrkūh and Saladin after the destruction of 1168. Casanova points out that as part of the fortifications of Fusṭāṭ initiated by Saladin, there was a Bāb al Qanṭara, which is much farther south than the point where the great aqueduct which served the Citadel met the Nile. It might be that this is the starting point of the aqueduct system (of which ours is a section) for a revived Fusṭāṭ; *op. cit.*, p. xxviii and Plan I, where it can be seen south of the island of Rawḍa.

[24] Cf. *Fustat: '65 I*, Plan III for a cross section of that part of this gutter system which runs beneath the street, and Plate V–a for a view of the mews and the turning of the gutter to run along the N–S street and thence into the cess-pool R′ in quadrant XVI–11, visible in Plan II of this article.

Plan III

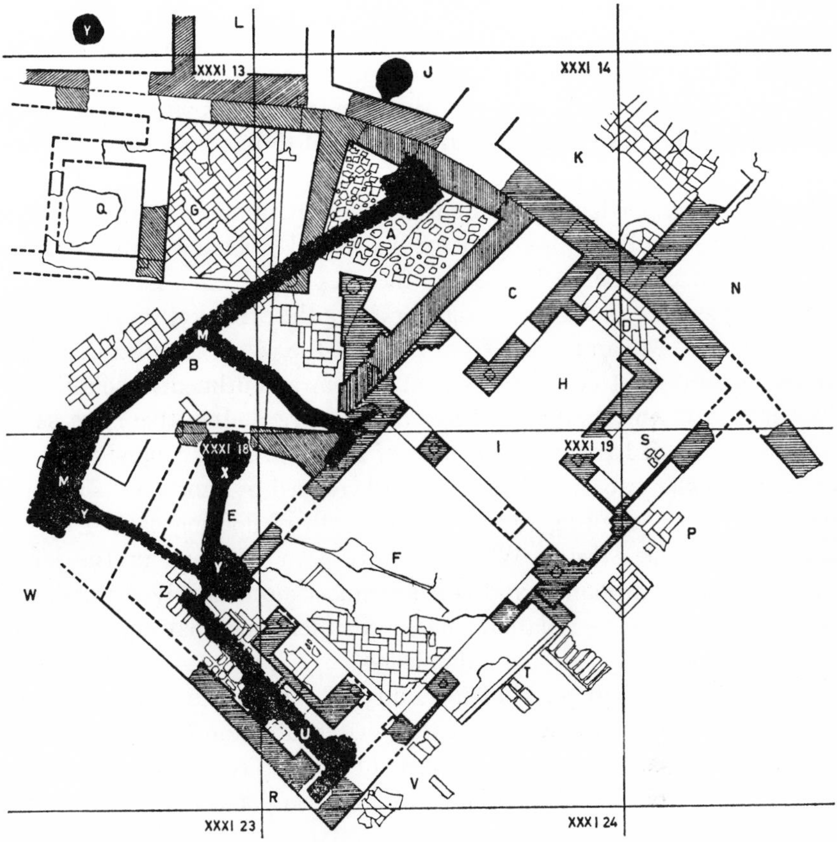

the gutter into it estopped, bricked up to the level of new flooring and used as a storage pit for cleaning water, or water for animals, if the parallel rooms to the left were used as stables. (See pit C in XVI–2 on Plan II and *Fustat: '65 I*, Plate XXXIII, fig. 15.) Thirty-four pits of all types were hewn in this part of Fusṭāṭ, a part containing three complete and parts of two other domestic complexes, a factory for making glass ingots, a pottery, and what appears to be a public fountain system.[25] (It should

[25] The dark grey area in the upper right section of Plan II (XI, 20) and Pl. II–a. The huge storage pits can be seen to the right and below the basin system, and the sharp break in the *gabal* at this eastern end of the excavated area may well mark the edge of habitation in this particular quarter. The dome and minaret belong to the mosque of Abū Su'ūd. All evidence of the 1965 and 1966 campaigns leads to the conclusion that we are in the Kōm al-Jāriḥ area. Cf. Casanova, *op. cit.*, pp. 51–63 and Plan I; Bahgat, p. 21, fig. 2; and *Fustat: '65 I*, p. 83, note 4.

be noted, too, that in medieval Fusṭāṭ, there was a complete intermingling of domestic and industrial entities.)

The complex with what appears to be a radial ground-plan in Plan III was not completely excavated at the conclusion of the 1965 campaign. However there is sufficient revealed evidence to point to a single " tenement " built around a paved countryard (F in quadrant XXXI–19) with a typical Sāmarrā-style " *bayt* " arrangement of rooms (C–H–S) entered from a porticoed, recessed passage (I) running perpendicular to them. To the south of the courtyard is a room U, which was the latrine of the ground floor. Beneath this was the deep canal, whose south-eastern terminus was the exit for a wide flue servicing the privies of the four to five stories above. As can be seen from Plan III the whole complex depended on the intricate gutter-sump-cesspool system as outlined in solid black. For an area of just under four hundred square metres there are seven sanitation pits and thirty-two metres of interconnected canals, all of the latter just under two metres in depth, all covered by sandstone slabs and up to a metre of flooring (difference in depth of flooring caused by the undulance of the *gabal*). What we have seen obtained in the larger complexes noted in Plans I and II is here most meticulously corroborated for the single, possible isolated, smaller complex, one unattended by any craft atelier, a purely " living " domicile.[26]

Why such a high pitch of ingenuity in the service of urban architecture? There seems little doubt that medieval Islam (with Byzantium serving as the link) was the direct heir of the highly developed sanitary engineering of the Roman Empire, and one even perceives refinements of inherited principles. These refinements involved variations in housing and urban services, points where topography and psychology fused to give each city its peculiar uniqueness. Fusṭāṭ was different because of the *gabal* shelf and the problem of how to relate the city to its source of water. The solutions reached by the builders and citizens of this teeming city, and the life lived in terms of these solutions produced something worthily unique in the world of medieval Islam.

---

[26] See Pl. II–b where the radial plan is apparent, and where stone columns can be seen engaged in the thick masonry of plastered walls. The room in the lower left of the picture is room C (XXXI–14) of the " bayt ". It should be pointed out that while architecturally the complex conforms to the Ṭūlūnid pattern, most of the artifacts recovered from undisturbed areas were of Fāṭimid provenance, which points to the durability of models in the Middle Eastern world. This is quite important for the history of the Islamic architecture of Egypt, for in the Fāṭimid Royal Quarter of al-Qāhira, not very far to the north, an entirely new mode of architecture was being employed, one in which dressed stone was coming to replace brick.

MUSLIM URBAN SOCIETY IN MAMLŪK SYRIA

by

Ira M. Lapidus

One problem which has long perplexed students of the Muslim world, and only recently has begun to yield to investigation, is the social structure and political and social organization of medieval Muslim cities.[1] It is difficult to imagine how, without associations of the citizens or communes to manage local affairs, these cities had any sort of common public life. Not governing themselves, they were governed by outside regimes. Deprived of autonomy, their populations, it is alleged, were not truly communities, but just dense agglomerations of isolated souls or dispersed families subject to the rule of the military elites, often foreign, who governed the territories in which the cities lay.

We now know that this view falls short of appreciating the inner organization of Muslim urban society. To help develop a more adequate interpretation, I would like in this paper to describe the forms of social life in Damascus and Aleppo in the late Middle Ages, specifically in the Mamlūk period from 1260 to 1517, and see in what ways these cities were integrated communities, and also some of the reasons why they were nonetheless without political autonomy.

I

The populations of Damascus and Aleppo fell into three broad classes: the Mamlūk military elite which commanded the armies and administered the state; the local notability distinguished by some measure of political power, religious learning, and wealth which included the *'ulamā'*, merchants and professionals; and the majority of the populace who possessed none of the crucial values.

---

[1] More complete discussions and full documentation for this topic and related issues is published in the author's *Muslim Cities in the Later Middle Ages*, Harvard University Press, Cambridge 1967.

The common people, the *'āmma*, included shopkeepers, artisans and workers with diverse situations and interests. There were rich retailers and poor peddlers, skilled and highly paid master craftsmen of luxuries, and humble artisans and workers producing the goods of everyday life. What made this part of the population an identifiable entity was the contrast with the notables, on the one hand, and with another part of the common population of the towns which we might call the lumpenproletarians, on the other. These were people outside the nexus of family, occupational, and religious ties by which the social life of the cities was organized. They were called *awbāsh, arādhil, ghawghā'*—vagabonds, migrant peasants and bedouins, beggars, and people without employment or family. Slaves and servants of the emirs, kitchen help, huntsmen, grooms, stable hands, as well as thieves and criminals also belonged to this class, and the rest of society would also have relegated the most menial and despised workers, scavengers, burial workers, waste removers, and poor and dirty tanners and weavers to the body of the disinherited. Even though we cannot draw a sharp boundary between the respectable working people and the lumpenproletarians and cannot always see in particular cases which part of the population is in question, the distinction is important for understanding the social organization and politics of the cities.

II

Neither the working people nor the lumpenproletarians of Damascus and Aleppo were amorphous masses. They were organized into communities, the most important being neighborhood solidarities called quarters. The names in Arabic are various—*maḥalla, ḥāra*. They refer to residential districts with small local markets and possibly workshops for weaving, but districts isolated from the bustle of the central bazaars. The quarters were relatively small communities, and I estimate on the basis of Ottoman census statistics of the early sixteenth century and the almost contemporary lists of quarters prepared by various authors that a population of the order of a thousand people was characteristic. Of course, districts both larger and smaller were also true units of social life, but the figure of a thousand has the correct order of magnitude and conveys the quality of face-to-face intimacy between the members. These quarters were often homogeneous communities and their solidarity, in some cases, was based on religious identity. Jews and Christians, and the various sorts of each, had their own districts. Among the Muslims different ethnic groups—Arabs, Kurds, Turkomans—lived apart. So too in the Arab Muslim majority population affiliation with the different Muslim schools of law was the basis for district quarters, as were common or presumed ancestry, clan ties, or common village origin. Migrants to the big cities from smaller towns and villages tried to recreate the old life inside the new walls. There were, for example, communities of people from Ḥarrān in Damascus. Other quarters were based on the clienteles of notable families, and the homogeneity of still others was economically based. Some quarters specialized in certain types of weaving, tanning, and other manufactures, but there is no evidence that distinctions of class or wealth were a basis of social cohesion. Of course, to a degree, some quarters were richer and some poorer, but basically they were whole communities made up of notables and commoners both, rich and poor. Economic, religious, and social life were not so differentiated as to create quarters by class distinctions.

Quarters were not only socially homogeneous, they were also collectivities for administrative purposes, and performed a host of police and fiscal functions. Each quarter had a chief called a *shaykh* or *'arīf* of the *ḥāra* who was its spokesman and governor. They were local notables chosen by the Mamlūk governors of the cities to supervise local affairs. The *shaykhs* also enforced minor police ordinances, and were responsible for the suppression of certain kinds of criminal activity. Each quarter was collectively responsible for the apprehension of criminals and/or the payment of blood money and indemnities. Furthermore, the quarters were units of taxation. When global fees were levied by the state, the *shaykhs* negotiated the tax and probably themselves divided and collected it within the districts. They thus had an important role as intermediaries between the demands of the regime and the resources of the people. Finally, the quarters acted in their own defence. In time of troubles they organized patrols to secure the districts and set up barricades. However, in the Mamlūk period, the gates of the quarters—now an established part of our image of the Islamic city—were not yet a permanent part of the structure of the quarters. Gates frequently had to be rebuilt in times of danger, and this means that, however cohesive within, the quarters were not isolated ghettoes, but adjacent streets and districts in the larger city. Not in their daily lives but only when threatened did they seal themselves off from each other. To understand the quarters we have to strike a balance between their self-sufficiency and isolation and their belonging to the larger city.

Of course, we cannot say that every quarter was a closely knit community of this sort, but in Damascus and Aleppo a very large number of them clearly were. One of the indications of the intensity of quarter solidarity was that in some cases it led to hostilities between different groups. In Damascus, feuds and pitched battles were not uncommon, especially towards the end of the fifteenth century, when the state was weak and the Mamlūks often encouraged hostilities to serve their own purposes. Mamlūk factions recruited auxiliaries from enemy quarters or encouraged quarters to attack each other as a punishment for disputes between the Mamlūks and the populace. The details of this fighting are not important enough to describe now, but at Aleppo, where there were similar feuds, the structure of the situation was more complex and warrants further discussion. In Aleppo the populace was divided into two hostile groups; one called Banāqisa, the people of the Bānaqūsā district lying outside the old walls and to the east of the city; and the other, al-Ḥawrānī, who lived in a southern sector near the Bāb Maqām. Their name indicates that they may have migrated to Aleppo from a region south of Damascus, and they are also said to have been butchers; thus people whose solidarity may have been based on common occupation as well as common origin and residence. The Banāqisa and al-Ḥawrānī fought a number of times in the fourteenth and fifteenth centuries, often when Mamlūk civil wars polarized the city populace.

Although this type of factionalism demonstrates the intensity of quarter loyalties, its basic causes remain obscure. Some clues, however, suggest interesting possibilities. In both Damascus and Aleppo these feuds centred mainly in quarters outside the walls of the cities, where physical isolation intensified social isolation. Inside the cities, where streets ran into each other, adjacent quarters more readily fused into the larger agglomeration. Moreover, in both cities the factions involved are sometimes identified not only by the name of their quarter or group, but also as Qays and Yaman. These are the names of enemy Arab bedouin tribal confederations whose histories go back to the first century of the Arab conquests, and their use suggests that the quarters involved had large populations of relatively recent rural origin. Bedouins and villagers were migrating into the cities, and sometimes whole villages were incorporated into the fabric of a continuously built-up urban area by the physical expansion of a city. Al-Qubaybāt in Damascus is a case in point.

Such rural populations brought pre-urban or proto-urban types of community organization to the cities, social patterns ultimately characteristic of bedouins who lived in tight kinship groups for the sake of their fierce competition over grazing lands and for protection against a more sophisticated and menacing outside environment, the *'aṣabiyya* of the desert so famous in Islamic history and literature. Villages in Syria, though differing in economic civilization, were often social analogues of the exclusive and mutually hostile bedouin groups, perhaps because of the sedentarization of bedouins or alliances between bedouins and villagers. In turn, the settlement of rural peoples in the cities preserved habits of social organization more appropriate to the nomadic than the sedentary way of life.[2]

In short, the quarters were small integrated communities. Their close family ties, ethnic or religious homogeneity, economic and administrative unity, quasi-physical isolation and the character of their mediating elites made them villages or village-like communities within the larger cities.

III

The inordinate importance of the quarters in the social life of Muslim cities is to be emphasized because of the weakness or even the absence of other forms of popular association commonly found in medieval or premodern cities. In particular, independent professional associations or guilds were very little developed in the Mamlūk period. Tradesmen and craftsmen were located in the markets by occupation, but there is no evidence that they formed religious fraternities, mutual benefit associations, or unions to regulate the economy of their trades. Whatever cohesion or organization may be discerned was the result of state regulation or control by the *muḥtasib* and his agents, including some of the artisans and merchants who assisted him in his regulatory and fiscal duties.

The absence of independent economic associations coupled with strong communal ties in the quarters helps explain the possibilities of mass political action and its limitation. The absence of independent economic associations deprived the towns of the means to articulate and negotiate economic grievances. This fact, coupled with the fact that rule by a foreign caste further inhibited political communication, meant that street demonstrations and other violence became common forms of economic protest. Food shortages or abusive taxation provoked closures of the markets, clamours, assaults on officials, pillage of the shops, and so on. I do not mean to imply that violent demonstrations were the only means of protest, for the people appealed for relief in a much less obstreperous way through the representations of their notables. Nonetheless they were common enough and characteristic of the unorganized populace of the markets.

---

[2] It may be worthwhile in light of migrations from rural to urban areas in Mamlūk and later in Ottoman times, and the evidence of the Qays-Yaman antagonisms in the towns, to open to question what we mean when we speak of Islam as an urban civilization.

Correspondingly, the strength of the quarters also had an important effect on the objectives and consequences of mass popular political activity. The quarters were the locus of a more determined and organized sort of resistance to the Mamlūk regime than the sporadic strikes and riots which could be ignited in the markets. When communal interests were vitally affected, resistance to Mamlūk abuses often reached the scale of rebellion and even of city-wide rebellion to expel rapacious governors and garrisons. Still, however large the scale of this type of action, it was always limited in purposes. The object of popular rebellions based on the quarters was usually to ameliorate some specific grievance, to remove some particular source of hardship, and usually to have abusive officials replaced by people who would, presumably, be more congenial. In other words, rebellions based on the quarters never rose to the level of rebellion in the usual sense of an effort to change the personnel of the government generally, and certainly not to that of revolution against the form of government itself. I think one reason for this limitation is simply that the communities which sustained this type of resistance were much too parochial in membership and concept to serve political purposes on a city-wide, much less on an empire-wide basis. Small neighbourhoods could defend immediate interests, but they could not conceive and execute revolutions. In the long run, the common people were both dangerous and politically impotent.

IV

The balance of quarter and market organization is but one element in the picture of Muslim urban organization. To see the configuration of the whole we have to look at another form of associational life, the fraternal societies. In Mamlūk Damascus and Aleppo, the two most important kinds were young mens' gangs and Ṣūfī orders. I would like to describe one example of each of these types of associations, which although not typical, will serve as paradigms for the impact of fraternal bodies on the structure of urban social life and the urban potential for autonomous political activity.

The first example is the case of Damascus youth gangs called *zuʿar*. The name, meaning scoundrels or troublemakers, appears only at the very end of the fifteenth century, but the phenomenon under different names is evidently much older. The *zuʿar* were the Mamlūk period counterparts of the *aḥdāth*, self-consciously organized groups of young men, most probably bachelors, with recognized chiefs, called *kabīrs*, some of whom claimed to be descendants of the prophet. They wore uniforms and a distinctive head-dress called the *qar'ānī*. The *zu'ar* were recruited from the working population and possibly the very minor religious functionaries. Carpenters, criers, shopkeepers, and spinners were among them. They were organized by quarter and mostly in the turbulent quarters lying outside the walls of Damascus, those with rural backgrounds and rural ideas of community life. The *zu'ar*, however, were not completely identified with the quarters either in membership or interests; rather, the quarters were the natural boundaries of their recruitment and organization. They were organized by quarters because the quarters were the field of action in which men were sure of each other, but they were not wholly of them.

These *zu'ar* fraternities had a very important part to play. First, they were defenders of the quarters. They resisted what they regarded as unwarranted or excessive taxation, assassinated abusive Mamlūks and tax collectors, and even fought pitched battles in defence of their interests. The *zu'ar* were the core of late fifteenth century and early sixteenth century popular resistance to the Mamlūk regime. Another of their roles, however, seems a contradiction, for their special interests sometimes led them to abuse as well as defend the quarters. The *zu'ar* were criminals, pillagers, thieves and assassins. They ran a protection racket in the markets and exploited the populace by evading taxes while forcing others to take up their share of the burden. Pursuing their self-interest, the *zu'ar* took on what would otherwise seem a paradoxical third role. Defenders of the quarters, criminal predators, they also served as paramilitary auxiliaries to the Mamlūks. The Mamlūks cultivated the *zu'ar* as clienteles whom they protected, armed, paid, and honoured by reviews in military formation. They employed them in wars, in repression of bedouin or village violence, as personal following in disputes the Mamlūks had with each other, and in their efforts to control and extort money from the population of the city. As far as the *zu'ar* were concerned, their object was to maximize personal advantages by playing all possibilities against each other. They simultaneously defended the quarters and served the Mamluk state, not because of any social or ideological purpose, but to exploit the weaknesses of both the state and the urban society at a time of great tension and the incipient collapse of the Mamlūk regime. They were parasites devoted to an apolitical violence which cut across the lines of community organization and served no social or political purpose except a very limited self-interest.

The second illustration of the roles of urban fraternities is an example of a totally different sort—a kind of Ṣūfī fraternity. The Ṣūfīs were the mystics of Islam who lived life in common as small bands of devotees around revered *shaykhs* and teachers. These groups were affiliated into orders with branches throughout the Muslim world. They represented not one but many tendencies of social life and religious feeling. Some were closely associated with the Muslim religious elites. Others belonged to the low-life of the cities and inspired divergent and " un-Islamic " religious views among the common people. It is one of these lower class Ṣūfī fraternities, an association of Ṣūfī beggars, which I should like to mention.

They are the *ḥarāfīsh,* beggars who lived on the charity of the Sultans and the emirs and on whatever people in the streets would give them. They were not beggars in any simple sense, however, for the *ḥarāfīsh* were also the vagabond entertainers and the menials of the city. They often did hard common labour on the canals or despised tasks such as burial work. The respectable people regarded them as barbarous, depraved and dangerous as well, for they were feared as plunderers and often took part in Mamlūk civil wars as auxiliaries, using the occasions to fight and pillage.

This may seem a strange description for mystics, but it seems certain that the *ḥarāfīsh* represented a debased form of Ṣūfism. They were organized into *ṭā'ifa,* groups led by *shaykhs* or sultans, and these groups were, from the description of their ceremonials and descriptions of individual *ḥarfūsh,* dervish orders. In a remote way, they were the counterparts of the begging friars of the European medieval towns.

The *zu'ar* and the *ḥarāfīsh* were totally different elements of the society, but what they had in common was their stance toward the rest of the population and the part they took in the political and social life of the cities. In some respects both groups were tied to the life of the rest of the community, and belonged, however remotely, to the world of Islam and the dominant norms of the society. They were recognized by the larger society which sought to organize, discipline and use their cohesion for its own purposes; in some cases to exploit their physical power, or to organize the distribution of alms or to use them for ceremonials; in some cases to keep touch between the notable and working classes and the very lowest reaches of society. Be this as it may, the *zu'ar* and the *ḥarāfīsh* nevertheless represented marginal elements, a lumpenproletarian part of the populace, because of the disapproved character of their rituals, dress, behaviour, and their violent and mercurial political roles as plunderers and Mamlūk auxiliaries.

Moreover, both of these non-communal fraternities reveal a tendency for the marginal elements of the population to be relatively highly organized as compared with the populace in general. Not only did the *zu'ar* and disreputable types of Ṣūfīs have a group life, but plain criminals and even runaway slaves were also organized into large gangs. I think it characteristic of the structure of Arab Muslim urban society in this period that the merchant and working populations be so ill organized and the lumpen-proletariat so well organized. The further one moved from the social and political realms dominated by the notables and the values and the pressures of the mass of society, the stronger did the tendencies to associational life become. In consequence, where associational ties were strong in Muslim cities, they were apolitical. *Zuʿar* and *ḥarāfīsh* violence was criminal in intent, seeking money without commitment to any other part of the society. Associations in Muslim cities did not serve, as they did in Europe, to integrate society, but only to further fragment the population by consolidating partial and divisive inclinations.

Thus, we are brought back to the central issue to which I have alluded. If this was the social order of Muslim cities, may we speak of an urban Muslim society? If the society was so divided into exclusive communities and so plagued by only partially assimilated fraternal associations, may we speak, in the social sense, of the city?

V

I think that we may for there were more comprehensive groupings than these quarters and fraternities. However, to understand what made Damascus and Aleppo whole communities we have to imagine an integrated social life without government and without centralized coordinating bodies of any sort. The way in which people acted in public affairs formed a pattern which made integrated societies out of the city populations despite the absence of formal political institutions.

First of all, however divided, the society had a common normative basis in acceptance of the principles of Islam. It is true that these values were not interpreted in the same way at every level of society, but because Islam makes no fundamental distinctions of class, caste, or of ethnic, sacerdotal, or legal status, most people shared the same expectations about the nature of community life and the approved ways of acting.

Secondly, the cohesion lent by a common normative order was reinforced by the activities of the elite which interpreted, elaborated and preserved Islamic values, and in doing so served the whole community without distinctions of class or sub-community. These people were called the '*ulamā*', the people learned in the literature, doctrines and laws of Islam. Their purpose was to preserve knowledge of the divine will, sustain the community as an Islamic community and give it religious and moral guidance. Thus they were *par excellence* prayer leaders, scholars, teachers, judges, consultants on the law, functionaries of mosques, and so on. But they were an administrative as well as a religious elite. The religion they interpreted is expressed essentially in the form of law, in the form of prescriptions of proper behaviour in virtually every aspect of a Muslim's existence. As the interpreters of the law, the *'ulamā'* were intimately involved in its application in everyday social and economic life. They were the judges and lawyers of the cities. Family life was under their jurisdiction. Commercial transactions, property transfers and contracts in general to be legally binding had to be witnessed and registered by people competent in Islamic law. The regulation of the markets was entrusted to the *'ulamā'* and they were in addition the managers of the cities' educational, religious and philanthropic institutions. All community interests were thus represented by this unspecialized, multicompetent body which was the religious, professional, commercial and managerial elite all in one, *al-a'yān*, the spokesmen, the leaders of the people.

Moreover, even though the *'ulamā'* were the urban elite, they were socially undifferentiated from the rest of the populace. They were not a separate class, but all the people recognized for competence in learning, and as such they came from every class and profession. Some of them were bureaucrats, some were merchants, and some were artisans. They were recruited from all the sub-communities. Intergenerationally, strong currents of social mobility also served to keep the *'ulamā'* from becoming differentiated from the rest of the population. They formed a core of people through whom the populace could communicate—one elite representing all persons and managing all communal affairs.

Furthermore, the *'ulamā'* served to create more comprehensive communities by crystallizing around themselves a higher order of associational life which cut across the lesser communal divisions and made for much larger unities than those based on the quarters. These were the loosely organized schools of law, which were at heart groupings of scholars. They were made up of *'ulamā'* study groups, teachers, disciples, interested members of the community, and patrons; and *'ulamā'* administrative clienteles such as the multitude of deputies, witnesses, orderlies, clerks, and agents grouped around the important judges, clienteles which radiated their influence and were to a limited degree an ordering force in the lives of the common people.

The schools, however, were more than just groups of *'ulamā'*. They were also the foci of mass affiliation, for everyone was considered to be a member of one of the four schools on the basis of birth or the traditional membership of his quarter, city or region. The scholars elaborated the law. The common people belonged to the schools in that they practised Islam according to the interpretation of their school and looked to its judges, witnesses and teachers for authoritative guidance. The schools were not highly organized associations, but rather loosely developed affiliations through which the influence of the *'ulamā'* was communicated and in which people found a common identity. They were the most comprehensive associations to which people belonged, and even though no one school organized the whole of an urban population into one body, they were far more inclusive than the other intra-urban communities and fraternities. Thus the affiliation of the common people to Islam, to its norms, to the *'ulamā'* elites, and to the widely based schools of law, formed what common basis of organization and action there was in these Mamlūk Muslim cities.

The form of this city-wide society had important political ramifications just as did the organization of associations on a lesser scale. *'Ulamā'* society was too little organized, too little specialized, and too little developed to cope with all of the concerns of the cities. The schools gave a certain measure of cohesion in family, commercial, educational, and religious life, but they could not really take the place of a government. Means still had to be found for the integration of the populace into a political whole which could manage such ultimate matters of public concern as defence against invasion from without and against massive violence within; as control of the economy to mobilize resources needed for the maintenance of the urban physical infrastructure and the provision of communal institutions such as mosques and schools. Without adequate internal community organization such major functions had to be entrusted to the Mamlūk regime. The consequence of community life based on the schools of law was that Mamlūk domination and indeed the rule of foreigners in the Arab world both before and since has its basis in an order of society in which towns like Damascus and Aleppo cannot fully govern themselves. The foreign Mamlūk elites were indispensable to complete the integration of urban communities begun by the activities of the *'ulamā'*. For the moment, suffice it to say that the Mamlūks used their ultimate powers of arms and money in dealing with the *'ulamā'* and the common people to create clienteles which helped serve the needs of city-wide administration, and to control and channel violent popular outbursts so that the equilibrium of the society would be preserved. Thus medieval Damascus and Aleppo were characterized by a pattern of community structures—cohesive quarters, the absence of guilds or economic associations, strong anti-social fraternities, and diffuse identification with the *'ulamā'* and the schools of law—which helps us understand why they were not and could not be autonomous and self-governing cities, but how their people nevertheless shared a common society.

THE ILLUSTRATED MAQĀMĀT OF THE THIRTEENTH CENTURY: THE BOURGEOISIE AND THE ARTS[1]

by

Oleg Grabar

It is only too rarely that evidence provided by the arts other than architecture is used for the study of a social or geographical problem such as that of the city. It is even rarer that a historian of art be led, during the investigation of documents like miniatures, which seem to be meant primarily for aesthetic appreciation, to problems of possible consequence to social history. However, the preparation of what is expected to be a complete corpus with commentaries of the illustrations of the *Maqāmāt* of al-Ḥarīrī has led me to a series of questions which go beyond technical problems of stylistic and iconographic analyses or of relationships between manuscripts; and, as I will attempt to show, some of these questions are central to the problem of the colloquium, for they may permit the definition of certain intellectual and historical coordinates of a precisely identifiable segment of a city's population. In other words, this paper starts from a methodological premise which is quite different from the premises of most papers presented at the colloquium. Instead of beginning with some specific urban centre or with some institution or problem which can be assumed to have existed in the Muslim city, the series of investigations which led to the foregoing remarks began with an attempt to solve in traditional techniques of the history or art a classic type of problem, i.e. the identification of the meaning of a body of images. But it soon became apparent, in the course of our investigations, that the illustrated *Maqāmāt* can also be seen as a rather curious document on the *taste* of their time and

[1] It will be apparent that this paper should be fully illustrated, as it was when presented. However, various considerations ranging from cost to permits made it impossible to provide a complete documentation, and the eight figures provided are no more than mere specimens. The matter is all the more regrettable since some of the main documents, especially the Leningrad manuscript, are still unpublished. Whenever essential, the precise reference to codices and folios is given. I simply hope that the lack of visual proof will not detract too much from whatever theoretical value the paper may have. In order to emphasize the latter, I have eliminated from the printed text those points mentioned in the lecture itself which are not understandable without pictures.

that this taste leads us directly into the problem of the intellectual and spiritual configuration of the urban order of Islam in the Middle Ages.

The very fact of the existence of illustrated manuscripts of the *Maqāmāt* raises three central questions which may serve to focus more clearly their documentary significance or what Max van Berchem would have called their " archaeological index ".

The first one is that of the actual reasons for their creation. For, while it is true that al-Ḥarīrī picked his stories from a vast store of literary and folk sources, the central characteristic of his work and the principal reason for its success was its purely artificial, even if at times fascinating, " acrobatie verbale ", as it has recently been called by Professor Blachère.[2] Examples of this are familiar to all Arabists but for our purposes their central significance is that almost by definition these linguistic pyrotechnics cannot be illustrated. Hence, in almost all instances, the illustrations are dealing with the frame of events which serves as an excuse for speeches, poems, artful descriptions, puns, and the like. The extent of this frame varies from story to story, at times considerably; yet it is also true that, if we except half a dozen involved narratives, the general feeling of a reader is one of contrived repetitiousness. It is clear that the function of the events which were illustrated is secondary to the point of the book or at least to the reasons for its success. We have thus a paradox of illustrations which at first glance miss the most significant aspect of the book they illustrate. It would not be far-fetched to suggest that there is as much outward need to illustrate the *Maqāmāt* as there is to illustrate a Platonic dialogue. In both cases there is a cast of personages and an audience; stories or adventures may be told or related, but these bear comparatively little relation to the main purpose of the work.

The few instances in which an illustrator of the *Maqāmāt* attempted to go beyond the simple story and to depict a more abstract idea or a more complex emotion are usually failures in the sense that the image by itself fails to convey its purpose without thorough awareness on the part of the viewer of details of the text. To give but one instance, fol. 6^{v} of the so-called Schefer *Maqāmāt*, illustrates the departure of Abū Zayd in the second *maqāma* from the crowd he has just entertained; " then he rose and departed from his place, and carried away our hearts with him." (*Fig. 1.*) All that appears on the miniature is al-Ḥārith and a group of seated personages showing with the gesture of their hands and, in spite of retouches, with their facial expressions, their sorrow at the departure of an invisible Abū Zayd. The open composition is rather daring for a

[2] R. Blachère and P. Masnou, *Al-Hamadāni, de Choix Maqāmāt*, Paris 1957, p. 46.

medieval miniature, but the point is that an image with a limited attempt at expressing an emotion does not automatically identify itself visually as an illustration of the precise passage it illustrates. Furthermore, its specific depiction of sorrow is weak because no ready-made and understandable visual language existed for this purpose, as it did for instance in a Christian Pietà; elsewhere the same gestures and facial features express a different emotion, surprise, for instance. If as simple a subject and one as close to the narrative as this one finds it difficult to project its specific meaning, how much more unlikely is it that the more abstract values of the book as a whole could have been translated into images?

Therefore some reason must exist for the development of *Maqāmāt* illustrations which is to a degree independent of the reasons for the actual success of al-Ḥarīrī's masterpiece, a success which was by its very nature different from that of *Kalīla and Dimna* or of the *Shāh-nāma* where, regardless of the moral or esoteric meanings given to stories or heroes, an element of purely narrative entertainment always existed. Some explanation must clearly be found for the *fact* of the existence of these particular cycles of images.

A second problem posed by the illustrations of the *Maqāmāt* is chronological. Of the twelve known manuscripts, eleven were made within about 120 years. The earliest dated one is 1222 and the latest 1337.[3] Of these manuscripts four are fourteenth century and can be shown to have a primarily derivative illustration, i.e. one based on earlier models. The six thirteenth-century manuscripts[4] on the other hand do not show obvious earlier models, at least not at first glance, and we may properly conclude that *prima facie* the illustration of the *Maqāmāt* is a phenomenon which grew in the first half of the thirteenth century. Although it is dangerous to judge from negative evidence, the point is strengthened by the fact that a number of twelfth-century manuscripts of the work are known, including two dated before al-Ḥarīrī's death, and none shows any sign of having been illustrated. It seems likely therefore that we are dealing with a fairly precisely definable moment of time. Its upward limit is the second half of the fourteenth century when there occurred a general decline in artistic creativity within the Arab world. Its lower limit may be put around 1200

[3] A complete and up-to-date list with a discussion of each manuscript will be found in D. S. Rice, " The oldest illustrated Arabic manuscript ", *BSOAS*, xxii (1959), 215. To these should be added the manuscript discovered by R. Ettinghausen and published by O. Grabar, " A newly discovered manuscript ", *Ars Orientalis*, v (1963).

[4] These are three manuscripts in Paris (Bibliothèque Nationale *Arabe* 3929, 5847, 6094), one in Leningrad (Academy of Sciences S 23), one in Istanbul (Süleymaniye, Esad Efendi 2916), and one in London (British Museum, *Oriental* 1200).

and some explanation must be found for the apparently sudden popularity of illustrations of the book about 100 years after its appearance as one of the most spectacular best-sellers of the medieval world.

The third problem is somewhat more complex to define. We may establish as a premise that the appreciation and appeal of a book of al-Ḥarīrī's *Maqāmāt* was limited to a highly literate Arab milieu.[5] Because of the presumption of elevated literary interest and because of the inherent financial investment involved in an illustrated book, this milieu may be, at least hypothetically, defined as that of the mercantile, artisanal, and scholarly bourgeoisie of the larger Arabic-speaking cities. Thus the illustrations depict an element of the taste of a comparatively limited social stratum within the urban setting. And the problem then is: How did this particular Arab milieu create an imagery? In other words what components went into the making of a visual language whose meaningfulness in its time we must as a working hypothesis at least assume? A definition of the language can on the other hand provide us with a unique instance of what may be called a self-view as well as a world-view of the literate Arab world of the thirteenth century.

Such then are the questions which are raised by the mere existence of illustrations to the *Maqāmāt*. The answers to them have to be sought almost entirely within the manuscripts themselves, since to my knowledge, there is no outside literary source which even acknowledges the existence of these images, while such sources do exist for the book of *Kalīla and Dimna* or for the *Shāh-nāma*.[6] The methods which I have followed are essentially an attempt to adapt certain practices developed in linguistics or ethnography by which one tries first to define the *structure* of the images in describing and explaining in as much detail as possible every element which appears in the 800-odd known illustrations. Then a first synthesis is put together in which the general characteristics of the visual language are identified and these are then related to other artistic traditions in order to make up what may be called the dialectal position of the *Maqāmāt*

[5] The very Arab character of the audience can be shown, for instance, in the transformation of the preserved frontispieces of one of the manuscripts (Paris 5847) from the usual princely subject matter to a depiction of a group of personages listening to a story. For a description and discussion (but with a somewhat different interpretation), see R. Ettinghausen, *Arab Painting*, Geneva 1962, pp. 110–15.

[6] For *Kalīla and Dimna*, see, for instance, the celebrated text discussed by T. Arnold, *Painting in Islam* (reprinted edition, New York 1965), p. 26. For the *Shāh-nāma*, the matter still awaits full elucidation, but the presumption of illustrated manuscripts is suggested by such objects as the Freer Gallery goblet, G. D. Guest, " Notes on the Miniatures on a thirteenth century beaker ", *Ars Islamica*, x (1943).

miniatures within contemporary Islamic art as well as within other traditions of medieval Mediterranean art.

Since much of this work is still unfinished and many of its aspects concern technical problems of the history of art such as the identification of meaningful forms, the nature of narrative illustration, the relationship between pre-established typological models and specific needs of the text, and the internal characteristics of individual manuscripts, what I propose to do here is to concentrate on three separate questions which are particularly pertinent to the subject of the colloquium: (1) Can one define, from the miniatures, the ways in which the bourgeois milieu for which the pictures were made saw the city? (2) Is the art of the *Maqāmāt* the only available evidence of an art of the bourgeoisie? (3) Can one determine the ways in which this artistic tradition formed itself from other traditions of images? In conclusion I shall try to suggest an explanation for the existence of this unusual cycle of illustrations and ask a question which I am unable at the moment to answer.

To answer our first question, that of the way in which the artist of the *Maqāmāt* saw the city, the images provide us with three elements: landscape and natural setting, architecture, personages. There is not much to glean out of the first element, since it can be shown that almost all features of natural landscape are part of an artificial convention probably belonging to a general vocabulary of Mediterranean origin used almost exclusively for compositional purposes. It would seem, on the whole, that the milieu with which we are dealing did not go out to look at nature or for that matter at the animal world for its own sake. The few instances to the contrary are either small details probably part of otherwise definable iconographic entities or quite unusual, such as the celebrated drove of camels in the Schefer manuscript.[7]

The representation of architecture, on the other hand, suggests far more interesting conclusions. The three major manuscripts of the thirteenth century—one in Paris (5847) one in Istanbul, and one in Leningrad—have developed three more or less standardized architectural settings which occur throughout with only minor variations from one miniature to the other, although more significant ones from one manuscript to the other.

The first type may be broadly called the *house* type. At its most common it occurs in the Leningrad manuscript and shows usually a large central area covered with a wooden conical dome which can be opened up by having a section of the dome rolled to the side or by folding up mats set

[7] Illustrated quite often, lastly in Ettinghausen, *Arab Painting*, p. 117.

over a wooden frame. This house also has chimneys for ventilation which can be turned in different directions, a stairway also used as a cooling place for water jars, and a heavy door with knockers generally sculpted. In most instances there is also a second floor but it is rarely depicted. Details of internal arrangements are few and usually only brought in when required by the text. Altogether this general type is an artificial combination of features which can be assumed to identify a bourgeois *dār* in the city.[8] (*Fig. 2.*)

The second general type is that of the mosque. Variations occur here fairly often in the degree of elaboration but the most common system includes a *riwāq*, a *miḥrāb*, a *minbar*, at times a sort of *maqṣūra* railing, a dome on the axis of the building, and more rarely a minaret. Additional details of construction are found occasionally, but as a rule they do not alter the basic type which is essentially that of the early Islamic hypostyle mosque and not the new centrally planned *īwān*-mosques or dome-mosques spreading from Iran in the twelfth century.[9] (*Fig. 3.*)

The third general type is of lesser significance to our purpose here but I shall mention it because it is a particularly fascinating one and because its origins still puzzle me. It is the type of the caravan at rest and its most remarkable utilization is found in the Leningrad manuscript. There, almost always regardless of the precise needs of the story, we find the same groups of tents: large square ones, circular ones, and an ubiquitous small blue and white tent-like object, which it is tempting to interpret as a *maḥmal* or as a *markab*,[10] in which case we could formulate the hypothesis that it is the specific practice of the pilgrimage that created the general type for the depiction of the caravan. It should be added, however, that the tent type shows greater variations from manuscript to manuscript than the house type and that any final conclusions about its origin and significance must await a more complete analysis that can be made here.

However interesting each of these three types may be in identifying some aspects of the material setting of the thirteenth-century world as seen by the Arab bourgeoisie, it is dangerous to go too far in utilizing them as

---

[8] For typical examples, see Ettinghausen, pp. 105, 107, 113 (unfortunately the examples chosen here had to be chosen on the basis of aesthetic merit as well as state of preservation and do not show all the characteristic features of the house); O. Grabar, *Ars Orientalis*, v figs. 1, 7, 37, 41. (Fig. 7 is reproduced here as Fig. 2.)

[9] For examples see O. Grabar, figs. 20, 23, 42. (Fig. 20 = Fig. 3 here.)

[10] Ettinghausen, p. 112. Exceptions occur either in such cases when a specifically Bedouin setting is required (Ettinghausen, p. 111) and the traditional wide and low black tent appears, or when, in the 26th *maqāma*, the tent is supposed to be a luxurious one and a princely model is used (O. Grabar, fig. 17 for the only published example; f. p. 101).

historical documents because to a degree they were iconographic types whose compositional significance as settings for a precise subject-matter often overshadowed any attempt at verisimilitude. What is more significant is to relate the type to incidents or settings required by the text or to note exceptional compositions of architecture.

It may be noted first of all that what I have called the house type is not limited in its use to instances when the text requires a private dwelling. It is particularly interesting to note that it occurs consistently as an illustration of the courts of the *qāḍi* and of various officials, *wālis* or heads of *diwāns,* in front of whom Abū Zayd has occasion to perform. In other words—at least within the precise optical system with which we are involved—there does not seem to be an identifiable architectural vision of the publicly accessible official building or else, we should assume that these institutions did not have an architecturally identifiable setting different from the house. Such is likely to be the case of the school which forms the setting of the 46th *maqāma;* it is architecturally undistinguishable from the house type and, like the court of the judge or of the governor, it is only identified by the actions which take place within it.

This point acquires its full significance, however, when it is related to the fact that certain other kinds of buildings were clearly and systematically shown as different. The most obvious instance occurs in the 29th *maqāma* where all manuscripts without exception have introduced an architectural construction identifiable by its monumental proportions, two superimposed floors with rooms opening on a balcony, an exterior stairway, in one instance a well.[11] It is a *khān* and it may be worthwhile mentioning that the twelfth–thirteenth centuries are the first centuries for which we have clear architectural evidence of the existence of superb new caravanserais from Iran to Anatolia and Syria. (*Fig. 4.*)

A second modification of the architectural norm occurs in representations of the *sūq,* of markets in general. In the 47th *maqāma,* the celebrated representation of the barbershop-cupping place shows a very small narrow building around which a crowd has gathered.[12] In the 15th *maqāma* the shop of a seller of milk and dates is also shown suddenly as a small opening cut out of a wall and, in the Istanbul manuscript, it appears even in a unique profile elevation.[13] It seems clear that there was an original visual expression of the small shops in narrow covered streets which characterized the mercantile context: one may mention the slave-

---

[11] Grabar, fig. 21; E. Blochet, *Musulman Painting,* London 1929, pl. XXX (=Fig 4 here).

[12] Grabar, fig. 39.

[13] Grabar, fig. 8.

market, which in two manuscripts is shown with a wooden architecture and a tiled roof quite different from other types of roofs,[14] and the representation of a tavern in the Leningrad manuscript. In the same context of a unique imagery dealing with a precise urban feature one should mention the well-known series of cemeteries discussed by the late D. S. Rice.[15]

A unique type of architectural background is provided in the illustrations of the 43rd *maqāma*. There, for reasons that are not entirely clear, the illustrators of the three principal manuscripts decided to represent a panorama of a small village characterized in the text as a Beotian village of stupid people. Two manuscripts, and especially the Schefer one, used the opportunity to give us a curious glimpse of the simpler people of a small town as they appeared to the large city's visitor: small houses and shops, pools of water, a few primitive activities like spinning, the silhouette of a mosque on the unusual central domical plan and not the proper traditional hypostyle one, and especially a mass of animals everywhere.[16] The very originality of this image testifies to its meaningful character as a document. (*Fig. 5*.)

Finally an original architecture occurs in the representation of a mysterious palace in a far-away island as illustrated in the 39th *maqāma*. Projecting balconies, high walls, highly decorated exteriors, and a garden illustrate an idealized vision of a palace, like a sort of kiosk for which we have evidence in texts but no remaining instances.[17] (*Fig. 6*.)

The conclusion to draw from this brief analysis is then that, however one is to explain the establishment of a generalized typology of architectural settings, the exceptions to it may serve better to illustrate a precise concern of those for whom the manuscripts were made. And it would be primarily the city's mercantile features, markets, caravanserais which were sufficiently significant to the users of the manuscripts that their interpretation had to be specific. Secondary subjects similarly treated were those which involved imagination of a higher life and a rather more earthy view of a socially lower setting. But therein also lies the limitation of the evidence provided by these images dealing with major architectural features. For they can only be used as archaeological documents when they depart from an iconographic norm. It is only then that we can be assured that they are meant to have the concrete meaning demanded by

[14] Blochet, pl. XXVII.

[15] Above, note 3.

[16] Ettinghausen, p. 116 (=Fig. 5 here); Grabar, figs. 33–4 and pp. 105–6.

[17] Grabar, fig. 30, pp. 104–5; E. Blochet, *Les Enluminaures des Manuscrits Orientaux*, Paris 1926, pl. XIII (=Fig. 6 here).

the text. Elsewhere the task of deciding between iconographic significance and standard typology is fraught with danger and can never be pursued safely. The problem exists, however, of the origins of the *topoi* and of their exact index and to this I shall return below.

The same type of analysis can be used in attempting to discuss and define the documentary value of the representation of personages, although there matters are somewhat more complicated by the individual stylistic peculiarities of each manuscript. The analysis may begin with the realization of the existence of one personage basically common to all manuscripts. Dressed in a long robe, the head covered with a simple turban, the face usually provided with a beard and large eyes, he may be called the typical Arab male figure.[18] (*Fig. 7.*) His ubiquity in all manuscripts makes him an iconographic type without precise documentary value and here again the departures from the norm are more significant in identifying the world recognized by the milieu for whom the *Maqāmāt* were illustrated. Minor changes such as a veil around the face identify the Bedouin. Slaves and servants are shown as youths, usually with short robes and at times in high boots and braided hair. Dark colours and a mere loin cloth depict Indian sailors. Women and children are rarely successfully represented but in one instance illustrating the 18th *maqāma* we see the image of a paragon of beauty, a sort of Miss Arab World of the thirteenth century.[19] (*Fig. 8.*) More interesting are the representations of officials, judges wearing long *taylasāns* and long beards, otherwise quite indistinguishable from the Arab crowds, or *wālīs*, usually in pseudo-military garb and accompanied by attendants; in most of the better miniatures these personages are always made to look a bit ridiculous thereby illustrating the satirical intent of the author.[20] Within this motley crowd there is yet another essential personage, the beggar or the *ṣūfī*, either in tattered clothes, or, more often, in a short robe, long tight trousers, a headgear with a long and usually pointed *qalansuwa* and a narrow long scarf around the neck, perhaps in imitation of the *ṭarḥa* or of the *ṭaylasān* of the official *qāḍī*. It is the costume under which Abū Zayd is shown when he cannot clearly be identified by his action, although it is worthwhile to note that there is nowhere a clear iconographic identification of the hero of the stories.

The main significance of this rapid enumeration is, it seems to me, the very narrow range of its typology of human beings. To a degree, of course,

---

[18] Typical example in central figure is illustration on p. 114 of Ettinghausen's book.

[19] This is a hitherto unpublished miniature of Paris 3929, fol. 151.

[20] Ettinghausen, p. 115.

no medieval art, in the Islamic world or in Christendom, has seen fit, before the Renaissance, to translate into visual terms the variety of human types which existed in the large urban centres and of which we have written evidence. There was a general medieval tendency to cast all human types into a small number of optically perceived images. The variants on the basic type that do exist and the clear satiric intent of some of the representations of authority would suggest the secondary conclusion that the human vision of the particular world of this bourgeoisie was limited to a few precise groups with which it dealt personally and which would have been meaningless without some vestimentary or facial identification. The touch of exoticism which appears in a few instances revolved around unusual themes such as that of the fantastic island from the 39th *maqāma*.[21] In that sense the limited character of the world provided to the reader of the *Maqāmāt* is reflected in the poverty of the human types found in the illustrations.

Even though it may be regretted that the illustrations of the *Maqāmāt* do not provide us with a vaster panorama of a visually perceived Near East in the first half of the thirteenth century, still they do give us a specifically defined view of the scope and of the visual vocabulary which can clearly be assigned to the Arab bourgeoisie of the thirteenth century. Is this the only evidence we have at that time for an art of this particular segment of the population?

As far as architecture is concerned it is extremely difficult to evaluate the evidence properly. This is true both of the archaeological evidence and of the literary, and one should avoid the temptation of generalizing on the basis of the considerable information available for Fāṭimid and Mamlūk Cairo or for Aleppo and Damascus. To limit myself to archaeological evidence, it seems clear that the large number of caravanserais found in Anatolia certainly bear some relation to mercantile activities, as do bridges and *sūqs* there and elsewhere and also the numerous commercial and industrial enterprises created as *waqfs* for religious institutions. Together with baths and warehouses they formed a major part of the official architecture of the city but too little is known about them at that time to define their character with any degree of certitude.[22] In any event, the

---

[21] I have discussed the illustrations of this story in a paper presented at the XXVth International Congress of Orientalists in Moscow; cf. *Proceedings* (Moscow 1963), ii, 46–7. Typical illustrations in Ettinghausen, p. 122.

[22] The precise typology of all these buildings is still to be done. For carvanserais, see K. Erdmann, *Das Anatolische Karavanserai*, Berlin 1961, and Sauvaget's articles in *Ars Islamica*, vi and vii (1939 and 1940). For other buildings the best introduction is Sauvaget's *Alep*, Paris 1941.

mercantile function of a building like a caravanserai need not mean that it reflects an architectural taste or style properly to be associated with the bourgeoisie. A greater impact of a social patronage other than that of princes seems to have made itself felt in two other areas: first, in the growth of small sanctuaries, the *mashhads* which at this time begin to identify cities and quarters but whose significance is usually strictly local and whose sponsorship may come from a lower level than that of the bourgeoisie, at least at this time;[23] and second, in city planning or, more correctly, the directions in which cities grew.

Herzfeld noted many years ago that a peculiarity of the twelfth- and thirteenth-century monuments of Syria is their small and sometimes odd size, as though they had to be fitted within immovable existing architectural entities.[24] And he had suggested that this was due to the impact of the local landowners, presumably the very type of rich bourgeois who would appreciate the *Maqāmāt*. Or in Cairo the transformation of the *sharī'at bayn al-qaṣrayn* into a sort of Fifth Avenue or a rue de la Paix probably reflected internal social and economic transformations in Cairo itself as much as the impact of the newly arrived military aristocracy. Altogether, however, as far as architecture is concerned, the exact impact of the bourgeois component, seen as a taste-making social unit and not merely as a partaker of wider cultural trends, in the stylistic and formal changes brought in the twelfth and thirteenth centuries seems to me to be still very difficult to assess properly.

The matter is far more complex and far more suggestive when we turn to the work of artisans, ceramicists, metalworkers, glass-makers. The evidence there of the existence of a powerful city-bred bourgeois art, on several different levels of quality, is so vast that I should like to limit myself to three points illustrating three different ways in which this art can be approached.

The first point is that the typically Islamic transformation of the common utensil—a plate, a jug, a basin, a glass—into a work of aesthetic quality is a phenomenon which can clearly be attributed to the urban bourgeoisie of the Islamic world. It appeared first in eastern Iran, developed in Fāṭimid Egypt (not necessarily under the impact of the East), was acknowledged in theoretical writing by the *Ikhwān al-Ṣafā'*, and grew to its most impressive heights in the twelfth and thirteenth centuries, to dwindle away as a mere appendix to princely workshops after the Mongol

---

[23] Some preliminary remarks in O. Grabar, " The earliest Islamic commemorative buildings ", *Ars Orientalis*, vi (1967).

[24] E. Herzfeld, " Damascus, Studies in Architecture ", *Ars Islamica*, xi–xii (1946), 37.

conquest. The demonstration of this point would require a lecture by itself and need not be made here.

The second point concerns more particularly the twelfth and thirteenth centuries. During this time, and especially after 1150, two major changes took place in the art of the object. One is the growth of numbers of signed and dated pieces which suggests the increase in marketable value of an individual's work and the opportunity for the artisan to express his pride in his craft; at the same time we have a number of major pieces in metal (usually thought to be a princely medium) specifically made for merchants, like the celebrated Bobrinski bucket in the Hermitage.[25] The other change is the rather sudden tremendous spread of figural representations in all media, more especially in Iran than in other parts of the Muslim world, although it characterizes all eastern provinces. There occurred a sort of revolution in the visual vocabulary available to and understood by a larger social unit than the court of the prince, until then the major patron of representational arts. The consistent use on objects of figural themes was paralleled with the animation of every part of the object, as in the so-called animated scripts, as though at that time value could only be expressed properly through figures.[26] These changes in themselves need not all be necessarily connected with an urban art, although *a priori* the character of the objects on which they occurred and the fact that a large number of bronzes and almost all the early ones in the new techniques bear inscriptions with the names of merchants suggests the possibility.

But this is where my third point comes in. A study of the inscriptions and of the iconography actually does indicate that it is only within the urban world that these changes can be explained. Three examples may suffice. Giuzalian's study of a series of *Shāh-nāma* fragments found on pieces of ceramic has shown that the texts used were popular, spoken versions of the epic rather than courtly written ones.[27] In itself this fact only tells us something about the character and literary make-up of the artisan, but it also suggests the new appropriateness of the less sophisticated as creators of major works of industrial arts. Further, the existence of a large number of luxury objects with Christian subject-matter—and perhaps with heterodox overtones although this particular matter still demands further investigation—suggests the participation of non-Muslims among

---

[25] R. Ettinghausen, "The Bobrinski kettle", *Gazette des Beaux-Arts*, 6th ser., vol. 24 (1943).

[26] A definitive study of this theme is being prepared by R. Ettinghausen. In the meantime, see D. S. Rice, *The Wade Cup*, Paris 1955.

[27] Series of articles in *Epigrafika Vostoka*, iii, iv, v (1949–51).

the users and patrons of the objects, a participation otherwise documented in the Geniza documents and which makes sense only within the context of the city. Finally, as a recent study by Ettinghausen has suggested,[28] the imagery on a large group of ceramics may be related to the imagery of Ṣūfism and it is once again in the towns with their guilds and associations, that we can best imagine the impact of the new vocabulary of a mystical movement whose social overtones have often been recognized.

It would appear then that, except for the ill-documented or improperly studied area of architecture, the illustrated *Maqāmāt* seen here as an expression of bourgeois art did not appear within a vacuum. In other parts of the Muslim world, however, quite different techniques seem to have been used for its expression and so far the illustrations of the *Maqāmāt* form the only major cycle of paintings which cannot be explained outside of the specific milieu of the bourgeoisie.

The problem of the relations between the *Maqāmāt* and the rest of what may be called bourgeois art lies elsewhere. It is that almost never can one show a clear contact between them. Here and there a tile or a glass object does show some stylistic or iconographic resemblance to the miniatures in the *Maqāmāt*[29] and one rather odd image in the late Oxford manuscript represents a *jāriya* just given as a gift to Abū Zayd in the odd shape of a nursing woman which recalls a still unexplained group of objects in the same shape.[30] But these parallels are few and the sources of the illustrations made for the Arabic *Maqāmāt* are not the same as those of the Iranian ceramics, even though both can be associated with a related social milieu.

What then are the sources of the Arabic images? Three strands may easily be identified. One is Christian art, most probably Oriental Christian art rather than high Byzantine art. Obvious in one of the Paris manuscripts, this Christian influence is less immediately visible in the other manuscripts but it is certainly there as has been demonstrated by Professor Buchthal.[31] A second source is Islamic princely art. A scene in the Schefer *Maqāmāt* illustrating the 12th *maqāma* shows Abū Zayd drinking in a tavern.[32] Since the act of drinking was a central mode for the

[28] R. Ettinghausen, " The Iconography of a Kashan Luster Plate ", *Ars Orientalis*, iv (1961).

[29] For instance two tiles in the Walters Art Gallery illustrated, among other places, in Ettinghausen, *op. cit.*, figs. 71 and 72.

[30] Folio 65v.

[31] H. Buchthal, " Hellenistic Miniatures in Early Islamic Manuscripts ", *Ars Islamica*, vii (1940).

[32] This miniature was discussed in a totally different context by D. S. Rice, " Deacon or Drink ", *Arabica*, v (1958), pl. VI.

representation of the prince, Abū Zayd has been transformed into a prince in pose and composition. Another scene from the Istanbul codex is supposed to represent Abū Zayd wealthy and powerful and shows him seated in majesty in his tent and surrounded on each side by a military man and by a cleric, representing the *ahl al-sayf* and *ahl al-qalam* of a princely image.[33] Drinking and power have been so fully associated visually with royal images that it is only in such terms that Abū Zayd could properly be represented in these activities. A similar type of relationship exists between the *Maqāmāt* and a few other identified artistic traditions: the Dioscorides one for plants, travel tales for certain features of foreigners, and perhaps a few others.

The third source is more difficult to define. It has often been called realism in the sense of observation of nature and of man. There is little doubt that such observations played a part in the creation of the *Maqāmāt* of the thirteenth century. They appear in the formation of the physical type of the Arab, in the reproduction of a multiplicity of telling gestures or characteristic details, and in the many " genre " scenes. Yet, even though there is something tempting about positing a realism of intent, if not always of execution, in these paintings made for a bourgeois milieu—as in Flanders and Holland in the sixteenth and seventeenth centuries—the term should be used carefully. In the crucial areas of anatomical verisimilitude, formal compositions, or spatial representations, the art of the *Maqāmāt* shows very few signs of moving towards any sort of realism. The vision of the painters and of their patrons was still that of a very conventional ideographic system in which the viewer recognized and reinterpreted in his own mind separate visual units which he could understand because he knew the text. The few exceptions found almost exclusively in al-Wāsiṭī's work to the contrary, the art of the *Maqāmāt* was not an attempt to capture the life and world of the Arab bourgeoisie but to illustrate the setting of the book of the *Maqāmāt*. Just as the book itself has elements of satire and is a significant source for the social and intellectual history of its time, so are the illustrations, but the point of the book was not to be a satire and it is only in a relatively small number of images from three manuscripts that one can clearly see attempts to copy directly the physical reality of the contemporary world by differentiating certain elements from the standardized mass of images.

But then how can we explain what I have called the underlying typology of the images, that is the very standard forms in the representation of architecture, landscape or man which are repeated from image to image

[33] O. Grabar, fig. 17.

with minor modifications and without necessarily fitting with the requirements of the text? It would be tempting to assume an iconographic background for these features outside of the *Maqāmāt* themselves and in the case of two of the manuscripts, we can do so. Paris 6094 clearly derives from Christian art and the figures of Paris 3929 bear striking resemblances to the little that is known of popular shadow plays;[34] in both instances, it is standard types rather than specific exceptions which are definable as closely related to an external tradition. But no such interpretation of an outside imagery suggests itself for the mass of illustrations in the greater manuscripts in Leningrad, Istanbul, and Paris, except in the instance of landscape. In line with the explanation I have suggested for the illustrations in general—i.e. that they illustrate a book and not life—I should like to propose the following hypothesis for the formation of the typology. Just as the setting of each *maqāma* shifts from Cairo to Samarqand without alteration of its specifically Arab character, so it is that in a small group of manuscripts a setting was created which reflects at the same time two characteristics of the text's setting: precisely Arab features but also abstract and repetitious formulas like those of literature. It is the standardized typology far more than the exceptions to it which succeeds in illustrating the book itself, but it is the two together which define the vision of the world of the Arab bourgeoisie of the early thirteenth century. To keep to our architectural examples, the novelty of the *khān* was recorded because of its particular meaning to the mercantile class, but the *maison bourgeoise*, the traditional early Islamic mosque, the ancient organization of a caravan were seen as obvious abstract entities identifiable by certain characteristic details but not specific representations of a given house, mosque, or caravan. It is perhaps tempting to imagine that the peculiarities of the typology of the house—and in particular its elaborate system for ventilation—suggest a particularly warm part of the Arab world, namely southern ʻIrāq, and thus that the term School of Baghdad for these manuscripts is justified. Yet I hesitate in doing so precisely because the basic character of the typology, of the standard forms, seems to me to be more clearly identifiable with a social level than with a precise land. It remains, however, that of all the known expressions of an art of urban centres, this specific group of Arabic manuscripts is the only one which has clearly been interested in reproducing something of the world which surrounded it. Their limitations both as historical documents and as illustrations of the text bring us back to our original question of why it is that they were illustrated altogether. Chronological evidence suggests

[34] Ettinghausen, *Arab Painting*, pp. 82–3.

that around 1150 almost all the arts of the Islamic world—outside of the West—underwent changes which can be attributed to the impact of the needs and tastes of the bourgeoisie. A most significant general characteristic of these changes is that they involved the development of representational images in all media.

Thus the *Maqāmāt* were illustrated because the milieu which had read them and appreciated them before 1200 developed at that time in a way that demanded a visual expression, just as today a slow-moving novel by F. Sagan or the *Leopard* of Lampedusa are automatically made into a film, whether they lend themselves to it particularly well or not. The Arab literate milieu of the city aristocracy, which did not have a tradition of meaningful images, chose its own best-seller, its favourite reading matter, and had it illustrated, because it wanted illustrations, not because this particular book especially lent itself to them.

But what change took place in the character of the urban bourgeoisie some time in the middle of the twelfth century that it suddenly demanded a new and quite revolutionary artistic expression? This I am unable to answer and it is the main question I should like to have answered by social historians. Is there any evidence in other sources which would justify the obvious changes in taste and in creativity?

Aside, then, from this or that archaeologically or historically significant detail provided by the miniatures, the major significance of the *Maqāmāt* to the historian is that its existence reveals one unusual facet of the complex world of the city in the Arab world of the Near East: its interest for and involvement in images for the sake of images even more than as an illustration of life. That, at the same time, a limited but definable vision of the world seen by a precise group in the city does emerge is due to the character of the book rather than to the character of the men who had it illustrated. All that they expected was a literarily faithful, imaginative, and meaningful visual translation of their favourite text and thus an appropriate status symbol for their position. This interest for images did not remain for long. Just as the Iranian ceramic types of the thirteenth century disappear shortly after the Mongol conquest, so the *Maqāmāt* of the early Mamlūk period show great artistic merit but are iconographically almost meaningless or copy earlier models or else are mere compendia. The original impetus for the illustrations was no longer there and the images tended toward dried up formal compositions, thus closing an original chapter of Islamic art.

Plates

1a. Sandstone column inserted in the wall of a house

1b. Internal Water Supply

2a. Area represented on plan II (XI-20, 25)

2b. Complex with radial groundplan represented on plan III (XXXI-14)

Photo Bibliothèque Nationale,

1. Abū Zayd departing
Paris, arabe 5847

2. House
Istanbul Manuscript

3. *Mosque*
Istanbul Manuscript

Photo Bibliothèque Nationale, Paris

4. Khān

Paris, arabe 5847

Photo Bibliothèque Nationale, Paris

5. Village
Paris, arabe 5847

Photo Bibliothèque Nationale, Paris

6. Palace

Paris, arabe 5847

Photo Bibliothèque Nationale, P

7. Arab types with qāḍī

Paris, arabe 5847

Photo Bibliothèque Nationale, Paris

8. Woman

Paris, arabe 3929